MY JOURNEY

MY JOURNEY

How One Woman
Survived Stalin's Gulag

OLGA ADAMOVA-SLIOZBERG

*Translated from the Russian
by Katharine Gratwick Baker*

NORTHWESTERN UNIVERSITY PRESS
EVANSTON, ILLINOIS

Northwestern University Press
www.nupress.northwestern.edu

Printed in the United States of America

10 9 8 7 6 5 4 3 2 1

Library of Congress Cataloging-in-Publication Data
Adamova-Sliozberg, O. L. (Ol'ga L'vovna), 1902–1991.
    [Put'. English]
    My journey : how one woman survived Stalin's gulag / Olga Adamova-Sliozberg ;
translated from the Russian and with an introduction by Katharine Gratwick Baker.
    p. cm.
    "First published in Russian in 2002 under the title Put' by Vozvrashcheniye Press."
    Includes bibliographical references.
    ISBN 978-0-8101-2739-5 (pbk. : alk. paper)
    1. Adamova-Sliozberg, O. L. (Ol'ga L'vovna), 1902–1991. 2. Women political
prisoners—Soviet Union—Personal narratives. 3. Political persecution—Soviet
Union. 4. Soviet Union—History—1925–1953. I. Title.
DK268.A27A33 2011
365'.45092—dc22
    [B]

                                                                    2011000505

∞ The paper used in this publication meets the minimum requirements
of the American National Standard for Information Sciences—Permanence
of Paper for Printed Library Materials, ANSI Z39.48-1992.

I shall bear witness.

—OLGA ADAMOVA-SLIOZBERG

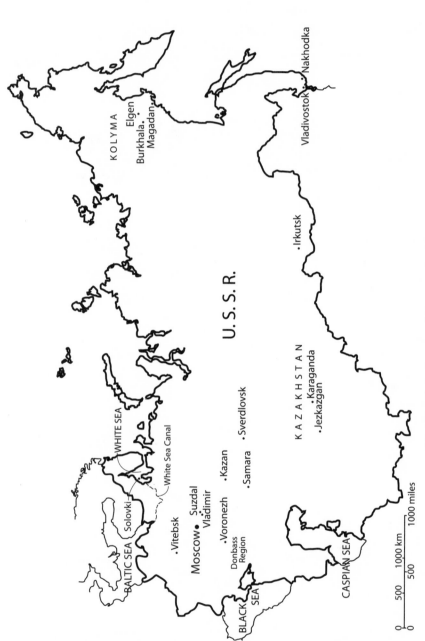

Sliozberg's Prison and Camp Locations

CONTENTS

~

~

KOLYMA

~

STORIES ABOUT MY FAMILY

Gallery follows page 124.

Translator's Acknowledgments

~

My most profound gratitude goes to Olga Lvovna Adamova-Sliozberg, whose extraordinary courage, determination, and vision inspired her to write her story, and to her family who sustained her throughout her twenty-year imprisonment in the Gulag and for thirty-five years after her return to Moscow.

Many colleagues, friends, and family members were helpful in encouraging me to complete the translation of Olga Sliozberg's memoir, and I am extremely appreciative of their efforts and support. Inna Petrovna Babionisheva was my closest colleague and friend throughout the first round of the translation.

Cathy A. Frierson has been enormously helpful because of her scholarly relationship with Simeon S. Vilensky, the Russian publisher of Sliozberg's memoir. She carefully reviewed my translation, helped me connect with Sliozberg's children, guided me through the challenges of moving a book toward publication, and recommended books that would enrich my understanding of the Gulag and the memoir literature. She also shares my love of Vinalhaven Island, where all the best work gets accomplished.

I am particularly grateful to John Crowfoot, who generously contributed time, ideas, and hands-on editing from the other side of the Atlantic.

Jane Taubman from Amherst College's Russian Department read through early drafts of the translation, and Diane Nemec Ignashev helpfully connected me with Mother Antonia Kolakova in Moscow, who also reviewed the translation.

I am indebted to Julia Borisovna Gippenreiter, professor of psychology at Moscow State University and my research partner in our study of the impact of Stalin's Purge on three generations of Russian families.

My dear friends and colleagues Boris Masterov and Irina Makarova provided a home for me in Moscow, and Anna Varga gave me repeated opportunities to sharpen my thinking about Soviet history and Russia today during my visits to that city. I am also deeply grateful to Simeon S. Vilensky and to Olga Sliozberg's children, Elga Silina and Aleksandr Zakgeim, for granting permission to have the memoir published in English and for their assistance with my work.

I would like to express special appreciation to Joseph Condon, Anita Gratwick, Philip Gratwick, Mary Janney, Robert L. Jackson, Caroline Moorehead, Marina Solovyova, and Kathy Van Praag, faithful friends and relatives who have read through various versions of the translation.

Leslie Fox and Keith Shay led me through Twitter to Northwestern University Press, where Mike Levine has been a supportive editor, and two anonymous readers made many helpful suggestions.

I am grateful to Eric Weber for creating a map of the Soviet Union that shows all the Gulag prison and camp locations in which Sliozberg was an inmate from 1936 to 1956.

My husband, Peter Titelman, has always been understanding and encouraging, as he pressed me onward toward the completion of this project.

INTRODUCTION

～

Olga Lvovna Adamova-Sliozberg was born in 1902 in the Russian town of Samara on the Volga River. Her parents were successful Jewish tailors, and she was the second daughter of their four children. She received an excellent education at the local gymnasium, and when she was sixteen the family moved to Moscow where she received further education in economics. Her husband, Yudel Ruvimovich Zakgeim, was born in Vitebsk (originally located in Lithuania but now in Belarus) in 1898. At the turn of the twentieth century, this ancient town was a shtetl in the Russian Empire's Pale of Settlement with about half of Vitebsk's population being, like the Zakgeims, Orthodox Jews. Yudel's family was evacuated to Samara during the First World War, and he and Olga may have met there as members of the Jewish community. They were married in Moscow in 1928.

They both grew up in traditional, nonpolitical, Jewish families but were not religious as young adults. In her memoir Sliozberg describes her husband as coming from a very religious family. She writes that he knew the Bible and religious history thoroughly, "although he had become a convinced atheist" as a young adult. She herself strongly resisted her father-in-law's pressure to have their infant son circumcised in 1930, writing that "it seemed to me completely unimportant whether my son was Jewish or Chinese, as long as he lived under Communism!"

Neither Sliozberg nor her husband was directly involved in the Russian Revolution of 1917, though of course the whole society was hugely affected by it. Neither of them was ever a member of the Communist Party—in fact, their daughter told me in 2005 that there were no Party members even in the extended family—but as a young couple they were sympathetic to the goals of the Revolution. Like many intellectuals of the time, they believed in Communism as a way of overcoming the social and economic problems of Russia in the early twentieth century, but they never joined the Party nor became political activists. Zakgeim was an instructor in basic politics in 1925, at the beginning of his career on the faculty of Moscow State University. By 1931, he was a professor in two university departments—the Department of Dialectics of Nature and the Department of History and Philosophy—and, according to Sliozberg, he also ran the offices of the Natural Sciences Department. He was apparently a gifted teacher. She was an economist. They lived comfortably in Moscow, where they were part of a highly cultured and relatively privileged elite intellectual community. In 1935 they were affluent enough to be able to hire a nanny to take care of their two small children while they both went to work.

In the spring of 1936, they were arrested (first Zakgeim and a short time later Sliozberg) by the NKVD (Soviet secret police) as part of a wide swath of political repression following the assassination of Leningrad Communist Party leader Kirov in 1934.[1] Sliozberg did not discover until many years later that her husband was shot within twenty-four hours of his arrest,[2] but she herself was immediately swept off into Soviet prisons, interrogation rooms, and slave labor camps during a period of Soviet history that came to be known as the Great Terror or the Stalin Purge. Innocent of any crime, Sliozberg lost her husband and was separated from her children, parents, profession, and home for twenty years. Unlike the millions who died in the camps, she survived, was eventually absolved of having committed a crime, and was officially rehabilitated in 1956.

Of her trial on November 12, 1936, Sliozberg wrote, "The written accusation against me was astonishingly stupid. It stated that . . . [a colleague of my husband at the university] had . . . recruited me into a terrorist organization that had the goal of murdering Kaganovich . . .[3] I had violated article 58, points 8 through 17,[4] which meant I was a terrorist . . . The indictment was signed by Vyshinsky."[5] Her certificate of rehabilitation, dated June 6, 1956, stated that the charges against her were "canceled, and the case is terminated for lack of evidence."

Sliozberg's children were four and six years old when she and her husband were arrested. As she writes in her memoir, she told them that their father had gone on a business trip when he disappeared. When the NKVD came to pick her up several weeks later, she explained her abrupt departure in the same way. The children were fortunate to be cared for by their grandparents, aunts, and uncles while their mother was in the prisons and camps, and they later told an interviewer that the reason they had avoided being sent to an orphanage was because their parents "were not 'the most important people' among those arrested."[6] As Sliozberg found out later, her parents' first task was to save their grandchildren; many young children of those arrested were placed in children's homes, their names were changed, and their families lost them forever.

Her mother quickly managed to exchange the Zakgeims' two-room apartment for an eleven-square-meter room in a large communal apartment on Petrovka Street where they had been living with their older daughter Elena and her son. "In this way," wrote Sliozberg, "my children were saved and never knew what it would have been like to have been orphans. They grew up among loving people who took the place of parents for them."

The children were not discriminated against during their school years but "were shocked when they were denied admission in 1948 and 1949 to the institutions of higher education they had chosen, and which by law they had the right to enter as [academic] gold medalists."[7] There was an intensification of antisemitism in the Soviet Union during the late 1940s and early 1950s, and the discrimination Sliozberg's children experienced at that time, and later when they were looking for professional employment, probably was the result of their being Jewish as well as of their being the offspring of political prisoners. Eventually, however, after Stalin's death in 1953 and their parents' rehabilitation in 1956, they were both able to enter graduate school and pursue professional careers.

Sliozberg was reunited with her parents and children in 1946, when her ten-year prison sentence came to an end, and she was permitted a short visit with her family in Moscow. She remained with them illegally until 1949, when she was rearrested and sent into exile in Kazakhstan. By then her parents were quite frail, and her children were seventeen and nineteen years old. Her daughter, Ella, later described their relationship during that time as one of exceptional closeness, recalling how her mother helped with her homework and the way they cuddled together at night, making up for the many years of mothering she had lost while Olga was in the camps.

After Sliozberg's second arrest, her children were permitted to visit her in exile in Kazakhstan during the summers, and after she was finally rehabilitated in 1956, she lived for the rest of her life with her by-then adult, married children in Moscow. Her daughter remembers Sliozberg's happy response to the birth of her grandchildren and her joy at being involved in raising them, since Sliozberg had lost that opportunity with her own small children when she was taken away in 1936.[8] After Sliozberg died in December 1991, her picture hung in a special place of honor on the wall in her daughter's apartment. In response to Sliozberg's years of imprisonment, her daughter became involved with the Memorial Society, a grassroots citizens' initiative established to honor and rehabilitate the victims of Stalin's political repressions.

The Gulag

Sliozberg, like millions of others in Stalin's Soviet Union, was a victim of state terrorism. An enormous network of slave labor camps was established throughout the country to maintain political control. Estimates vary widely regarding the number of people that passed through the labor camp system from 1929, when the camps first began to proliferate, until Stalin's death in 1953. It's probable that millions of people died as a result of political repression during Stalin's rule, including those who died during the famine following agricultural collectivization in the early 1930s and those who were victims of political repression from 1934 to 1953. It is generally agreed that complete certainty about the number of casualties is impossible since so many records were lost or perhaps never existed. But millions were directly affected, and even more family members were indirectly affected by the violence, intimidation, and losses caused by Stalin's Great Terror.

Concentration camps were first created by the British during the Boer War in South Africa around 1900. The Russian czars used imprisonment and exile as tools for political control and maintenance of power, but the systematic use of concentration camps for ethnic cleansing or political repression on a large scale was a twentieth-century phenomenon perfected by Nazi Germany and the USSR. The Soviet camps were created to contain even *potential* political dissidents who had done nothing wrong, and the camps rapidly became a way of perpetually intimidating the wider Soviet population. Active opponents of Stalin's rule were summarily put to death, and many people, such as Sliozberg's husband, were executed without any specific charges. Many innocent people were denounced by envious neighbors, coworkers, and even spurned lovers. Widespread suspicion and fear permeated human relationships, and there were no legal guarantees of basic human rights that could protect those who were falsely accused.

The network of slave labor camps in the Soviet Union during Stalin's reign is referred to as the Gulag. Initially GULAG was a simple acronym for *Glavnoe Upravlenie Lagerei,* or Main Camp Administration, but by the mid-1930s, Solzhenitsyn and others observed that the Gulag "was a country within a country." The camps reflected the paranoia, fear, degradation, and abuse that permeated the country as a whole during that period. The camps were filthy, interrogations were brutal, and work brigades were ineffective because life in the Soviet Union was generally filthy, brutal, and ineffective. The culture and mentality of the Gulag reflected the broader culture of Soviet society.

Between 10 and 15 percent of Gulag inmates were women, and they were held separately from the male prisoners. In the men's camps a culture of harsh competition for food and other resources prevailed. In the women's camps relationships could be equally hostile and competitive, depending often on differences in the women's political and social backgrounds. Sliozberg, however, made many deep friendships in the Gulag that continued in Moscow long after her rehabilitation. Other women Gulag memoirists, such as Ginzburg, also describe warm personal relationships with their fellow sufferers.[9]

Women prisoners, like men, found their own ways to survive, and often this included prostitution or attachment to a camp husband in order to avoid rape and other forms of sexual brutality and exploitation. Sliozberg observed that women who compromised their values in this way lost a sense of meaning and self-respect, and they were then more vulnerable to falling ill and dying under the harsh conditions of the Gulag.

When permitted a choice, prisoners often divided themselves into social groups based on their ethnicity, and many (but not all) of Sliozberg's closest friends in the camps were Jewish. Antisemitism had been deeply ingrained in Russian culture for centuries, but in the Gulag it was especially intense. A fresh wave of antisemitism swept through the country as well as the Gulag after the Second World War and during the period of the Doctors' Plot just before Stalin's death in 1953, when a group of prominent Jewish doctors in Moscow was accused of attempting to assassinate Soviet leaders. Sliozberg, then in exile in Kazakhstan, reported being a frequent target of antisemitic comments from fellow prisoners and coworkers.

The Memoir Literature

Many Gulag memoirists started recording their experiences so that their family members and friends would know what had happened to them. It did not at first occur to them that their work might someday be published. But gradually they began to take on the responsibility of bearing witness for all those who had not survived the camps; memoirists came to recognize that they were writing for future generations. Their writings emerged as archival documents at a time when Soviet officials were systematically destroying or distorting the evidence of what had happened to the innocent victims of political repression. Because many of them were cut off from their own families and many of their husbands had been shot, widowed women memoirists recorded nonfictional eyewitness accounts that honored the lives, the suffering, and the enormous strength of the millions who had not survived. Memoirists also generated a sense of community among themselves, as many returned westward with a tremendous sense of alienation from their former lives and even from their families, who could not understand what they had lived through in the Gulag.

Most Gulag memoirs have a fairly predictable structure. They usually start with a brief description of work and family life before the arrest. This establishes the normality and innocence of the writer's daily activities. The heart of the memoir begins with a detailed account of the arrest, the nighttime raids that devastate home and family, and the brutality of the police that contrasts dramatically with the personal dignity and kindness of their fellow political prisoners. The memoirs usually describe separations from friends, long journeys, and adjustments to new prisons or camps.

Most memoirs also include detailed descriptions of the *zone,* or the area of the camp inside the barbed wire, implying that the whole of the Soviet Union was a kind of larger zone—an enormous prison with a similar lack of freedom and individual rights. This section of many memoirs includes descriptions of the brutality, crudity, and moral laxity of the guards and the nonpolitical prisoners (true criminals who set the tone for the social environment of the camps) in contrast to the nobility and generosity of spirit among the political prisoners.

Some memoirs written by men describe efforts to escape, whereas women's memoirs tend to include occasional quiet moments of connection with new friends, experiences of mutual support, expressions of caring, conversations about their families and former lives, and even an appreciation of passing natural beauty. Both men and women often write about the incredible luck of randomly finding an indoor job that may give them an opportunity to recover their physical strength while enhancing their chances of survival.

The memoir literature also frequently describes the experience of exile. Too much physical closeness, a lack of privacy, and sustained levels of deprivation even in exile could and often did destroy friendships forged through shared suffering in the camps.

By the end of most memoirs the anecdotes begin to flag, and the details of being set free and returning home are somewhat condensed, although for some individuals, as Vasily Grossman observed, the "barbed wire was no longer necessary . . . Life outside the barbed wire had been assimilated in its inner essence into life in camp."[10] A recurring preoccupation throughout almost all Gulag memoirs is "the relationship between 'physical' and 'moral' survival—what it takes to stave off death, what is at stake, what price may be paid, and in what ways the physical and moral needs support each other or clash."[11] Some are sustained by their religious faith. Those without religious faith, like Sliozberg, are sustained by a sense of responsibility for their fellow sufferers and by the unforgotten dream of returning to their families.

Ginzburg's Memoir

Eugenia Semyonovna Ginzburg (1904–1977) wrote a two-volume Gulag memoir that was translated into English and published in the United States in 1967 (*Journey into the Whirlwind*) and 1979 (*Within the Whirlwind*). A powerfully novelistic narrative, her memoir has been the subject of considerable scholarly study and offers parallels as well as contrasts to Sliozberg's work. Unlike Sliozberg, Ginzburg was a loyal Party member. She worked at the Teacher Training Institute in the city of Kazan before her arrest. Ginzburg was arrested a year later than Sliozberg but on equally trumped-up charges. Like Sliozberg she was imprisoned, interrogated, and sent to Siberia, where she lived out an equally brutal but somewhat shorter sentence. Ginzburg started to write her memoir while she was still in Kolyma, and she continued to work on it after she had left the camps and returned to Moscow. She initially wrote it for her son, but the work took on a much broader literary scope as it progressed. Ginzburg's writing style is more polished than Sliozberg's, and she uses a more artistic pre-revolutionary Russian novelistic approach to her Gulag experience.

According to Sliozberg's daughter, Elga Silina, Ginzburg and Sliozberg met each other in passing during their time in the camps of Kolyma, once even riding in adjoining cars of a transport train. After they had served their prison sentences and returned to life in Moscow, they continued to be acquaintances, but they never developed a close friendship like that of many women who had been together in the camps. It is impossible to know how many Gulag experiences Ginzburg and Sliozberg may have shared with each other, but there are interesting overlaps in their stories. Some scenes in both Ginzburg's and Sliozberg's memoirs are actually the same, as when each of them sees her mother's face in a mirror in a bathhouse and then realizes it is her own or when fellow prisoners recite long novels and poetry to one another in the freight trains carrying them to Siberia.

Both of them loved Russian poetry, had memorized a great deal of it, wrote their own poetry about their Gulag experiences, and found that poetry sustained them through their worst suffering. They also both expressed a love for natural beauty and the arts, including music. As Viktor

Frankl writes of his own experience in the Nazi camps, "There is an inten-sification of inner life and an appreciation of the beauty of art and nature in order to forget one's present circumstances."[12]

Sliozberg's Memoir

For twenty years, until the political amnesty of 1956, Sliozberg lived first in the concentration camps of far-eastern Siberia and then later in exile in Kazakhstan, where she always felt she was in imminent danger of being sent back to the Siberian camps. She suffered from the drastic physical environment of Siberia, from the debasement of her personal humanity through false accusations and brutal interrogations, from occasional se-vere illness brought on by starvation and cold, from the pervasive crimi-nality around her, and from forced physical labor in the camps. In 1936 she was a beautiful, delicate intellectual, as evidenced by a family photo-graph from that period. How did she ever survive? In her memoir she tells the day-to-day story of her own survival as well as the stories of the many men and women who suffered with her.

Sliozberg decided to record her Gulag experiences while she was in the transit prison in Kazan a year after her arrest and, as she says in her mem-oir, she "wrote" them in her head (paper and pencils were not available to prisoners) every night for years because she wanted to be able to explain to her children what had happened to their parents. When she came back to Moscow in 1946 after her first criminal sentence had come to an end, she wrote the memoir on paper for the first time, put it into a metal can, and buried it in the garden of the family dacha. After her rearrest and seven years of exile in Kazakhstan, she returned to the dacha to dig up the buried memoir but could not find it. So she sat down and wrote it all over again. In 1964 it was complete, although in her later years she also added to the book a collection of stories about her family.

Sliozberg's memoir is one of the best known of all Gulag memoirs and was widely distributed in the Soviet Union through samizdat during her lifetime.[13] She undoubtedly hoped that it would be published in the 1960s after Solzhenitsyn's *One Day in the Life of Ivan Denisovich* appeared in the journal *Novy Mir,* but the political climate changed when Brezhnev deposed Khrushchev in late 1964, and publication became impossible. The memoir never made its way to the West until after Sliozberg's death in 1991, and it was eventually published for the first time in its entirety in Russian by Simeon Vilensky's Vozvrashcheniye (The Return) Press in 2002.

Sliozberg's memoir was particularly well received by other Russian writers during the 1960s. She was one of the approximately one hundred sixty former Gulag inmates interviewed by Solzhenitsyn for his extraordinarily comprehensive *Gulag Archipelago*, and she was one of only four interviewees who were brave enough to permit Solzhenitsyn to use their names when including their stories in his narrative.

Stylistically Sliozberg's memoir is simpler than Ginzburg's and more documentary in tone because it is testimony rather than reminiscence. Sliozberg tells her story through anecdotes and reflections as she defines the historical and moral worth of her Gulag experience. It is an educated woman's account of extraordinary times, but the true heart of the memoir lies in her empathic human connection with the many men and women she meets in prisons, on transports, in the camps, and in exile. She is an honest and powerfully observant witness who finds her own strength in the relationships she forms with others who are suffering.

Sliozberg tells readers what it is like for a small woman to do hard physical labor when the temperature is fifty degrees below zero. She describes cruel prison guards and sadistic camp commanders as well as an occasional kindly guard who could be quietly compassionate toward the political prisoners. She describes fragile young women who cling to her motherliness through years of suffering. She describes warm friendships with cultured intellectual women from Moscow and Leningrad as well as friendships with simple peasant women who helped her survive—who taught her through shared experience to dig into her own soul for resources she didn't know she had and to maintain her own integrity in spite of the brutality around her.

As is evident from Sliozberg's frequent references to nineteenth- and twentieth-century Russian, French, and German poets, novelists, composers, dancers, and artists, she—like many of the other men and women she encountered in the camps—was highly educated. Recitation of poetry and fiction gave people who were politically repressed an opportunity to express their feelings through great literary works. A traditional Russian education, with its emphasis on memorization, gave prisoners access to an interiority of the mind that may have helped some of them survive. In addition, many political prisoners like Sliozberg began to write their own poetry while in the Gulag, and the lines that appear at particularly emotional moments in her memoir express the universality of her experience, providing an artistic perspective that lifts her above her daily suffering.

The memoir also shows Sliozberg's evolution as a maturing woman. When, at the age of thirty-four, she first arrived in Lubyanka prison, the

NKVD's pretrial and interrogation center in Moscow, she was in a state of shock about what had happened to her. In the memoir she is quick to acknowledge that she was initially somewhat arrogant and insensitive in her assessment of the other women prisoners. She assumed that they were criminals whereas she was only there because of a "mistake" that would soon be corrected.

Gradually Sliozberg formed relationships with her fellow prisoners, began to understand that they too were the victims of "mistakes," had suffered, and had been torn from their beloved parents, husbands, and children. She began to question her earlier positive assumptions about the excellence of the Soviet political system as she tried to understand the situation in which she found herself. At the same time she developed deep compassion for her fellow prisoners and began to participate in the mutual support systems they had developed.

Two years after her 1936 arrest, in a cell in the far-northern Solovki prison, Sliozberg and three other prisoners implemented a regular daily exercise program while also teaching one another foreign languages and mathematics. Later, in a far-eastern labor camp, after several years of chopping down trees in the permafrost, Sliozberg was fortunate to land an indoor office job that was probably an important factor in her survival.

While in exile in Kazakhstan, she was able to organize a successful jacket production business based on principles of efficiency, accountability, and honesty that were previously unknown in that setting. Throughout her twenty years in the camps and in exile, she reached out with kindness and compassion to younger women—her "girls' club," whose members had lost their mothers, their lovers, and their hopes for the future. In her final years in the Gulag, she formed an intimate relationship with a fellow prisoner, Nikolai Vasilevich Adamov, who became her second husband. Though not from her intellectual or social class, he had a powerful personal integrity that resonated with her own. When the long agony of imprisonment, labor camps, and exile was over, Olga and Nikolai gradually went their separate ways, back into the worlds they had come from, and yet on a deep emotional level it is clear that they were the strongest of loving partners. Her sadness is palpable when she tells of hearing from Nikolai's niece that he had died in 1964 at the age of sixty-two from tuberculosis contracted in the Gulag.

Unlike many women prisoners in the Gulag, Sliozberg knew, throughout the twenty years of her imprisonment and exile, that her family was waiting for her back in Moscow. After completing the memoir, she wrote several additional chapters describing the history of her family and all they did to support her during her time in the Gulag. Her mother worked tirelessly on her behalf to arrange a judicial review of her case, her sisters sent her warm clothing and cared for her children, and those two maturing young people regularly wrote her loving letters, sharing their lives with her. She never felt abandoned by the people who cared for her, even though letters often took a year to arrive. This ongoing support and connection may have been another major explanation for her survival, although some women did survive the Gulag even though they had been permanently cut off from their families.[14]

When Sliozberg returned to Moscow, she was a woman from a strange, distant, and terrible land, but the whole family fully embraced the person she had become. Like other former Gulag prisoners, she was, as Grossman described the phenomenon, "someone from a foreign country [where they've] got their own customs, their own Middle Ages and modern history, their own proverbs . . ."[15] But she lived happily with her family, bringing her strange world back into theirs for another thirty-five years. According to her daughter, Elga, she was mentally alert, had a warm circle of friends, walked regularly, could hear clearly, and never used reading glasses even in her later years. She contracted pneumonia, fell asleep, and died quietly after a five-day illness in her son's home on December 9, 1991, at the age of eighty-nine.

The Translation

In the translation of the text, I have tried to be as accurate as possible, reflecting Sliozberg's clear writing style and preserving her occasional shifts to the present tense in order to convey a sense of the conversational fluidity with which she tells her stories and inserts her poetry into the narrative.[16] Small changes in sentence structure and colloquialisms are inserted only occasionally in order to clarify the meaning of Sliozberg's testimony for English-language readers. All explanatory footnotes are mine, except for Sliozberg's excerpt from Alexander Herzen's memoir, *My Past and Thoughts*. Occasionally Sliozberg uses simple peasant language when recording the comments and confessions of the less-educated women in the barracks with her. Written Russian can communicate social class through dialogue in a way that is impossible in American English. Such efforts in American English imply either crudity or a stylized ethnicity that would be jarring to readers, so I have not tried to create a "peasant" sound to the language in translating these conversations. But otherwise the translation is as faithful to her intention as I could make it.

My translation follows the Library of Congress transliteration system, although I have modified this system somewhat, eliminating Russian hard and soft signs, in order to make the text more readable, and using familiar English spelling of Russian names as appropriate.

The photographs included in the translation are family pictures from the 2002 text.

Notes

1. Sergei Mironovich Kirov, 1886–1934.

2. Like many men arrested during the Stalin Purge, Sliozberg's husband was said to have been sentenced to "ten years without the right to correspondence." This euphemism meant that he and others so sentenced had actually been shot within twenty-four hours of their arrest. Women, like Sliozberg, were more often brutally interrogated after being arrested and then sent to a series of prisons and labor camps.

3. Lazar Moiseyevich Kaganovich (1893–1991) was a member of the Politburo and a longtime crony of Stalin.

4. Article 58 of the Soviet Criminal Code covered all political crimes. It was broad enough to indict anyone the secret police wished to arrest.

5. Andrei Januaryevich Vyshinsky (1883–1954) was chief prosecutor of the Moscow Show Trials of 1936 to 1938.

6. C. A. Frierson and S. S. Vilensky, *Children of the Gulag* (New Haven, Conn.: Yale University Press, 2010), 162.

7. Ibid., 322.

8. Ibid., 367.

9. E. S. Ginzburg, *Journey into the Whirlwind*, trans. P. Stevenson and M. Hayward (New York: Harcourt, 1967).

10. V. Grossman, *Forever Flowing*, trans. T. P. Whitney (New York: Harper and Row, 1972), 63.

11. L. Toker, *Return from the Archipelago: Narratives of Gulag Survivors* (Bloomington: Indiana University Press, 2000), 96.

12. V. E. Frankl, *Man's Search for Meaning* (Boston: Beacon, 1959), 39.

13. Samizdat was the underground self-publishing and distribution of dissident writing during the Soviet period.

14. For other Gulag memoirs written by women, see S. S. Vilensky, ed., *Till My Tale Is Told: Women's Memoirs of the Gulag* (Bloomington: Indiana University Press, 1999).

15. V. Grossman, *Life and Fate*, trans. R. Chandler (New York: Harper and Row, 1980), 365.

16. Twelve additional poems written by Sliozberg during her imprisonment and exile are not included in this translation.

Bibliography

Adamova-Sliozberg, O. L. "My Journey." In *Till My Tale Is Told: Women's Memoirs of the Gulag*, edited by S. S. Vilensky, 1–89. Bloomington: Indiana University Press, 1999.

Adler, N. *Victims of Soviet Terror: The Story of the Memorial Movement*. Westport, Conn.: Praeger, 1993.

Applebaum, A. *Gulag: A History*. New York: Doubleday, 2003.

Asher, O. D. *Letters from the Gulag: The Life, Letters and Poetry of Michael Dray-Khmara*. New York: Robert Speller and Sons, 1983.

Baker, K. G., and J. B. Gippenreiter. "The Effects of Stalin's Purge on Three Generations of Russian Families." *Family Systems* 3 (Spring/Summer, 1996): 5–37.

Balina, M. "The Tale of Bygone Years: Reconstructing the Past in the Contemporary Russian Memoir." In *The Russian Memoir: History and Literature*, edited by B. Holmgren, 186–209. Evanston, Ill.: Northwestern University Press, 2003.

Chukovskaya, L. *The Akhmatova Journals*. Vol. 1, *1938–41*. Translated by M. Michalski and S. Rubashova. New York: Farrar, Straus and Giroux, 1994.

Conquest, R. *The Great Terror: A Reassessment*. New York: Oxford University Press, 1990.

Efron, A. *No Love Without Poetry: The Memoirs of Marina Tsvetaeva's Daughter*. Edited and translated by D. N. Ignashev. Evanston, Ill.: Northwestern University Press, 2009.

Frankl, V. E. *Man's Search for Meaning*. Boston: Beacon, 1959.

Frierson, C. A., and S. S. Vilensky. *Children of the Gulag*. New Haven, Conn.: Yale University Press, 2010.

Galler, M., and H. E. Marquess. *Soviet Prison Camp Speech: A Survivor's Glossary*. Madison: University of Wisconsin Press, 1972.

Ginzburg, E. S. *Journey into the Whirlwind*. Translated by P. Stevenson and M. Hayward. New York: Harcourt, 1967.

———. *Within the Whirlwind*. Translated by I. Boland. New York: Harcourt, Brace, Jovanovich, 1979.

Grossman, E. *Why Translation Matters*. New Haven, Conn.: Yale University Press, 2010.

Grossman, V. *Forever Flowing*. Translated by T. P. Whitney. New York: Harper and Row, 1972.

———. *Life and Fate*. Translated by R. Chandler. New York: Harper and Row, 1980.

Hoffman, B. *Inside Terrorism*. New York: Columbia University Press, 1998.

Holmgren, B., ed. *The Russian Memoir: History and Literature*. Evanston, Ill.: Northwestern University Press, 2003.

———. *Women's Works in Stalin's Time: On Lidiia Chukovskaia and Nadezhda Mandelstam*. Bloomington: Indiana University Press, 1993.

Kemball, R. "Translator's Introduction." In *Milestones: A Bilingual Edition*, by M. Tsvetaeva. Evanston, Ill.: Northwestern University Press, 2003.

Kerr, M. E., and M. Bowen. *Family Evaluation: An Approach Based on Bowen Theory*. New York: Norton, 1988.

Khlevniuk, O. V. *The History of the Gulag: From Collectivization to the Great Terror*. Translated by V. A. Staklo. New Haven, Conn.: Yale University Press, 2004.

Kolchevska, N. "The Art of Memory: Cultural Reverence as Political Critique in Evganiia Ginzburg's Writing of the Gulag." In *The Russian Memoir: History and Literature*, edited by B. Holmgren, 145–166. Evanston, Ill.: Northwestern University Press, 2003.

Kushner, H. Foreword to *Man's Search for Meaning*, by V. E. Frankl. Boston: Beacon, 2006.

Lermontov, M. *Major Poetical Works*. Translated by A. Liberman. Minneapolis: University of Minnesota Press, 1983.

Moberg, K. U. *The Oxytocin Factor: Tapping the Hormone of Calm, Love, and Healing*. Translated by R. W. Francis. New York: Da Capo Press, 2003.

Paperno, I. *Stories of the Soviet Experience: Memoirs, Diaries, Dreams*. Ithaca, N.Y.: Cornell University Press, 2009.

Shalamov, V. *Graphite*. Translated by J. Glad. New York: Norton, 1981.

Solzhenitsyn, A. I. *The Gulag Archipelago, 1918–1956*. Translated by T. P. Whitney. New York: Harper and Row, 1985.

Taylor, S. E. *The Tending Instinct: How Nurturing Is Essential for Who We Are and How We Live*. New York: Times Books, 2002.

Toker, L. *Return from the Archipelago: Narratives of Gulag Survivors*. Bloomington: Indiana University Press, 2000.

Tsvetaeva, M. *Milestones: A Bilingual Edition*. Translated by Robin Kemball. Evanston, Ill.: Northwestern University Press, 2003.

Vilensky, S. S., ed. *Till My Tale Is Told: Women's Memoirs of the Gulag*. Bloomington: Indiana University Press, 1999.

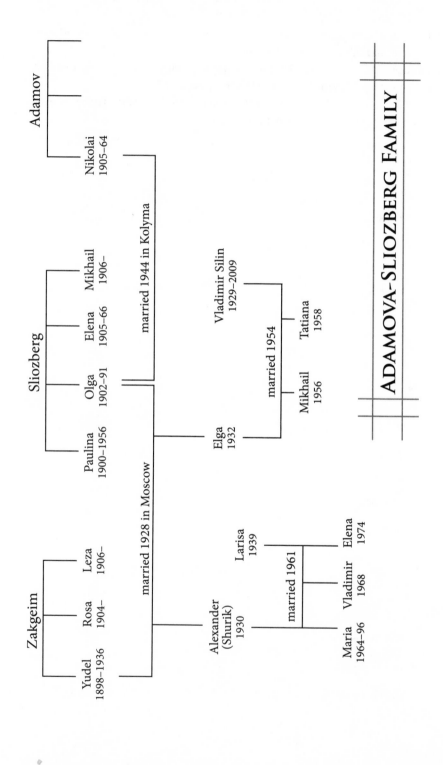

ADAMOVA-SLIOZBERG FAMILY

Zakgeim

Yudel 1898–1936
Rosa 1904–
Leza 1906–

married 1928 in Moscow

Sliozberg

Paulina 1900–1956
Olga 1902–91
Elena 1905–66
Mikhail 1906–

married 1944 in Kolyma

Adamov

Nikolai 1905–64

Alexander (Shurik) 1930
Larisa 1939

married 1961

Maria 1964–96
Vladimir 1968
Elena 1974

Elga 1932
Vladimir Silin 1929–2009

married 1954

Mikhail 1956
Tatiana 1958

A Chronology of
Olga Adamova-Sliozberg's Life
~

August 1, 1902: Born in the city of Samara on the Volga River

1928: Married Yudel Ruvimovich Zakgeim, senior lecturer at Moscow State University

1936: Husband arrested and shot within twenty-four hours

April 27, 1936: Arrested, incarcerated in Lubyanka prison, Moscow

September to November 1936: Confined in Butyrka prison, Moscow

November 12, 1936: Sentenced by the Military Board

1936: Sent by transport train from Moscow to the Solovki monastery prison

1938: Held at Kazan prison, Kazan, for ten months

May 10, 1939: Sent by transport train from Kazan to Vladimir and by truck from Vladimir to Suzdal

July 10, 1939: Sent by transport train from Suzdal to Vladivostok

August 14, 1939: Arrived in Vladivostok

April 27, 1944: Completed her sentence but had to remain in Kolyma

1944: Met and married Nikolai Vasilevich Adamov

June 1946: Traveled by steamship from Kolyma to Nakhodka, Vladivostok's port

July 1946: Train from Vladivostok to Moscow

August 6, 1946: Arrived in Moscow and stayed with her parents and with her sister, Elena, on Petrovka Street; Nikolai visited her there

August 29, 1949: Rearrested and incarcerated in Malaya Lubyanka prison, Moscow

October 1949: Confined in Butyrka prison, Moscow

December 1949: Sent by transport train from Moscow to Karaganda, Kazakhstan

April 29, 1951: Nikolai Adamov rearrested

March 5, 1953: Stalin's death

1954: Traveled to Jezkazgan, Kazakhstan, and lived there with Nikolai after her exile ended

1955: Took a train to Moscow in order to apply for rehabilitation

February 14, 1956: Khrushchev delivered his "Secret Speech" to the Twentieth Party Congress; he denounced Stalin's crimes of terror and repression

June 6, 1956: Sliozberg received her certificate of rehabilitation; her case was terminated for lack of evidence

1956 to 1991: Lived with her son and daughter in Moscow

1964: Nikolai Adamov died of tuberculosis in Voronezh at the age of sixty-two

1964: Sliozberg completed her memoir and began to distribute it through samizdat

1968: Solzhenitsyn completed *Gulag Archipelago,* which includes Sliozberg's testimony

1989: An excerpt from Sliozberg's memoir was published in *Dodnes' Tyagoteet,* a collection of women's memoirs from the Gulag

December 9, 1991: Olga Adamova-Sliozberg died in Moscow

2002: Vozvrashcheniye Press in Moscow published *Put' (My Journey)* in its entirety

NAMES OF PEOPLE MENTIONED IN THE MEMOIR

~

In Moscow Before Sliozberg's Arrest

Marusia, the family nanny in 1935

Yudel Ruvimovich Zakgeim, Olga's husband, a biologist and professor

Alexander/Shura/Shurik and Elga/Ella/Ellochka, their children

Cellmates in Lubyanka Prison

Zhenia Bykhovskaia

Alexandra Mikhailovna Rozhkova

Sonia

Zhenia Goltsman

Zina Stanitsyna

Tamara Konstantinovna

Tamara's mother

Cellmates from Cell 105 in Butyrka Prison

Zlata

Katia Nikolaeva, a weaver and the head woman of the cell

Ania

Zhenia Bykhovskaia, a cellmate from Lubyanka

Motia, a kulak peasant girl from Siberia

Nina and Valia, wives of bureaucrats

Pinson (Sophia Solomonovna), an old woman

Zhenia Volkova, a student from Gorky

Lira

Sonia Ashkenazi

Solovki Monastery Prison

Monakhov, the commandant of the prison

Zhenia Goltsman, a cellmate from Lubyanka

Lida Dmitrieva

Zina Stanitsyna, a cellmate from Lubyanka

Ania Bublik

Vinogradov, the chief guard for the building

Nema Rabinovich

Masha Yarovaia

Niura Ivanova

Shura Alekseeva

Cellmates in Kazan Prison

Katia Toive

Zina Stanitsyna, a cellmate from Lubyanka

Olga Ivanovna Nikitina

Maria Danielian

Liza

Cellmates from Suzdal Convent Prison

Zhenia Goltsman, a cellmate from Lubyanka and Solovki

Lida Dmitrieva, a cellmate from Solovki

Transport to Kolyma

Maria Danielian, a cellmate from Kazan

Nina Verestova, a cellmate from Butyrka

Liza Tsvetkova, a cellmate from Kazan

Olga Radovich

Askhab
Galia Ivanova
Natasha Onufrieva
Zavalishina

Magadan, Sliozberg's First Camp

Kolmogorsky, the foreman
Raia Ginzburg
Rosa Borova
Altunin
Galia Prozorovskaia
Basia
Prokhorov
Monia Lourye, married Basia
Polina Lvovna Gertzenberg, a member of the Polish parliament
Valia

Office Job as a Bookkeeper

Igor Adrianovich Khorin

Devil's Wheel Camp

Sashka Sokolov, a foreman
Alla Shvander
Kostia, Alla's suitor
Ania Orlova, the assistant brigade leader
Volodya
Grania, a religious woman
Ivan, Grania's husband
Sonka and Liubka
Mirra Kizilshtein
Liza Keshve

Masha Mino

Nina Gagen-Torn

Bird Island Camp

Sasha, the team leader

Elgen, Kolyma Environs

Galia Prozorovskaia, from Magadan

Raia Ginzburg, from Magadan

Onishchenko

Nadia (Nadezhda Vasilevna Grankina)

Vikenti Yakovlevich Tulitski

Kina Kinusia, Nadia's daughter

Nadia Fedorovich

Yagodny Camp in Kamchatka

Nikolai Vasilevich Adamov, married Sliozberg in 1944

Alexander Alexandrovich

Burkhala: At Home with Nikolai

Mikhail Lvovich Sliozberg, Olga's brother

Nikishov, director of Far East Construction

Vladimir Nikolaevich Novikov, deputy minister of defense

Steamship from Kolyma to the Port of Nakhodka

Sophia Mikhailovna, a doctor

Vera/Verochka, Sophia Mikhailovna's daughter

Julia, Vera's little sister

Olga Arseneva

Nadia

Andrei Petrovich Shelest

Simochka
Olga Ivanovna
Ofitzerov, an NKVD lieutenant
Ivan Kolosov

Return

Olga Radovich
Lipa Kaplan

Butyrka Prison Cell 105 (Second Time)

Wanda
Maria Ivanovna Sinitsyna
Olga Pavlovna Kantor
Aino
Valia
Vasia Petrov

Prisoners' Transport to Karaganda, Kazakhstan

Olga/Olia Kosenko
Vera Samoilovna Lokkerman
Maria Gertsevna

Exile in Karaganda

Valia Gerlin
Yura Aikhenvald, a writer who married Valia Gerlin
Anisia Vasilievna Korneva, director of the sewing shop
Satenov, local deputy director
Alik Volpin, the son of the poet Yesenin
Emanuel Mandel/Naum Korzhavin, poet
Vera P.
Kerta Nourten

Natasha Vakula

Maria Nikitichna Puzikova

Ida Markovna Reznikova

Gita Abramovna

Anna Petrovna

Stories About My Family

Polina, Olga's younger sister

Vladimir Arkadevich Tronin, Polina's husband, a Civil War hero and government official

Elena Lvovna Sliozberg, Olga's older sister and a doctor

Dima/Dimochka, Elena's son

Katia, a nurse at Elena's clinic

Petia

Anisia and her son Vasia, patients of Elena

Ruvim Yevseevich Zakgeim, Olga's father-in-law

Aaron Sliozberg, Olga's paternal grandfather

Misha, Olga's cousin

Lev, another cousin

Beiliss, a Jew accused of murdering a ten-year-old Christian boy in 1913

Tania, Olga's great-granddaughter

My Journey

Instead of an Introduction

I have been rehabilitated.

For twenty years this moment has seemed as though it would be a step into a radiant future. But with the joy has come the feeling of being an outcast, of being somehow inferior. No one can give back the best twenty years of my life. No one can bring my dead friends back to life. No one can tie together the broken, lifeless threads binding us to our closest relatives.

Returning to life is a painful process.

And here it is most important to add up your capital. What have you brought back with you? What do you possess?

You have no roof over your head, no money, no physical strength. Your place has been taken, because life abhors a vacuum, and the bloody wound that opened in the flesh of life when you were torn from it has healed over. Your parents have died and your children have grown up without you. For twenty years you have not worked in your profession. You have fallen behind and can only work as an apprentice while your comrades have become masters. And being an apprentice is difficult for someone fifty years old. It would seem that everything is very bad. It would seem as though you are bankrupt.

But if, through all those years, you kept earnestly thinking, observing, and trying to understand, and you can now share everything with people, then they will need you, because in the bustle of life, under the din of patriotic drums, amid the threats and the incense of flattery, people cannot always tell the lies from the truth.

And woe unto you if you failed to understand and failed to bring anything back from the abyss. You have been deprived of everything and no official scrap of paper can restore you to your place in life.

For you, all you are left with is what your soul has retained.

You are either destitute or you are rich.

This book was conceived in 1937, a year after I was arrested.

In the beginning I never thought of it as a book. I just thought about how to explain to my son and daughter that their mother and father had become "enemies of the people." I kept thinking about it night after night. In prison, the most difficult thing to learn is how to sleep. I tried to learn how to do this for three years. For three years I lay there quietly all night long, telling the story in my head. About everything. Not only about myself, but also about my comrades in misery with whom fate had connected me, about their bitter sufferings, and the tragic circumstances of their lives. When something horrible shocked me, I "wrote it down" at night in the story in my head. And it grew more and more voluminous.

That is how this book was created.

It has lived in me all these years.

A Wood Chip

In 1935, I hired a nanny to take care of my children. She was woman of about thirty, hardworking, tidy, and quite reserved. I wasn't in the habit of asking her about her personal life. Marusia seemed a bit dim-witted, indifferent, and not very affectionate with the children. She was stingy and tightfisted but quite efficient and honest.

We had lived together side by side for a whole year and were content with each other.

One day at lunchtime a letter came for Marusia. As she read it her face changed. She lay down on her bed saying she had a bad headache.

I felt that some misfortune had befallen Marusia. At first she wouldn't answer my questions and lay with her face to the wall. Then she sat up on the bed and in a harsh, bitter voice cried out:

"You want to know what's wrong with me? All right, but don't get mad at me. You say we've lived well here. But I too had a husband, and our life was no worse than yours. I had three children, better than yours. We slaved away day and night, trying to make it, raising animals. My husband could do anything with his hands. He could make felt boots and fur coats. In our home the cup was full. We had a woman who worked for us; there was nothing wrong with that—it wasn't forbidden. Look, you're allowed to keep a working girl, and so could I. I hired an old woman to help my mother with the house, and I broke my own back working in the fields.

"But in 1930 during the winter I went to Moscow to help my sister with her new baby, and while I was there they seized my family because we were kulaks. They sent my husband to the camps, my mother and the

5

children to Siberia. Mother sent me a letter telling me to find a way to stay in Moscow—'Maybe you can help us,' she wrote, 'because there's no way to set up housekeeping or earn money here. The children and I are living in a miserable mud hut.'

"Well, from that time on I've been doing housework. Whatever I earn I send to them. And now they write to tell me that my children have died . . ."

She handed me the letter. A neighbor had written, "Nothing has been heard from that guy of yours for three months. They say he's digging a canal. Your children lived with their grandmother, and they kept getting sick. The mud hut is damp and there isn't much to eat. But, never mind, they managed somehow. Your Mishka and my boy Lenka were friends. He was a nice kid. And then suddenly the children all came down with scarlatina, mine too. They came out of it, but God took yours. Your mother is out of her mind, she won't eat, she won't sleep, she moans all the time. She'll probably die soon, too."

That evening I couldn't wait for my husband to come home. He was an assistant professor at the university, a biologist, and in my eyes he was the wisest and most educated person on earth. I felt as if a heavy weight were pressing on my heart. The world that had been so clear, so intelligible, and so secure for me had been shaken. What had Marusia and her children done wrong? Could our life, so clean, so hardworking, and so upstanding, be based on the suffering and blood of innocent people?

My husband arrived, excited as always after his lectures, with the joyful feeling of a person who is content with his day's work and anticipates relaxing in the circle of his loved ones. The children threw themselves upon him, climbing on his back. I loved nothing in the world more than the sight of my children squealing with joy, scrambling up their father's broad back. But today I caught Marusia's painful glance and quickly interrupted this scene.

I called my husband to the other room and told him everything. He became very serious.

"You see, they can't make a revolution with white gloves. Annihilating the kulaks is a bloody and difficult process, but it has to be done. Marusia's tragedy isn't as simple as it seems to you. What was her husband sent to the camps for? It is hard to believe that he wasn't guilty of anything at all. You don't end up in the camps for nothing. Maybe we should think about getting rid of Marusia. There is much that is suspicious about her . . . Well, I don't insist," he added, seeing how my face changed. "I don't insist. After all she may be a good woman; perhaps in these circumstances there has been a mistake. But you know that when they cut down a forest, wood chips fly."

This was the first time I had heard this expression that held so much comfort for those who stood on the sidelines and so much pain for those who fell under the ax.

He said a lot more about the historical necessity of transforming the villages, about the enormous changes taking place before our very eyes, and about how we would have to reconcile ourselves to the inevitable victims . . . (Later I often noticed that this idea was especially easy for those who had not fallen victim themselves. But Marusia certainly did not want to reconcile.)

I believed him. All these horrors were a thousand miles away from me! I lived quite safely with my family in a world that seemed unshakable. I had to believe him in order to feel that I myself was a decent and significant person. And I was used to believing him. He was honest and wise.

And Marusia continued to take care of our children and do the housework, and only occasionally, while peeling potatoes or darning socks, would she stop and gaze fixedly at the wall, her hands motionless, and then a worm would creep into my heart again.

But I quickly calmed myself—when they cut down a forest, wood chips fly.

The Beginning of the Road to Calvary

Men were not merciful,
God did not save!
—MIKHAIL YURIEVICH LERMONTOV

One ordinary Saturday I came home full of thoughts of what we would do on Sunday, about how happy my daughter would be with the doll I was bringing her, and how enthusiastic my son would be about the elephant I would show him at the zoo the next day.

I had always said I was not delusional like other mothers and could see my children's inadequacies. But I lied. Deep in my heart I knew that no one else in the world had as intelligent, beautiful, charming children as I had.

And I came home after work, knowing that a splendid Saturday evening and a splendid Sunday were before us.

I opened the door. The awful smell of boots and tobacco struck me.

Marusia sat in the middle of complete devastation, telling the children a story. Piles of books and manuscripts were strewn on the floor. Wardrobes were open, and our underwear had been pulled out and then roughly stuffed back into them. I couldn't grasp the situation and not a single thought came into my head; but I felt terrified, and a premonition of misfortune turned my soul to ice. Marusia stood up. In a strange quiet voice she said:

"It's nothing. Don't fall apart!"

"Where is my husband? What has happened? Was he hit by a car?"

"Don't you understand? They took him."

No. This could not have happened to me or to him! True, there had been some rumors (but only rumors, because this was the beginning of 1936) that something had happened. There had been some arrests . . . But of course those things had happened to other people; it could in no way touch us, such peaceful, upstanding people . . .

"How did he react?"

"He was sitting there, quite pale, gave me his watch for you, and said you shouldn't worry, everything would be cleared up. He told the children he was going on a business trip."

"Yes, of course, it will be cleared up! Of course you do know, Marusia, what a fine, upstanding person he is!"

Marusia smiled bitterly and looked at me:

"Oh, you educated woman, you! Don't you realize that whoever ends up there never comes back? Do you think there is really any justice there?"

But surely I knew everything about him. I knew that he couldn't have done anything criminal.

No, I will be cheerful. I will show that I believe in the justice of our courts. He will come back, and this odious smell, this empty home will only be a terrible memory.

And then a strange life began for me. The children knew nothing. I played with them, laughed, and it seemed to me that nothing had happened, as if it had all been a terrible dream. And when I walked out into the street and went to work, I looked at everyone as if an invisible barrier separated me from them. They were normal, and I was doomed. And they spoke with me in a special tone of voice, and they were afraid of me. When they noticed me, they crossed to the other side of the street. There were also some who showed me special attention, but this was heroism on their part, and both they and I knew it.

One old man, a member of the Party since 1913, came to me and said, "Get your affairs in order; they may arrest you too. And remember, you should answer only the questions they ask, don't add anything extra, every superfluous word will only lead to another long interrogation."

"But he is completely innocent! Why do you give me such advice? You, a Bolshevik! Does that mean you don't believe in the justice of our courts? You're not worthy of your Party card!"

He looked at me and said, "Just remember my words, and in a year's time we'll have a serious talk about the situation, if possible."

I thought it beneath my dignity to listen to his advice, and I tried to live as if nothing had happened.

During this time there was a conference of the Stakhanovites from the brush industry where I worked. When we gathered in Vitebsk, it turned out that this was the first time the workers in this industry had met together since the beginning of the Soviet period. At the meeting we learned that in Tashkent they were trying to invent a machine that had already been in use for ten years in Nevele and that in Minsk they could only dream of the brilliant technology already developed in Ust-Sysolsk.

It was cheerful, effective, and gratifying work. I was the secretary of the meeting, worked all day, and completely forgot that I would return to an empty apartment when I came back to Moscow and that once more I would be carrying packages to the prison . . .

The day after I returned to Moscow, they came for me.

It's strange that my first thought was that I had all the materials from the conference: "The meeting cost fifty thousand rubles. All my work is on note cards. It will all go to waste. No one will be able to read my handwriting."

While they were making a four-hour search of my apartment, I put the materials from the conference in order. I couldn't seriously take in the fact that my life was over; and I was afraid to think that they would take my children away from me.

I wrote, pasted, and sorted the materials, and while I wrote, it seemed to me that nothing had happened. I am finishing my work and will hand it in, and then my boss will say to me, "Good job, you were not confused. You saw that it was just a misunderstanding!" I myself don't know what I was thinking of. The inertia of work or maybe the confusion from my fright was so enormous that I worked exactingly and effectively for four hours, as if I were at my workplace in the office of the People's Commissar.

The investigator conducting the search finally took pity on me: "You would do better to say good-bye to your children!" he said.

Oh, yes. Say good-bye to the children . . . I really have to leave them. Maybe for a long time . . . Everything will be cleared up. This cannot be happening.

I went into the children's room. My son was sitting up on his bed. I said to him:

"I have to go on a business trip, my little one. You'll stay with Marusia, be a good boy!"

His little lips twisted:

"How strange! First Papa went away on a business trip, now you are going away, pretty soon Marusia will go away—who shall we stay with?"

I kissed him on his thin little foot.

My daughter was sweetly sleeping and snuffling with her nose buried in her little pillow. I turned her over gently. She smiled and murmured something.

For the first time in my life I realized what it meant to be choked with tears. I could hardly breathe. But to this day I remember with pride that I did not let my son see my grief.

We left the building.

The door closed. We got into the car. In an instant normal human life ended for me.

Occasionally some tasks would flash into my brain for a moment through inertia. Something was left unfinished. I needed to fix something. I had been planning to putty the window. It's drafty. My son will catch cold. No, it isn't that. Something important. Oh, yes, Mama! I have been hiding from her all the danger hanging over me. I have been comforting her with invented news about my husband. Now she will find out.

I didn't embrace her when I said good-bye the last time I saw her, postponing conversation with her in order to prepare her . . . No. This is not the most important thing. There is something I haven't done. I wanted to go to Stalin, to try to arrange a meeting with him, in order to explain to him that my husband was innocent . . . No, not that . . . Something else I still haven't done . . .

It's over. My life is cut off. I am alone against an enormous machine, a terrible, evil machine that wants to crush me.

Lubyanka Prison

The cell inside Lubyanka prison looked like a hotel room. A polished parquet floor. A large window. Five beds occupied, and a sixth one empty. But the window is covered with a screen. In the corner there is a slop bucket. In the door they have cut out a small window and a peep hole.

They brought me there in the middle of the night when everyone in the cell was asleep, and they pointed out the bed to me. Lying down on it seemed as unthinkable as falling asleep on a red-hot stove. I was eager to talk with my neighbors immediately, to find out from them how the investigation would go and what lay ahead of me. I hadn't yet learned how to endure in silence. No one spoke to me. All of them turned toward the wall, away from the light, and continued to sleep. I sat down on the bed, and the night dragged on, and my heart was breaking . . .

There were still two hours to go until wake-up time, but I shall never forget them.

Finally at six o'clock they knocked on the door—time to get up.

I jump up, sure that today they will summon me and everything will be explained. I will manage to prove to them that my husband and I are not guilty. I will convince them that they cannot take away my children, that I am innocent . . .

The first truth I took in was that patience is the most important thing to learn in prison. They may summon me today or in a week or in a month, and no one, ever, will explain anything to me.

When I realized this (the first two or three days I expected they would summon me at any minute, but they only called me on the fifth day), I began to look around and get acquainted with my neighbors. I first turned my attention to Zhenia Bykhovskaia because of her foreign dress, which was black with red trim.

"Now here is a real spy!" I thought, seeing how she washed with a foreign sponge and wore some sort of elegant underwear. Zhenia had a nervous tick that spoiled her face.

"I myself won't despair," I thought. "For me everything will be explained, but you've landed in a mess, and it shows in your face."

As I later found out, Zhenia had worked in the underground in Fascist Germany and had to leave because of a serious illness that caused unexpected fainting spells and made it impossible for her to stay in the underground. Once she lost consciousness in the street with Party documents on her person. She was rescued by a Communist doctor to whom she was taken by chance. In 1934, they sent her to the Soviet Union for a cure, but in 1936, she was arrested. One of the main reasons for arresting her was that she had avoided the Gestapo too easily, especially by fainting in the street. Evidently she must have had connections there.

I didn't know all of that, and I looked at her with abhorrence and malicious pleasure.

I felt more at ease when comparing myself with *real* criminals. Compared with them, I seemed so innocent and clean that not only an intelligent and gifted investigator dealing with my case but even a child could see that I was guilty of nothing.

My neighbor on the right, Alexandra Mikhailovna Rozhkova, a sweet-faced woman of about thirty-five, already had a five-year sentence. She had already spent three years in a camp, and now she had been brought here for a new investigation because of her Trotskyite husband, whom they connected with the murder of Kirov.

In the morning Alexandra Mikhailovna carefully washed, dried, and sewed a white collar onto her blouse because she expected to be summoned for an interrogation that day.

She was telling me about the camp, where she hadn't lived badly because she was allowed to work as a doctor, and in passing mentioned her son, the same age as mine, who had been left with a woman friend.

"What! You had a son left behind? You haven't seen him for three years?"

How could this woman be so interested in her collar and ask me what was playing in the Moscow theaters!

I was horrified, since I hadn't yet been to the camps. I had the stupidity and cruelty to say to her:

"You probably don't love your son as much as I love mine. I wouldn't be able survive without him for three years."

She looked at me coldly and answered:

"Oh, you'll survive even ten years without him, and you too will only be interested in food and clothing, and you too will fight for a small basin in the bathhouse and for a warm corner in the barracks. And remember now that everyone suffers in the same way. Here last night you groaned and twisted and disturbed your neighbors' sleep, but Sonia (she was across from me) hadn't been allowed to sleep for ten nights in a row, and that was the only night she had gotten sleep. And you woke me up, and I couldn't fall back to sleep until the morning, and I thought about my son who, according to you, I don't love as much as you love yours, and for me it was terribly painful."

This was a good lesson. I have remembered my whole life that we all feel the same pain when our living flesh is cut.

Sonia, whom Alexandra Mikhailovna told me hadn't slept for ten nights, was a pleasant twenty-seven-year-old brunette from Riga. Fate had sent her to Berlin where she married the Trotskyite Olberg, who was also from Riga. She divorced him in 1932 and, with a new husband, a Soviet citizen, returned to Moscow. While she was Olberg's wife, she and he had led Russian-language circles for German engineers, who were going to work in Moscow. About a hundred people attended these conversation circles. They were unemployed, pro-Soviet people who dreamed of Russia as the Promised Land. They worked in Russia in 1932 and 1933. It's possible that there might have been real spies and terrorists among them, but Sonia would have been the last to know this. All the same she seemed to be the main witness against them. For three months she had been summoned for interrogation every night, had been kept with the investigator until five in the morning, had been given one hour to sleep, and was never permitted to lie down during the day. She was a rather weak-willed woman, without character, and not very bright. They argued with her using uncomplicated sophisms that seemed irrefutable to her. The interrogations went something like this:

"Was Olberg a Trotskyite?"

"Yes."

"Did he lead conversations in the Russian-language circles?"

"Yes, he gave his students practice in the Russian language."

"As a Trotskyite he couldn't help but explain all events from a Trotskyite point of view?"

"Yes."

"Are Trotskyites terrorists?"

"I don't know."

A fist banged on the table.

"You are protecting Trotskyites! You yourself must be a Trotskyite! Do you know what I am going to do with you? You will be happy when they finally shoot you! Your husband"—they meant her second, much-loved husband—"will be arrested for his connection with you. I advise you to bear in mind that you were in the Komsomol and you should help the investigation. And so—are Trotskyites terrorists?"

And Sonia signed.

"Yes."

And then face-to-face confrontations with the Germans would begin that went like this: They would bring her into the investigator's office where some Karl or Friedrich sat crazily, understanding nothing. He would throw himself toward her and say:

"Frau Olberg, please confirm that I was only studying the Russian language in your circle!"

The investigator would pose the question:

"You affirm that Karl so-and-so was a participant in the Olberg circle?"

Sonia would answer:

"Yes."

Karl would sign:

"Yes."

The face-to-face confrontation ended, a quiet Karl would go back to his cell without realizing that he had signed his own death warrant. Sonia would return to the cell in tears and say:

"That's the seventieth person for whom I gave false evidence, but I couldn't do anything else."

It was easy to get her to cooperate.

Zhenia Goltsman was thirty-eight years old. She had joined the Party in the early days of the Revolution.

Her husband, the writer Ivan Philipchenko, had been brought up by Maria Ilinichna Ulianova, and he was quite at home with the Ulianov family. He shared their dislike of Stalin. On this question there were endless collisions and battles between Zhenia and him, leading her to despair because only two people in the world were dearer than life to her: her husband, who brought her into the Revolution and whom she considered to be a most honest Communist and talented writer, and Stalin, whom she worshipped.

After Philipchenko's arrest, Zhenia was called in for an interrogation while she was still at liberty, but then they arrested her and began to interrogate her every day. She came back from the interrogations in a gloomy state, never telling her cellmates about anything that had happened. When my neighbors educated me about how to behave during the investigation, they told me not to say a lot, because you could get tangled up and not be able to get out of it. They advised me to pay attention to the way the investigator wrote down my answers, so that I wouldn't sign something that was completely different from what I had said. Zhenia would harshly interrupt them and tell me:

"Remember that if you are a true Soviet, you should help the investigation to uncover this terrible plot. It seems to me that insignificant things may often give a clue to the investigation. You must speak the whole truth and believe that they will not condemn the innocent."

But once Zhenia came back from the investigation in tears, with red blotches on her face, and asked for a piece of paper to write a letter to Stalin. On that day she didn't hold back and shared with me what had happened. Zhenia not only had advised me to speak the whole truth in the investigation but she herself considered it her Party duty not to hide anything from the investigator. Thus she passed on all Philipchenko's opinions about Stalin, as well as everything that was also said about Stalin in Gorki Leninskie. They jumped on what Zhenia said. She was given a very highly qualified investigator, who appealed to her at first as a Party member, invoking her Party conscience, and then when the investigator had heard all of Philipchenko's interesting opinions, he summarized them and composed a final protocol stating that Philipchenko planned to kill Stalin. This last protocol Zhenia would not sign because it was rather a long way from Philipchenko's stating the opinion that the country would breathe easier when Stalin was dead (as reflected in his frequent words, "if only he would vanish") to the intention of committing a terrorist act.

Now when Zhenia had signed all but this final evidence against Philipchenko, the investigator changed tactics and began to abuse her, yelling at her, and even hitting her. Zhenia was shocked by this and for several whole days wrote letters to Stalin about these violations of the rules of investigation.

Philipchenko, of course, was doomed, regardless of whether Zhenia signed the final protocol, but she couldn't bear the thought that they would show her evidence to him and that he would die in the conviction that she had betrayed him. Having voluntarily signed all the previous evidence, she struggled with them so as not to sign this last protocol. They also began to interrogate her at night, and during the day they wouldn't let her sleep and put her in a detention cell. Then suddenly they left her in peace, and after several days someone knocked on the wall, informing us that Philipchenko had been shot and had asked them to tell his comrades that he died an honest Communist. Zhenia was devastated. In addition to all the horrors that had occurred, she was most deeply tortured by the fact that he hadn't sent final greetings to her. That meant he knew she had reported that terrible evidence against him.

The fourth inhabitant of our cell was Zina Stanitsyna, a twenty-eight-year-old girl. Before her arrest she had taught mathematics in a college in Gorky.

I asked her what she had been accused of, and she told me she was justly arrested and was very guilty.

"What did you do?" I asked.

"I made a mistake about one of our teachers. He lived in Moscow and came to Gorky once a week to give a lecture on dialectical materialism. With me he was very outspoken and talked of many things very critically. To me this seemed a sign of the highest intelligence and concern for his country.

"He spent the night in a student dormitory and kept his things in my apartment. He also brought comrades around to visit. I was amazed at the weight of his suitcases. He had said there were books in them; however, in the investigation he said he was a Trotskyite, that there was Trotskyite literature in the suitcases, and that the people who came to see him were members of the opposition. So it turned out that my apartment had been a secret meeting place."

I listened to Zina with respect. She was principled and without self-pity. But the conclusion to her story filled me with amazement.

"I decided to bear the punishment and not let there be even the slightest stain on my conscience. I remembered that Professor N. (I don't remember his family name) presented a lecture for mathematics teachers. While he was showing a theorem on the blackboard, the electricity went out. There was neither kerosene lamp nor candles. I split a ruler and made a little torch of the kindling. The professor ended his demonstration by the light of a splinter and said, 'Life has become better, life has become more joyful now, thank God, as we work by the light of a splinter!' This was obviously a mocking joke against Stalin, meant to discredit him."

"And you communicated this to the investigator?"

"Of course!"

"And you didn't reproach yourself for his arrest?"

"Later when the professor was called into my investigation and we had a one-on-one confrontation, I felt quite uncomfortable."

"Did he acknowledge his guilt?

"At the beginning he denied it, but then he said he had completely forgotten this event, since it hadn't had any significance for him."

"But you ruined a human life for such a small thing!"

"In politics there are no small things. At the beginning I too didn't understand all the criminality in his remark, but later I recognized it!"

I was shaken. Alexandra Mikhailovna Rozhkova's rich experience added to this conversation (and she had already been in the camps for three years):

"Well, the main thing is to cast suspicion on a person, and then probably they will discover even more sins. If you are human, they'll make a case against you."

I didn't want to talk anymore with Zina, but a crack opened up in my decision to help the investigation and be fully open . . .

The Investigation

I spent five days waiting for my first interrogation.

Having seen and heard so much, I had lost some of the optimism with which I had prepared myself to show that my husband and I were completely innocent. But all the same I thought I was a completely different kind of person from my neighbors in the prison cell, who were connected with some very important people and had been drawn into the political struggle.

I am not a Party member, nor is my husband, whose major focus in life is science. Perhaps there is some kind of plot, but why do I have to answer for it?

I imagined the investigator would be intelligent and refined, like Porfiry from *Crime and Punishment*. I put myself in his position and was sure I would realize who was standing before me in two seconds and would quickly let that kind of person go free.

Finally they called me. I ended up with a completely nondescript investigator who was about twenty-five years old. The interrogation office was small and not at all luxurious. Probably during the day there was a real office here. Two fishing rods stood in the corner, since my investigator apparently planned to go fishing after his night's work.

After the first set of questions, the investigator wrote down: "I confess that my husband was a Trotskyite, and there were Trotskyite gatherings in our home."

I wrote: "No."

So we sat there all night long. The investigator said in a bored voice:

"Think about it, confess," and he looked at his watch. Within ten minutes he again said, "Think about it," and again looked at his watch. While I was thinking, he walked around the office, went up to the fishing rods several times, and adjusted something.

The investigator's next question was:

"What have you heard about the death of Allilueva? How did she die?"

I answered calmly and truthfully:

"She died of appendicitis. I read about it in *Pravda*."

The investigator pounded the table with his fist.

"You are lying! You heard something completely different! I have information!"

And suddenly I remembered with horror that a month or two ago I was visiting the old Bolshevik Tronin, whom I deeply respected. One of the guests, Rozovsky, told us that Allilueva had shot herself after Stalin coarsely interrupted her in front of guests when she stood up for Bukharin. This Rozovsky (he was the director of a department store) was arrested before me because of some sort of embezzlement of funds, so we thought. He could of course have told his interrogator that this conversation about Allilueva's death had taken place in my presence.

I felt terrified. Tronin and his family would be prosecuted for spreading anti-Soviet rumors. And then . . . "If you are human, they'll make a case against you." Yes, I already had said that I hadn't heard any conversation about Allilueva's death. And perhaps Rozovsky hadn't talked about it with the interrogator. My whole determination not to hide anything from the investigators completely vanished. I answered: "I read in *Pravda* that she died from appendicitis," and I trembled with fear that Rozovsky had talked about Allilueva's suicide in his investigation and that I would then seem like a liar.

Finally the investigator said:

"Think about it in your cell. You understand that only a pure-hearted confession will give you the chance to see your children again. Obstinate denial characterizes you as a professional political fighter. Go away and think about it."

I returned to the cell at five thirty in the morning.

Alexandra Mikhailovna and Sonia said that, according to all the signs, the authorities would view me as a very minor criminal, and I would receive a sentence of three to five years in the camps. Zhenia said they would free me. They argued over these possibilities, but I had turned to ice inside: all this was so far from the intelligent and fair-minded investigation I had expected! For the first time I realized the real possibility that they might condemn me and that I would lose my children.

And I again began to wish that they would call me back and that I could explain to them that I was innocent. The thought of Rozovsky and his version of Allilueva's death didn't go away. I couldn't sleep all night and trembled with fear.

Within two weeks they really did call me back, and everything repeated itself all over again, including the fishing poles, with which the investigator busied himself and which played on my nerves. There was no conversation about Rozovsky, and I realized that he had said nothing about me.

Two months later they called me back a third time, and the investigator showed me a protocol signed in my husband's hand where, in response to the question of whether he was a Trotskyite, my husband had answered, "Yes."

"How can this be!" I shrieked. "It is not true!"

"Of course it is true, but he certainly gave us a hard time before we beat the confession out of him!"

At this the investigator smiled a crooked smile, and I realized that they must have beaten and tortured my husband, if he had signed such a statement. I shuddered and for a moment I had the feeling I might faint. Then I realized one thing and it made me feel proud of him, full of love for him: he did not testify against me in any way, no matter how much the investigators beat him, no matter how much they tormented him! And I swore to myself that I would never sign a lying testimony against him, especially since, after his "confession," it would have no meaning.

Again I sat through six hours. This time the investigator shouted, beat his fist on the table, called me a political prostitute, promised me that I would never see my children again, and that they would be put in an orphanage to isolate them from the influence of my degenerate family. I feared this more than anything because in orphanages they changed the children's last names, and so they could never be found again. That was what they said in our cell. I think the investigators spread these rumors in order to threaten us even more.

And again I returned to the cell, and again waited, but they did not call me back.

The investigation had ended.

I had been *unmasked*.

The investigator presented materials to the court in which he proved that I was a criminal, liable for the most severe, the most agonizing punishment and expulsion from life.

He was younger than I. He lives somewhere today. His conscience probably does not trouble him. In fact he *fulfilled his duty*!

Methods of Investigation

Now I understand that I was very lucky in my investigation. It took place at the beginning of 1936, when women were beaten only if their crime was considered very important for the investigation. But in 1936 they didn't feel uncomfortable about manipulating maternal feelings to accomplish their despicable goals. They only threatened that they would put my children in different orphanages, they would change their last name, and I would never be able to find them again.

In 1937, investigative methods became even more brutal.

My friend Raia Ginzburg was the wife of an old Communist, an active participant in the October Revolution. She herself had joined the Party in 1917 and had taken part in the October uprising. Up until 1937, her husband was among the leaders in the Chelyabinsk region, where I think he was, in fact, the first secretary of the Party Committee for the region. In 1937, they arrested Raia and him, indicting them with the terrible crimes of treason, espionage, terror, and God knows what else. They tormented Raia, trying to make her sign testimony against her husband, but she stoically and categorically refused to do this. Finally they engaged her in the ultimate battle: one terrible night her seven-day questioning began (we called these interrogations *conveyor belts*). The investigators changed, but she had to endure seven days and nights without sleep, defending herself against their gang. On the seventh day the investigator went out but didn't close the door to the neighboring room. Raia heard the voice of her fourteen-year-old son, Alik, who was somehow trying to prove his innocence. The investigator yelled, "You lie, you scoundrel! Will you speak the truth? I will destroy you!" And more of the same. Then it seemed to her that they shut his mouth, and she heard the sound of blows. This went on for about ten minutes. Then the boss of the GPU came into the investigator's office where Raia sat, half dead and half alive. This person had been a frequent visitor to her home and had seemed to her to be a decent man. He said to her, "Raisa Grigorevna, you heard? Well, listen. Sign the testimony against your husband, and I give you my word that tomorrow I will send Alik to his aunt in Moscow. Otherwise I can't help either you or him."

Raia, driven almost to insanity after seven days and nights of interrogation and fear for her son, signed the testimony against her husband and herself without looking.

After 1956 I got together with Alik. I asked him what had happened to him in the NKVD office. He said they called him in and began to swear at him for going to the family of some friends of his arrested parents. He had cut wood, brought water, and generally helped them, distracting them from their grief. The investigator yelled at him, scolded him, and then drove him away. The next day they really did send him to his aunt in Moscow. Apparently they beat the sofa with a stick and not him.

I ask myself why was it necessary to torment people so, to commit such crimes against the human conscience, when they could have forged our signatures. Apparently it was important to preserve this testimony for posterity as a justification for their crimes. Not for nothing was it written in our files, "Keep forever."

In the Butyrka prison where they took me at the end of my interrogation, I met a young woman whose name was Zlata (I don't remember her last name). Three months earlier Zlata had given birth to twins. Her husband had been arrested. They let Zlata stay with the babies and feed them for three months. The little girls got sick, not surprisingly. (Their mother was constantly crying. What kind of milk could she give?) One of the twins died. She was two-and-a-half months old. The other was still sick. But then the three months were up, and they arrested Zlata. In the interrogation they demanded that she sign testimony against her husband that had nothing to do with how things really were. She continued to refuse. Zlata then asked the investigator to tell her if her little daughter was alive, if she had recovered or not. There was only one answer: "Sign the testimony against your husband, and then I will answer you."

Zlata signed nothing.

A Mother's Gift

A mother and a daughter arrived in our cell. This was the only time when for some reason they didn't separate relatives. The mother was seventy years old, and the daughter was forty.

The mother was the granddaughter of a Decembrist who was sent into exile in Siberia. The mother was a neat, clean old woman who was good at housework and was very religious. She looked around attentively and waved her hands in surprise. She would hear some grievous tale, shrug her shoulders, and say, "Listen, we'd better drink tea with rusk! I've dried it on the heater." And the bread was carefully cut with a thread (there are no knives in prison), dried out, and sprinkled with salt.

Her daughter, Tamara Konstantinovna, was a doctor. One felt her to be her mother's type in every way: contained, calm on the outside, always very neat and orderly. And holding onto herself was absolutely necessary: she was being charged with violating the eighth point (which relates to terrorism)—a serious offense. The investigator had sworn to force her to confess and turned the whole arsenal available to him onto her. They threatened her, beat her, and for five to eight days she sat in a cold cell with only bread and water as punishment for being rude in the investigation and not answering their questions. They called her every night, and by day they wouldn't let her sleep. Poor Tamara Konstantinovna would come in at eight o'clock in the morning and, sitting with her back against the door, would start to fall asleep. At that very moment came a cry, "Don't sleep!" She suffered that way for days on end. Her mother and all of us tried to screen her from the peephole, but they drove us away.

After lights-out in the evening, Tamara would only just have lain down when a key would clank and the voice of the duty officer would say, "Prepare yourself for the interrogation." In spite of all her self-control, her face changed, and tears fell from her eyes. And her mother blessed her and whispered, "Be brave!"

The affair of the daughter turned out badly, even though she had not signed a single protocol. There was much senseless testimony against her, clearly beaten out of the witnesses, but fully sufficient to give her fifteen years. (In the end that's what she got.)

But for some reason they decided to let the mother go free. Why that was, no one knew. The paths of interrogation are inscrutable. But through a whole series of signs it was clear that they were going to free her. And so one day the chief officer came into the cell and called for our old woman to gather her things. We realized that they were going to free her (and so it turned out). Our dear old woman gave away all her things—her comb to someone, her toothbrush to someone else, her warm socks to another. To her daughter she gave all the very best things, and then made the sign of the cross over her and said, "I bless you with a mother's blessing, and I permit you, if the situation turns out very badly, to take your own life. You don't have to torment yourself. I will answer to God for your sin!" Tamara Konstantinovna kissed her hand, and her mother made the sign of the cross over her, prayed, and her face was so wonderful and bright that it seemed as if she had given life to her daughter and not permission to die.

Butyrka Prison in 1936

One evening, after I had been at Lubyanka for four months, the little window in the door opened and the duty officer said:

"Sliozberg, get your things together."

Zhenia Goltsman came up to me: "You see, I was right, you are going free. I am happy for you. Remember the rest of us left behind here."

We kissed each other. Zhenia was a very good person. She was really happy, thinking I was going to be released. But the others were somewhat jealous. I know this from my own experience: I could be happy for a comrade who was lucky, and at the same time my heart hurt more for myself.

Zhenia Bykhovskaia wasn't in our cell anymore. Her investigation had ended, and they had taken her somewhere else.

Alexandra Mikhailovna was sure I was not being released but was being taken to another cell. Sonia was silent.

We said good-bye and I went out. I was escorted to the courtyard and put into a Black Maria. If you don't know what that is, I will explain: It is a closed green van for moving prisoners around. Inside, the van is divided into separate compartments for individuals; the compartments are so narrow that people with long legs have to pull them in. Otherwise they might get caught in the door. In 1937, these vans were so familiar that in one school when the first graders were asked, "What color is a crow?" they answered in unison, "Green."

And so the guards pushed me into a separate compartment. I couldn't see where we were going. I trembled all over. Somewhere deep inside me the foolish hope still flickered that they would take me home and set me free. The Black Maria stopped. We got out in the courtyard of Butyrka. It was a moonlit August evening. In the first courtyard there were several large linden trees whose leaves gleamed in the moonlight. It had only been four months since I had seen trees, and yet my heart ached so painfully that I almost collapsed. They led me to the second courtyard, bare and gloomy, and then into the prison building, where they handed over my documents in a closed packet, registered me, and led me into a cell.

The cell was enormous with water-stained, arched walls. On both sides of the narrow passage were wooden shelflike bunks, packed with bodies: between the bunks were ropes hanging with rags. Everything was dim in the smoky darkness. It was noisy; some voices fought and yelled, others cried.

I stopped in confusion, holding my suitcase and my bundled kerchief. A pregnant woman, the head woman of the cell, came up to me.

"Don't be afraid," she said. "Here almost everyone is a political prisoner just like you. I myself am a weaver from Trekhgorka. My name is Katia Nikolaeva."

We shook hands: "You must lie down near the slop bucket. Here that's the rule for newcomers."

In the corner stood a huge reeking wooden bucket. Around it on the bunks nearby was some free space. I was already settling in when I noticed two free spaces on both sides of a woman with long black braids who was sleeping in the opposite corner of the cell near a window.

"And would it be possible for me to lie near the window?" I asked Katia.

Katia hesitated slightly but answered:

"Well, why not, lie down, only the neighbor there is not very nice."

I went to the window and lay down.

My neighbor, Ania, apparently was glad to see me. At this moment they brought in a kettle of hot water. I had some sugar and biscuits; I invited her to share them with me and started asking her about the people lying on the bunks. Ania said something very nasty about each of them. In her opinion the cell was full of criminals.

Suddenly I noticed Zhenia Bykhovskaia on the opposite bunk. During the four months we had lived together I had come to love her, and nothing remained of my previous conviction that she was a spy.

"And do you know that woman?" I asked Ania.

"Oh, that is a despicable spy. I could kill her with my own hands."

After this conversation I walked over to Zhenia. From nearsightedness she had not noticed me earlier, but when she recognized me she kissed me and let me sleep near her. I quietly moved my things and lay down next to Zhenia. Ania looked at me maliciously and again was left alone with three bunks around her.

"What kind of a person is she?" I asked Zhenia.

"She is the former wife of K. He was a 'red professor,' a very interesting person. He left her and in recent years lived in Leningrad. Out of revenge she wrote a denunciation against him, saying that he was a secret Trotskyite and double-dealer. They arrested him and at the same time arrested her, too, because earlier she had not told them about his sins. Now she writes denunciations of everyone in the cell, and no one will speak to her. They brought you here, and that must mean your case is finished. Too bad. I had hoped they would free you. Now you'll have to wait for a sentence. For me I don't expect less than ten years. But with you the case is simpler. Probably you'll get away with five."

When Zhenia invited me to lie beside her, a neighbor, Motia, welcomed me in a friendly way. She pushed away two of her neighbors, Nina and Valia, saying:

"Never mind, we're crowded, but there's always room for one more, because, you see, these old friends just bumped into each other."

Thanks to Motia's interference, a gap of about forty centimeters opened up between the bodies on the bunk where I could squeeze in. This was sufficient for me, but one thing disturbed me: we lay like sardines, head to head, but on Motia's cheeks there were some terrible black spots, eliciting an involuntary repulsion. Although Zhenia told me they were not infectious, I couldn't help trying to cover my face with my shawl. Motia noticed this.

"Don't be afraid," she said to me. "I am not infectious. I got frostbite on my cheeks."

These spots were very grievous and depressing for Motia. For hours she massaged her face as Nina had taught her and then asked if the spots were paler, since of course we were not permitted to have mirrors.

Motia was able to read but, as she expressed it, she wasn't used to it. She felt sorry for me because I read all day long.

"But you should rest," she said, and was amazed when I assured her that I could only rest with a book. When she wasn't fussing with her cheeks, Motia herself lay on her bunk the whole day with closed eyes and listened to Nina and Valia's conversations. Both of them were beautiful and young—not more than thirty. Nina was the wife of an important military man, and Valia the wife of the regional Party Committee secretary. They had become very good friends, and all day they reminisced about their former lives, which seemed to them completely resplendent, as was often true for many arrested people. They forgot everything bad and forgot all the difficulties and pain that of course had occurred. They thought Motia was sleeping, but she listened intently, and from time to time she turned to me, communicating her observations in a whisper:

"And Nina had a maid; her mother-in-law stayed home and still they had a maid."

"But she worked and had a child at home."

"Well, an eight-year-old kid and a granny at home. No, they were simply spoiled people!"

Another time Valia described a funny situation when an important but undesirable guest had come to their home. She hid from him in the children's room, and her husband locked himself in his study and fell asleep. The guest drank tea with the mother-in-law, and then went out on the balcony to smoke, but her husband came out of his study at that moment and said, "Well, the old windbag finally left!" Motia laughed with everyone at this, her narrow black eyes glittering slyly, and she whispered into my ear:

"There were four rooms."

"Why four? There was a children's room, a study and a living room—that's three in all."

"No, the mother-in-law had a separate one. She told Nina that her mother-in-law was capricious and didn't want to sleep in the same room with the child. So they gave her their own bedroom, and they themselves had to sleep in the living room. That's the way the big shots lived!"

Nina told Valia that one time when she and her husband were at a resort, the nanny bought their daughter Nelli a long red velvet coat and a black fur cap, reflecting the nanny's own taste.

"I didn't recognize my daughter," said Nina. "She was such an elegant little girl, but here she had been turned into a real little Russian doll, a *matrioshka*. I went out right away and bought her a short fur coat, and I made the nanny give that ugly coat away to somebody so it wouldn't be in my house."

Motia whistled.

"Did you hear?" she whispered, "They gave away a new velvet coat and fur hat! That's how they lived! Nina had three fur coats: a sealskin, a white one, and she has a fox fur coat here. And Nina had a lover!"

"How do you know? Did she tell you?"

"She told Valia. She was at a resort without her husband, and the lover arrived, saying, 'I missed you. The city is empty without you!' But then her husband also arrived. And that other guy got back into his car in the middle of the night—and away he went. Look, one guy isn't enough. She had to have a lover. These bosses knew how to live!"

"Yes, but why do you call them all bosses? Couldn't I have been a boss too?"

"No, your husband is a teacher. That's a working man. But these guys are bosses."

She didn't like the bosses! I must say that she had several good reasons for this. Throughout the eighteen years of her life, she had had more than one run-in with bosses, and every time these collisions brought her no small amount of grief.

Motia was twelve years old when her peaceful childhood in a village near Tarusa came to an end. She remembered a childhood filled with mushrooms and strawberries—a childhood spent splashing all day in the river Oka with the other children and going for nighttime hayrides. She remembered a splendid grandmother, who was the best singer and story-teller in the village. She studied easily and happily in school.

"I was very bright in arithmetic and also good with my hands. I could fix the fuse box and the electric burner. I got water piped from the stream to the schoolyard. The teacher loved me and called me "Edisonchik, Edisonchik."

This life ended in 1929, when Motia's parents were identified as kulaks, and exiled to the northern Urals with three children, the oldest of whom was Motia. They were taken into the forest there in September, dropped off, and told to build a place to live. A slushy rain fell, the women wailed, and the children cried. Somehow or other they dug underground mud huts and put together clay ovens. There was no livestock, and there was nothing to feed the children. In the first year the middle girl died. Her father and mother went to work cutting down trees, and Motia was left doing the housework.

"It's boring there," said Motia. "The summer is rainy and short, and the winter is fierce. There's no school. Mother and father are working from morning until night, and I am looking after my little brother, keeping the oven warm, melting water from snow, but it's damp, dirty, and smoky in the mud hut. Not many children around, and all of them are working from morning to night, too. It gets dark early. There's no kerosene. I'm sitting there with a little torch and a small smoky lamp with a wick, and my little brother is constantly catching colds and coughing."

That's the way Motia survived until 1935, the year she turned seventeen, but, like all the other kulaks, she was refused a passport at that age. Things were bad at home. Her father walked around as gloomy as a cloud. Her mother and younger brother were always sick. Motia went to work cutting down trees with her father, and her mother stayed home with her brother. But in 1935, after the murder of Kirov, her father got drunk and said, "It wouldn't be so bad to bump off all the bosses so they wouldn't torment people anymore."

"They arrested my father, and my mother just coughed and coughed, and next winter both my mother and brother died. And then it got so sickening for me, so boring, that I decided to run away, back to my grandmother in her village. I didn't have a passport or money. Early in the spring of 1935, I got myself together. I took two pairs of shoes, a package of dry bread, and started off on foot."

In three months Motia walked almost two thousand kilometers. She stayed at night in villages and also in hayricks. At the very beginning of her trip, she spent the night in the forest, slept soundly, and in the morning her cheeks were frostbitten.

One pair of boots broke immediately, and later, if the road wasn't too rough, she went barefoot. In some villages they fed her out of Christian charity, and sometimes she worked for it. And then she arrived. Grandmother cried with joy and couldn't gaze at her Motia enough. And truly, if it weren't for her cheeks, Motia looked good at eighteen years of age. She was small, strong as a hazelnut, well built, with slyly glittering black eyes, a benign sense of humor, and a good spirit. Her grandmother fed her, caressed her, daubed her feet with warm lard, dressed her up, slept in the same bed with her, and wouldn't let her into the street, fearing that someone would see her who should not . . . And even so the authorities soon found out. She only lived with her grandmother for a week, and then they came and arrested her for a violation of passport regulations. She said:

"But all the same I'm not sorry I ran away. In the camps there are lots of people. There are even movies sometimes, and it won't be any worse there than it was in the forest!"

Yes, poor dear Motia! For you it won't be any worse anywhere.

So I came to live in cell 105 and wait for sentencing. I lived there for three months, took a closer look at things, and more or less figured out who its residents were.

Before it had seemed to me that if I lost my children, nothing else in life could interest me, but now the enormity of the pain surrounding me pulled me out of an immersion in my own fate and made me think about other people.

Of the hundred women in our cell, there was one old Socialist Revolutionary (SR), two Georgian Mensheviks, and two Trotskyites. All five of them had been in prisons and in exile for eight to fifteen years. Now they had been brought out of political isolation for reinvestigation. For these people the question of their relationship with the government and especially with the NKVD had been decided long ago: they were enemies with whom one must fight. For the Trotskyites, the most important enemy was Stalin, whom they called *Papulya*, and they would mockingly ask us, "Why doesn't *Papulya* help you, since you love him so much?"

The SR and the Mensheviks simply despised Stalin and considered him a fool, but they also detested Lenin who, in their opinion, had destroyed democracy and thus opened the path to all the lawlessness.

The year 1936, from their point of view, was only a detail. They were actually somewhat glad because their most terrible predictions were turning out to be true.

For them the situation was morally easier. Everything was clear and in its place. It was also easier for them because they had gotten used to the terrible daily existence of prison life. All their ties with freedom had been cut, they didn't have either children or parents, and their husbands had been killed long ago or, like them, were wandering around from prison to prison.

They talked about cities from the point of view of the prisons in them. For example:

"Do you like Orel?"

"Are you kidding! Stone floors and a high fence around the courtyard."

"And Samara?"

"The city isn't bad, but they only let you wash yourself for fifteen minutes in the bathhouse."

They knew how to stand up for their rights, they knew all the rules, and the prison authorities were a little bit afraid of them. The authorities would immediately put them on special diets and if necessary would send them to the hospital.

These women talked about politics as if it were all completely clear: the Revolution had died ten years ago (the Mensheviks and the SR said fifteen years ago), the country was going to collapse, and the faster it happened the better.

They laughed when people told them of the stupidities of industrial leaders. (I didn't tell them how in Tashkent a machine had been invented that had been in use for ten years in Nevele.) They were sure that if war broke out, Soviet power would tumble down like a house of cards.

With secret pleasure they met newly arrested groups of people, especially Communists, who had once persecuted them and now would have to share prison bunks with them.

Listening to their conversations I noticed how poorly they knew the Soviet people of our time and even the details of our daily life. But how could they know our life, since they had observed it from behind prison bars for so long?

I watched them but so much did not want to become like them. I was so afraid that my only memories would be of prisons and my only hopes would be for a nice political prison with a good library and a little courtyard to walk around in.

Except for these five women, the other ninety-five people in the cell were all convinced they were innocent. Just a few, the most seasoned Party members, refrained from talking about their cases. The rest had an irresistible need to talk, to tell, to advise, and to ask for opinions about what lay ahead for them.

A great many had simply been slandered. Others were guilty without being aware of it. Certainly it never entered anyone's head that telling or listening to a joke that was familiar to all Muscovites could in fact lead to a sentence, according to article 58, point 10, of the Criminal Code of the Soviet Constitution, in other words, *agitation against the Soviet government*, and was punishable by deprivation of freedom for up to ten years. No one thought that if a man were alone with his wife and spoke badly of, let's say, Kaganovich or Molotov or, God forbid, Stalin, his wife would be obligated to communicate this to the NKVD. If she did not, she had committed a crime according to article 58, point 12 (the crime of *not reporting*), and could be deprived of her freedom for eight years.

No one considered that there could be such consequences from acquaintance with former *oppositionists:* they were permitted to live and work again in Moscow, and many of them were even restored to membership in the Party, so why could one not mix with them?

At the beginning I tried not to believe the grievous tales told to me. Certainly if all of them were as innocent as I was, then horrible sabotage had taken place. That meant the newspapers lied, leaders lied in their speeches, and the judicial system lied. No, this could not be! Somewhere, in the buildings for solitary confinement, in the men's cells, these cursed conspirators were imprisoned. Because of them everything had gotten so mixed up, and now one could not distinguish between the innocent and the guilty. But I also could not disbelieve these people. I could not disbelieve it when the old woman Pinson told me how she had been brought face-to-face with Muratov:

"I demanded a confrontation with him. The investigator brought me to the office. A kind of old gray-haired man with darting eyes sat there.

Only when he began to speak did I realize this was Muratov. (Muratov was thirty-three years old.) I threw myself on him:

"'Andrei Alexeevich, say that all of this isn't true, say that I was never in a terrorist organization.'

"And suddenly, can you imagine, he says to me, 'Ah, Sophia Solomonovna, there is no use denying your guilt! I already confessed that you and I wanted to kill Kaganovich together. I advise you to confess it too.'

"Can you imagine? I wanted to kill Kaganovich! I couldn't kill a chicken, but I could kill Kaganovich?"

I couldn't disbelieve Zhenia Volkova.

They had sent her as a top student from Gorky to Moscow for the May Day demonstration. Back in Gorky she had the bad luck of being one of the best shots in her riflery school. Someone denounced her, saying that at the demonstration she was planning to kill Stalin. She did know how to shoot a rifle, but how she could have carried a rifle to the demonstration was completely incomprehensible.

Zhenia cried for days and feared for her mother, who had a weak heart. Politics had never interested Zhenia at all, and dialectical materialism was the most difficult subject in school for her because the teacher required that students read the newspaper. She was interested in music, her schoolwork, and one special boy, a very idealistic member of the Komsomol, who "will now despise me because he is ready to give up his life for his country, and they'll say I'm a traitor."

I couldn't disbelieve Sophia Solomonovna or Zhenia because I saw their eyes, heard their moans at night, felt their pain and confusion. And I gave up trying to be vigilant, which everyone recommended, even Zhenia Bykhovskaia, and I began to believe my eyes, my heart.

The most unhappy people in prison were the Communists.

They took upon themselves the role of voluntary defenders of the NKVD.

They assured everyone that there was a huge counterrevolutionary conspiracy in the country, and if there were admittedly mistakes with its liquidation, then *if you cut down a forest, wood chips fly*. They said one had to cut out the gangrenous section, along with the living tissue, in order to save the organism.

When they were asked why one had to beat people and force them to give false evidence during the investigations, they answered, "Well, it must be done," and there was no way to object to that.

All of them were sure that Stalin did not know what was happening in the prisons, and they wrote him endless letters.

Stalin was beyond suspicion; he seemed without sin. Of course he didn't know about all the horrors that were happening. And if he did know, that meant *it must be done.*

So they spoke and so they thought, and every fact of monstrous injustice that they encountered lay on their shoulders twice as heavily. Every fact hit them personally, and they felt obliged to defend its expedience before the non-Party members, before people who were outraged because those facts were so incompatible with Soviet power.

They said one could not believe everyone was innocent and that in this very cell there were many hidden enemies.

As for their own guilt, they accused themselves not of intentional crimes but of a criminal lack of vigilance.

It was very hard for them.

And the hardest of all was that in defending the justice and expediency of the government's activities, they themselves began to lose faith in this justice.

And their lives, from their youngest years on, had been given to the Party.

They were its children, its soldiers.

For them it was very hard.

And now I will tell you what I felt.

This is very important because it's the way that not only I felt but also many, many people who unexpectedly or unluckily ended up behind barbed wire as *enemies of the people.*

My husband always reproached me because I didn't read the newspapers attentively, didn't like social gatherings, and had little interest in politics.

To me the dearest of all were my children, my husband, my home, and literature, too, which I loved with an unreciprocated love. I always wanted to write, but I knew that a writer must somehow know or see more than a reader, and what did I know or see of life?

I frequently grumbled: the apartment is small, there isn't enough of this or that, foreign things are good, and ours are bad.

But now when everything in the world conspired to make me hate our life, when extreme injustice had been committed against me, I realized how well I had lived. How good it had been for me to work and know that I was doing essential, useful work. How good it was for me to raise my children and be sure that all roads were open to them. How confidently I walked on the earth and felt that it was my home, and if things were badly organized or shabby in my home, I was angry about it and complained because it was my home, and I wanted things to be good there, better than in all the rich foreign homes.

How simple, how easy I felt with people! How well I understood their yearnings and their lives. How I believed with all my being that our life was the most just, the most honest. Now all my friends, sisters, brothers, children—all those whom I loved—had remained behind in that life. They were doctors, teachers, engineers, and all of them would serve as soldiers if the time came for war. They built and defended that life, not sparing their strength and health.

Oh, if only at least in my thoughts I could hate that life, then I would be an internal emigrant, my connection broken with all those whom I loved and with all that had been my life.

And everything around me conspired to make me feel hatred. I searched for, but never found anything with which I could oppose the mighty arguments of those who so unjustly shattered my life, those who didn't seek the truth, but forced extortions and distortions, who kept us awake for weeks on end in order to force us to sign lies—they were all Party members. For this monstrous work they received awards and prizes.

Oh, how poorly armed I am! How little I know, how hard it is for me to struggle with the arguments of those who disparage our life and wish for its destruction.

And I kept quiet, painfully reflected, painfully did not want to become an enemy, painfully hoped that justice would triumph, that once again word and deed would be one, that once again I would be able to love our life without conflict or doubt.

One day while I was exercising, an ordinary convict who had been cleaning the yard came up to me and whispered:

"Yagoda has been arrested. Yezhov has taken his place."

I took this news back to the cell, and what hopes it awoke! How excited they became, all those who had predicted that justice would prevail! How everyone began to wait for them to set us free!

But time went by and people received even heavier sentences. Those who would have received three to five years under Yagoda began to receive ten to twelve years. There were even rumors of sentences of twenty-five years.

Gradually the optimists became quieter, and our groundless hopes faded away.

One morning they opened the door and led a young woman into the cell. She had an unusual name—Lira.

Lira came in with confidence, looked around with a sharp glance, and went directly up to Ania.

Someone tried to warn her about Ania, but Lira said boldly, "But I like her."

For three days the new friends conversed all day long. Lira had many tasty bits of food, and she generously shared them with Ania. Ania simply came back to life. A person had finally appeared who valued her.

But within three days Lira collected her things and moved over to a free place not far from Zhenia and me.

She stood on the bunk, shapely, beautiful, provocative, and in a voice that could be heard throughout the cell said to Ania:

"Keep in mind that I have spent three days with you in order to find out what nastiness you wrote about my dear K., who had the misfortune of having once been your husband. You denounced him out of jealousy! Oh, you were right. He exchanged you for me! Ah, how he loved me! What a splendid man he was! Although I ended up in prison because of him, I do not regret that I met him."

Ania threw herself at Lira like a cat, but they stopped her, and she wheezed hoarsely, growled, and snarled, unable to utter a single word.

And Lira threw her arms akimbo, laughed, and even did a little dance.

"Oh, he too does not regret that he threw you over for me! Better to die in prison than to live with such an evil cat! And he loved me for three whole years, and we were happy."

Ania beat herself, snarled, and threw herself around so much that they had to take her to the hospital.

Three days later she came back much quieter, and for days on end she lay there with her eyes closed covering her ears.

It was the evening of November 6, 1936.

They kept bringing newly arrested women into our overcrowded cell. They lay on tables, on the floor under the bunks, and in the passageway.

The majority came in with the usual words: "I'll stay here on the edge of the bunk. They arrested me by mistake and will quickly release me. It's a misunderstanding."

No one paid any attention to these words. Everyone was busy with her own concerns.

They brought in a woman with a huge belly, probably in her ninth month, and made room for her on the bunks. Someone gave her a shawl and another gave her a coat, in order to make the bed softer for her. She lay there with a dark face and gazed in one direction. Around midnight she began to groan and bite her fingers. The birth had begun, so they took her to the hospital.

This made a disturbing impression on everyone. Almost all of us were mothers and could imagine how hard it would be to give birth under such conditions.

And at two in the morning, the door opened, and a thirty-five-year-old woman noisily entered, wearing a flimsy low-cut pink dress, a pretty hairdo, and a flower in her hair.

The woman was sobbing loudly and talking nonstop. From her words we realized that her first husband had been a Trotskyite. He disappeared from her life nine years ago, leaving her with a son, Levochka. The son was a weak, crippled child. For nine years she had waited for her husband, fearing to marry another because he might offend miserable little Levochka.

Finally she decided to get married. On November 5, she moved in with her new husband, and on November 6, they arrested her right at her wedding table.

She rattled on, cried, and screamed incessantly:

"My Levochka, Levochka!"

We were already excited because tomorrow was a holiday, they were bringing in more and more new people, and a birth had begun in our cell. And here was this bride in a pink dress with a flower in her hair, crying out, "My Levochka, Levochka!" Suddenly from a corner of the cell, a woman became hysterical and began to wail:

"My Yura, Yura, my own!"

Immediately other voices began to lament:

"My Irochka!"

"My Mishenka!"

Half the cell broke into hysterics. I covered my head with a kerchief. I fought the almost irrepressible desire to cry out: "My Shurik, my Ellochka!"

But I bit my hand until it bled, covered my ears, and closed my eyes. Next to me Zhenia Bykhovskaia was shaking hard and also kept quiet. We nestled close to each other.

The door opened, the supervisor yelled and dragged away the women who were in hysterics—one to the detention cell, one to the hospital, and one to an empty cell. Within two hours everything had calmed down, and all lay quietly.

November 7, 1936, had arrived.

And on November 9, a notice was delivered to me. I was summoned to the military tribunal of the Supreme Court. Everyone was surprised. My case had seemed so mild, and suddenly I was to be judged by the Supreme Court!

I understood how serious my position was by the change in the faces of the most experienced cellmates. Sonia Ashkenazi was in the cell with us. She was a Trotskyite. I haven't talked about her because she was so quiet all the time, and I didn't know what she was thinking. She was in the last stages of tuberculosis. She tried very carefully not to infect her neighbors, and she ate from separate dishes. After she coughed, she spat in a box and lay facing the wall, turned away from everyone else. And suddenly this Sonia came up to me, looked at me with her beautiful eyes, and kissed me on the lips. I realized that Sonia thought it wouldn't be so bad anymore for me to be infected, now that it was all the same for me. As if half asleep, I collected my things and left the cell. They led me to Pugachev's Tower (it was said that Pugachev had been imprisoned there) and delivered the accusation.

Within three days, on November 12, the trial began.

The Trial

If they accuse me of stealing the bells of Notre Dame and
carrying them off in my waistcoat pocket, I will first cross
the border, and then I will defend my innocence.

—HEINRICH HEINE

The written accusation against me was astonishingly stupid. It stated
that Muratov (a colleague of my husband at the university) had told a certain Morenko that he had recruited me into a terrorist organization that
had the goal of murdering Kaganovich, and that I *might have heard* some
sort of conversation between Muratov and my husband on December 5,
1935.

This was so fantastic and vague. But it was the crime of which I was
accused. I had violated article 58, points 8 through 17, which meant I was
a terrorist. I was threatened with a loss of freedom for not less than eight
years or even with execution. Some colonel explained all this when the
accusation was delivered to me. The indictment was signed by Vyshinsky
and ended with the words, "she responded to the investigation with stub-
born resistance and never acknowledged anything."

I sat in Pugachev's Tower and thought about the fact that Pugachev had
been here and now I sat here and that politics had indeed been ground
into very fine particles.

I hoped I would meet my husband at the trial, that he also might be
awaiting trial, and that he felt just as I did.

As always I thought of the children, of the fact that now it would be decided whether I would ever see them again.

I sat in the round tower for three full days and nights, and again a determination to struggle grew in my soul. I was even glad that a court would judge me and not an invisible troika. I was glad that I could speak and argue. In my mind I reviewed the arguments for my innocence, the absurdity and lack of evidence of guilt.

On November 12, they took me to Lubyanka in the Black Maria. There they left me in the prison hairdresser's room where there was a table with a mirror and an armchair. I was alone. For the first time in seven months I saw myself in a mirror. I liked what I saw. The eyes shone with decisiveness in a very thin face. I thought that now I would see my husband, and I wanted to encourage him with my appearance.

The wait was rather long, around two hours. Somewhere a clock struck twelve. They brought me lunch. Everything is carved in my memory: I remember that they gave me pea soup with a piece of meat in it and buckwheat kasha with meat. It was not a prisoner's meal but probably came from a workers' cafeteria in Lubyanka. I didn't have time to eat the soup because they came for me. They led me into the room where the Court met.

There were no defendants there besides me. In the places for the public the investigators sat in uniform on a platform. There was a long table covered with a piece of red woolen cloth.

To the right of this table stood a bench for the defendants behind a barrier of pale polished wood.

I sat on the bench. Behind me stood two guards with rifles and the director of the prison, Popov, a thin tall man with a huge mustache sticking out in all directions.

Directly opposite the bench hung a round clock. The hands on it showed 12:45.

"The trial shall begin. All rise."

I jumped up. About twelve judges came in. Ulrikh presided. I looked at these men in uniforms decorated with medals. The majority of them were elderly people, about my father's age. A tall man with a gray head and medals on his uniform began to read the accusation. I already knew it by heart, and therefore I looked at the judges and thought, "Can it be that these men are the Bolsheviks whom I am used to treating with respect? Can it be that they are the men on whom I would throw myself for protection from any danger? Can it be that they will not understand that I am innocent and will condemn me?"

The chief asked if I wanted to speak. I leaned forward:

"Yes, I want to speak!"

I delivered an excellent speech. I said it was not necessary or possible to prove my innocence but that they had to prove my guilt. My accuser was, in the words of the investigator, a *Trotskyite bandit*, but my record was clean. Why believe him and not me? Muratov had given evidence that he had privately proposed we kill Kaganovich and that I allegedly agreed to that!

The only way in which I could oppose this wild assertion was to state the fact that I had lived very well and was satisfied with my life. There was no reason why I should suddenly get mixed up in such a crime, the more so because I could never expect any advantage from a change of government. It had absolutely nothing to do with me!

And what kind of formulation is it that "Sliozberg might have overheard a conversation"? I could have heard it, but I did not hear it. It is forbidden to punish a person for something she *might have heard*! I finished by asking the judges to remember when deciding my fate that I had two small children.

I delivered an excellent speech, but it did not help me. At a certain point I realized that no one was listening to me:

"The Court will withdraw into conference."

The judges stood up and went out. When the door opened, I saw a table in the next room covered with bowls of fruit and glasses.

The clock struck one o'clock.

Within five minutes the judges returned, and the chairman read:

"You are sentenced to eight years of strict incarceration in prison and four years' deprivation of rights."

For me it was as if boiling water had been poured on me. I turned around and saw Popov in a crazy pose with his arms open as if for an embrace. (Later I realized that women often fainted, and Popov caught them.) I did not faint. I pushed away Popov and ran down the corridor. I think I wanted to escape. Then the thought pierced me: "Incarceration in prison." I didn't even know there were such sentences. I stopped and turned back to Popov, who was at my heels.

"I heard the words *incarceration in prison*. Does that mean I'll be in prison for eight years?"

"Yes, that's your sentence."

"Ah, why did I lower myself and tell them about my children!" I exclaimed.

"It was well done. They had intended that you get five years' deprivation of rights, but it was reduced to four years."

(Later I realized that everyone was routinely deprived of rights for five years).

They led me to a big hall where there were about ten convicted people. Among them I ran into Zhenia Goltsman and Zhenia Bykhovskaia. Both had received sentences of ten years in prison. Zhenia Bykhovskaia had been sentenced to solitary confinement without the right of correspondence.

All sat quietly, beaten. No one cried.

In this one day they had condemned about a hundred women. The Court was in session for sixteen hours, with an average of ten minutes for each person.

I had taken up fifteen minutes with my speech.

That means they condemned some people in five minutes.

Solovki

After the trial they took us to a big room with bunks that had been hastily knocked together (earlier there had probably been a club located here), and we stayed there for two days. All I remember of these two days are groans, cries, and requests for visits with our children and relatives.

As for a visit with my children, I rejected the possibility because I considered that bringing them here would wound them for the rest of their lives. I hadn't yet decided whether I had the strength to see my mother and father, but the authorities made the decision for us. They didn't permit any visits. They loaded us onto a train and sent us to Solovki. We traveled for four days. In the compartment with me was the writer Vilensky-Sibiriakov. He was terribly sick with a stomach ulcer. His wife, Marfa Mitrofanovna Vilenskaia, had been in our cell 105. I remembered all kinds of details about her and told them to him. He listened greedily. It was the last news he had of his wife with whom he had lived for thirty years. Before the Revolution they had lived together in exile in Siberia, from which he had taken the pseudonym Sibiriakov. He died later in Solovki. I ran into his daughter in Kolyma.

They took us across the White Sea in the steamship *SLON* (*Solovki Camp of Special Designation*). Everyone said this would bring us good luck, but in fact all the prisoners were transported on this steamship, and it is doubtful that it could have brought any of them great good luck!

At Solovki the cells were not ready for us and for a time they put us into a big room, a former dining hall. The stoves there were enormous. They took up half the wall and were very warm. The floors were of good quality, made of thick wide boards. The walls were whitewashed and the benches were wooden with backs. They gave us a dinner that wasn't half bad.

Several times the commandant of the prison, Monakhov, came in. He was tall and heavy. He had a good-natured face.

Apparently he took great interest in us. On one of his visits he said: "And what have you done to get such sentences?"

And then the next time he suddenly said:

"Well, you'll be sitting here for eight or even ten years. Divide yourselves up into groups of four or five people, and choose the company you wish."

This was extraordinary. Never had anyone done such a thing. Just the opposite—if people had made friends, they separated them. Everyone was excited. It wasn't easy to choose your friends for the next eight years.

For me it was clear whom I did not want to be with. I was very afraid of people who cried and groaned. I did not want to be in a cell with Mensheviks and Trotskyites. Zhenia Bykhovskaia was closest to me, but I was not permitted to join her, since she had been sentenced to solitary confinement.

Zhenia sat in a corner and was already detached from everyone. She had nothing to say to those of us who were full of plans for joint living, since she could only expect solitude. My heart was pierced with sharp pain, but I had to organize my life. I went past her, not looking at her, and went up to Zhenia Goltsman.

She sat next to a pretty young girl who nestled against her. I knew this girl. She was the stepdaughter of Professor D. Her name was Lida.

Zhenia and I decided to take Lida with us into our cell. We felt very sorry for her and, besides that, we wanted to give her an education, since her schooling had ended at the elementary level.

The fourth person who asked to be in the cell with us was Zina Stanitsyna, whom I knew from Lubyanka. I had gotten close to Zina because Muratov had sent her to prison. He was a colleague of my husband and had also slandered us.

Zhenia said she had one condition for our living together. We could not break prison rules and communicate with other prisoners through tapping on the walls. She was a Communist and wherever possible she would abide by Soviet laws. We organized ourselves according to the following routine: we got up at eight o'clock, and for an hour we exercised with the window open. Then we had breakfast and sat down to our studies. For two hours each day Zhenia taught us English, and for two hours Zina taught us mathematics. For one hour I taught Zhenia French, and for an hour I taught Lida Russian. Then I read French books, of which there were two hundred fifty volumes in the library and all of them very good.

Lida was very musical and sometimes sang in a pure, tender coloratura.

Zhenia read Lenin and Marx, Zina studied vector analysis, and Lida toiled at her mathematics, Russian, and English homework. Zhenia was very strict in making sure that we read *Pravda,* which was sent to us, from beginning to end. She didn't let me off when I glanced through the paper instead of reading it carefully.

One hour a day we walked in the old cemetery, which was overgrown with grass and lilacs. Between two birch trees there was a gravestone that always made me sad and thoughtful: "A Cossack Commander from Zaporozhskaia Sech [I have forgotten his name] was born [at some time or other]. At age seventy-five, he was shut up in the monastery because of *unruly behavior* and lived there until he was a hundred and three years old. Then he was released, but his soul having grown humble [at a hundred and three years old!], he wanted to live out his days in quietness and prayer. He died at age one hundred and ten."

I read "his soul having grown humble" in the inscription on the gravestone of this Cossack commander and thought about the fact that I would be getting my freedom when I was forty-two years old and that then I would probably live on and look back on these eight years as just an episode in my long life. But I was never really able to believe that.

At eight o'clock in the evening we again got undressed and did exercises with the window open. Then we drank tea and our daily work was done.

We never lay down on our beds or slept during the day so that we would be tired out and would sleep at night.

This was a very good regime, and it seems that ours was the only cell that organized itself that way. In the other cells many people wept, lay on the bunks, read, and reminisced about their former lives. Later when we joined the others after about a year and a half, we were very different from them and looked as if we had been at a resort.

Monakhov often dropped in on us. He probably watched us through the peephole in the door of our cell because once he came in, seeing that we were reading an article in English, and said:

"Amazing how much progress you have made! And I'll never master it. I've tried three times."

Zhenia said to him jokingly:

"You can join our circle. We'll teach you quickly."

He waved her away:

"No thanks, no way. I'd rather live without English."

But he did not live for long, poor thing! At the end of 1937, he was arrested for liberalism in his contact with *enemies of the people.* They say that Monakhov died in a transit camp in Vladivostok.

He made our lives more pleasant for a year in prison. He was a very good man.

The nights were difficult. Being tired, I would fall fast asleep, but at two o'clock I would wake up feeling as if my heart had been stabbed. I could not fall back to sleep, and the hours until dawn were unbelievably agonizing. To get up or read was not permitted, and to turn over was not allowed. Zhenia was a very light sleeper, and it would have been too bad to wake her. I lay there quietly with closed eyes and taught myself not to remember. The least weakening of will and the faces of my children, husband, and mother would float to the surface. It can't be, it can't be, and then you begin to cry out.

During these nights I recognized that it *was* possible to govern your thoughts: Some thoughts you permit and others you drive away. It *was* possible not to remember, not to regret, not to torment yourself with feelings of guilt about yourself, your husband, your mother, what you accused yourself of—not having loved enough, having hurt someone, or not having had enough compassion. Possible . . . But very hard.

> The white night is restless.
> Shadows of towers hang over the windows.
> I am so tired of turning over such
> Heavy thoughts in my mind.
>
> The moment I remember that distant world
> It's as if my heart has been stung with pain.
> Among the stones I step carefully,
> Trying to lead myself away out of sleeplessness.
>
> The thirst for life struggles with sadness
> Driving away unwanted thoughts.
> This means that great grief
> Hangs like a millstone around my neck.
>
> This means that with clenched teeth
> I have decided to endure and wait.
> Gulls scream loudly, rudely,
> The night passes, so I must sleep.

In the morning I would get up feeling as if I had been beaten and only would return to normal after an hour of exercise in front of the open window.

One time a medical assistant came in to give us medicine. As always a guard was behind him. (The medical assistant was a prisoner.) While putting drops in Lida's eyes, he whispered:

"Sergei Lukovetsky died. He asked that people in the free world be told that he was not guilty. He said, 'I die a Communist.'"

Another time he whispered:

"Sonia Ashkenazi died. They found her this morning."

I remembered her beautiful eyes and how she kissed me before the trial. She had died.

A pale emaciated girl came into our cell.

"I am from a special punishment cell," she said. "My name is Ania Bublik."

There was a free bunk near me. Ania lay down on it and very quickly fell asleep. She coughed deeply. Apparently she was so worn out that she did not wake up until evening. In the evening the doctor, Vostokov, came to see her. Like us he was a prisoner and cared for us with attention and compassion. Unfortunately he wasn't with us for long. They quickly exchanged him for a civilian with a bureaucratic attitude. Vostokov listened to Ania and asked:

"Have you had tuberculosis?"

"In childhood, but then I recovered."

He gave her some sort of powder and then said to me:

"Don't breathe very close to her."

So we realized she had tuberculosis. Ania also realized this. Of the five women in our cell, most were afraid to talk with her and were afraid of becoming infected, but I wasn't afraid. I felt so nauseated at this time that I wanted to die. And besides how could I leave this girl alone at a time that was so terrible for her? I talked whole long days with Ania, and she told me her story.

She had been born in Harbin, China, where her father worked on the railroad. When the railroad was transferred to the Chinese, the employees were given a choice: either they could become Chinese citizens and continue to work on the Chinese Eastern Railroad (CER), or they could go back to the USSR and retain their Soviet citizenship. Ania's parents stayed in Harbin, but as an enthusiastic member of the Komsomol, she dreamed of going to Russia. Her mother begged her on her knees to stay. Many were frightened by the hard conditions of life in the USSR, but Ania was unbending. She arrived in Moscow and entered the Institute for Foreign Languages. (She had known English from childhood.) She lived in a dormitory and was very enthusiastic about Moscow and the institute where she studied.

But within three months they arrested her for suspicion of espionage. There was an amazing statute referred to as SE. She was sent to Solovki with a ten-year sentence. (Later in Kolyma I met many victims of this statute who were former employees of the CER.) Her outrage knew no limits. She struggled in her own way. She demonstratively would not stand when a commandant entered, she spoke loudly, and she opened the small window without permission. Naturally she was thrown into a punishment cell. And conditions in the punishment cell were like this: First of all one had to take all one's clothes off and then put on a dirty prison smock. The cell had no windows. Food consisted of four hundred grams of bread a day and two mugs of hot water. A cot was brought into the cell for six hours. The rest of the time one had to stand or walk around the two-square-meter cell or sit on the floor that was flooded with water. They put people in the punishment cell for four or five to twenty days. She must have very deeply angered the commandant of the prison because he gave this poor girl twenty days. It was the first time in my prison life that I had witnessed such a severe punishment. Usually prisoners became sick after five days.

Ania lived in our cell for a month. She got worse and worse, and one sad night she began to bleed from her throat. They took Ania to the hospital where she died two days later. She was twenty-one years old.

Strangely enough I did not get infected.

And so we lived for the whole year. In the fall of 1937 they suddenly stopped lending us books from the library. We lived for months without books, and finally they gave us a new catalog in which there were textbooks at the high school level; there were absolutely no foreign or scholarly books. The catalog section for fiction consisted of five typed pages. We were permitted to take out one book a week. This was a terrible blow. We cried as if we had all had our sentences doubled. We wondered why they had done it, and Zhenia suggested that the prisoners had been communicating with each other through the books—we prisoners were ourselves guilty.

It was especially upsetting when they gave us pages of our most beloved books cut up for use as toilet paper. That was how I received half a page of Heine's poetry, and another time a little piece of Tolstoy's *The Cossacks*.

At the same time they stopped giving us newspapers. During those days I had a quarrel with Zhenia for the first time.

Vinogradov, the chief guard for the whole building, came into our cell. He was a member of the Komsomol and not a very bright fellow, but we liked him. Apparently he wanted to imitate Monakhov because he tried to reeducate us. If we complained that it was cold, he would answer, "They will be warming up the stove. A Soviet prison does not punish people, but it reeducates them." Or he would come into our cell, give us a short lecture about the Stakhanovites, and then end reproachfully, "You see how hard most people work, but you have done something wrong, so here you sit in your cell."

In recent times, Monakhov hadn't been seen, and Vinogradov hadn't visited us for two months. Today he came in acting totally different from his usual self.

"Stand up!"

We stood.

"Do you have any grievances?"

"No."

He turned to go out. At that moment I asked him why they weren't giving us newspapers.

"There was an order on that."

"You yourself said that the purpose of a Soviet prison is to reeducate people, but how can we be reeducated without newspapers?"

He became confused. And suddenly Zhenia came to his aid. In a lecturing tone, she said:

"They are to educate those who are politically ignorant, but people like us should be responsible for our own actions!"

Vinogradov cheered up and nodded his head:

"Exactly, exactly!"

And he stepped out of the door to avoid further discussion.

I flew at Zhenia:

"How dare you interfere when I am asking the guard a question?"

She was somewhat embarrassed.

"Well, you could see that he didn't know how to answer."

We began to have time on our hands. We made chessmen out of pieces of bread and began to play. For three days we enjoyed ourselves with chess, but on the fourth day Vinogradov came in, grabbed the chess pieces, and said:

"It's forbidden."

"Well, and why this?" I asked Zhenia. "Simply to torment us?"

"I ask you not to say anything that borders on slander. It means that someone has been sending political documents through chessmen made from bread."

I waved her away and said nothing more. She was having a hard time finding rationalizations.

For two days they didn't take us outside to walk, and when we did go for a walk, we were shocked. Our dear cemetery had been divided into separate yards with high walls. Not a single blade of grass or shrub remained on the ground. Two birch trees had been cut down. The gravestone lay like an orphan in the middle of the courtyard.

One day when we were doing exercises in long prison underpants and handmade bras, the door opened and a whole commission came in. We were certainly a pitiful sight. Grayish underpants made of rough cotton hung to our knees, and our bras were made of coarse bands of cloth. With the open window and the door now open, it was freezing, and we stood there in the draft, blue with cold.

First the colonel came in wearing a gray lamb's wool hat and sheepskin coat with a collar of the same fur. He had a ruddy face and smelled of hair tonic and wine. Four military people followed him into the cell, and behind them all was our Vinogradov.

"What's this?" the colonel asked Vinogradov while squeamishly pointing to us.

"What is this? I ask you. Is this a health resort or a prison? At resorts people do sports, but in prison they serve their sentences. This is outrageous! Stop this immediately!"

We made a movement to dress ourselves.

"Stand still! Why aren't the bunks made according to the rules? Why is the window open? This is not a gym but a cell!"

On the table lay a book—Yelisarova's memoirs of Lenin.

Suddenly I said:

"But Lenin sat in a czarist prison, and he did exercises two times a day. That was also a prison."

The colonel shouted, "Shut up!"

He turned around and walked out.

All of them left. They locked the door. Within five minutes Vinogradov returned, saying:

"It is forbidden to do exercises." He took Yelisarova's memoirs and went out.

Once they gave us a copy of *Stalin* by Barbusse from the library. There was a large portrait of Stalin in it. Lida for some reason expressed admiration for his face.

"And do you like his looks?" she asked me.

My rage had been accumulating for so long that I burst out:

"No, I don't like faces with low foreheads."

Zhenia boiled up:

"I consider that a political comment!"

"I don't like people with low foreheads. I don't like men with brown hair. I prefer fair-haired men with blue eyes, high brows, blue-eyed fair-haired men, no matter what you may do to me!"

Zhenia turned away and stopped talking with me.

In the cell things got so tense that I was glad when Vinogradov told me to collect my things a week later.

I said good-bye to everyone. Zhenia came up, kissed me, and said:

"I think you are going to have a review of your case. With you it was all so trivial! I wish you good luck!"

Oh, what an optimist she was.

I went out.

They took me to a cell where four women were imprisoned. When we got to know one another I found out that all of them had had three-year sentences according to article 58, point 10, and had been in a camp until now, but their sentences had ended. So when they were taken from the camp to the prison, they were sure they were being sent to the mainland to freedom.

The delay greatly disturbed them. They tried to comfort themselves with the idea that navigation from the island to the mainland had been suspended.

Then they asked me about myself and discovered with horror that I was a terrorist who had been sentenced to eight years of imprisonment.

When I tried to explain to them that all of us were now either terrorists or spies and had sentences of eight to ten years, they clearly did not believe me. And of course three years ago when you got a sentence like that you had to have done something.

This conversation took place during the first evening after my arrival, and the next day I noticed that all of them were embarrassed, whispered among themselves, and wanted to say something to me. Finally Nema Rabinovich, the oldest of them, spoke to me:

"We have already served our sentences, and we are ready to start a new life. Our cases were minor and we got here by accident, but your case is completely different. I hope that you won't take offense, if just for the few days we are here, we don't communicate with you."

How ridiculous! This I had never expected.

And we began to live in a small cell—about fifteen square meters—the five of us, with me sitting in one corner, and the four of them in another. I think it was even worse for them than for me, since they were terribly ashamed. But I envied them excruciatingly. They talked among themselves, sometimes laughed, played guessing games or solved riddles, and ate all together.

I sat alone. I had no books or paper, and the only thing I could do was mentally compose poetry and smoke one cigarette after another. In this way five days went by. Finally I was given a book. (The others were given four books and they could exchange them with one another.) I read my book in portions, thirty pages a day, and for me thirty pages was like one tiny bite. And I looked around with envy at how their books lay there un-read, since they were busy discussing their future lives.

Three more days passed by. And suddenly the director of the prison build-ing came in and took out Nema Rabinovich, telling her to leave her things behind! Everyone decided that meant she was getting her freedom. Fifteen minutes went by. The director of the prison building then took out Masha Yarovaia also without her things, and Nema appeared in the doorway, white as a sheet. Masha went out. Nema was still speechless. Then she said:

"They extended my sentence to ten years. I have to serve another seven years."

She sat on a bunk and began to smoke one cigarette after another.

The door opened. Masha ran in sobbing and threw herself on the bed:

"They added seven. God must have punished us for what we did to poor Olga. All these eight days my heart was breaking as I looked at her. They added, added. Seven, seven, seven years!"

The remaining two went out and came back also crying and shrieking. It was painful to see how life had destroyed all their plans and dreams. Nema and Masha were longing for their children, who had been left with complete strangers. Niura Ivanova had planned to join up with a camp convict who was completing an eight-year sentence. She had wanted to wait for him and had created plans about how she would support him until spring by sending him parcels.

Shura Alekseeva's mother had been waiting for her. She had barely sur-vived until the end of her only daughter's sentence. She wrote Shura every week: "Now only twelve weeks are left, now eleven, now ten. I am waiting, waiting, waiting."

Several hours went by; they brought in hot water. I had a few candies. I went over to their half of the cell.

"Let's make up. Here's a treat for you." I put the candies on the table. "I am not angry with you. How could you know? But now it's probably dan-gerous for me to be with you. I have eight years, but you have ten."

People live through such things! In the evening all five of us sat on Masha Yarovaia's bed, and I told them the story from the French novel *In the Abyss* by Georges Honnet. It was one of the most sentimental novels I had ever borrowed from the prison library for practice in French. These novels served me well. I retold them with variations and became famous in prison and in the camps as a great storyteller.

In the spring of 1938 two women came into our cell who had gotten sick and fallen behind their Gulag transport. From them I learned that the women's prison at Solovki was going to be closed and all the prisoners sent to the mainland. That is what awaited us.

Kazan Prison

In the Kazan prison the regime was calculated to crush us completely, both physically and psychologically.

A bell would awaken us at six o'clock in the morning. At five minutes after six the guard on duty would burst into the cell in order to lift and screw our bunks up onto the wall. If the bunks weren't already made, he would scream and threaten to send us all to the special punishment cell. We feared him terribly and hurried, although it was clear that he arrived so soon after the bell just to yell at us, threaten us, and set a tone for the whole day.

Seven minutes after six. The bunks are screwed to the walls, and we six women find ourselves in an empty cell with a stone floor, stone arched walls, and a twenty-watt lightbulb in the ceiling. (These were bulbs that burned with a red filament, leaving the whole cell almost in darkness.)

The window was shielded with a wooden panel on the outside, and the top was covered with a thick wire net. The sky was not visible. The furniture consisted of six little benches, about forty centimeters long, screwed to the wall, a table a half meter long and thirty centimeters wide that was also screwed to the wall, and a slop bucket in the corner.

It was difficult to walk around the cell because they gave us coarse men's boots, size forty-four, and if they clopped on the stone floor, the voice of the guard on duty immediately hissed:

"Do you want to end up in the special punishment cell? Don't make noise!"

One could only speak in whispers. In fact one could be sent to special punishment even for speaking in a half whisper.

An endless prison day began. The day was broken into segments: toilet, breakfast, dinner, supper, a fifteen-minute walk, evening toilet, and sleep.

You waited and waited for any interruption to this killing monotony.

They didn't give us needles or thread; they didn't permit any kind of game. For creating chess pieces out of bread you could be sent to special punishment for a week. Once a week they gave us one book. Now I can't imagine how we managed to read in such half-darkness. One of us, Katia Toive, even went blind.

Books were the only distraction, the only happiness—they were air, bread, and water for a mind that was suffocating, dying from lack of nourishment. When I was reading, I felt human again. They hammered us on the head so long and so stubbornly with the idea that we were not people but just trash. Not only the guards whom we despised did this but also the newspapers (which we hadn't lost the habit of believing), leaders of the Party, and the country. So we ourselves began to feel that we were somehow guilty of something.

But here Tolstoy and Dostoevsky spoke to me, and I felt equal to them in my human essence. I understood them with my whole soul, as they probably wished to be understood.

How offensive it was when they gave us a book that had to serve as my nourishment for two weeks, and that book turned out to be a mere collection of platitudes.

I remember one novel I received. The author was a Soviet writer—actually not a bad one. I don't want to hurt his feelings, but the novel he wrote was abominable. No matter how hard I tried, I couldn't read through this book. I felt so badly. A fat book was lying there, but I couldn't possibly read it! I literally cried. I wished that the author had gone to prison for ten years and had been given that sort of book to read. I repeated, like a schoolgirl:

> His gaze was like a silent moan,
> A piece of bread was all he needed,
> But someone gave the man a stone
> Instead of food, for which he pleaded.

The rule from the good old days that political prisoners should be given textbooks had not been abolished. But they gave us alphabet primers and elementary arithmetic books probably to mock us. The director of the prison building was very irritated by our university degrees.

You sit on your forty-centimeter-wide stool that is screwed to the wall, and you think and think. It is very difficult to find a theme to think about, a theme that won't break your heart.

Shall I dream? But what about? The sentence—eight years—seems endless. A remission of the sentence can only be brought about through a general political change. But the force of hypnosis was so enormous that even in this tomb, privately by myself, I could not, for example, dream for very long of Stalin's death or his overthrow. It seemed like a ruination, like a return to capitalism.

Only in the depths of my brain, in the deepest depths where thoughts arise as yet unformed into words, did a feeling of protest begin to form.

If *he* was infallible and a genius, that meant that I and hundreds of thousands of others like me were supposed to sit in these odious cells, and thousands of other people were supposed to look through the peepholes to be sure that we were not diverted for a minute from our pressing grief, and for this base work they would receive awards and would believe they were doing important work for the government, leading the country toward Communism.

Remember? That was out of the question. You would go out of your mind. You try to drive away every shade of memory. You immediately try switching your brain to mechanical work: counting, reciting poetry, making up words from the letters of one bigger word. But sometimes memories take possession of your heart and you lose your will. Oh, how painful it is.

The walls of the Kazan prison were one and a half meters thick, but all the same we could hear the drone of steamships. And after all, I'm a woman of the Volga! Those sounds overwhelmed my soul. I immediately imagined the Volga, its breadth, its ships, and my youth.

You try not to listen, not to believe that right now while I sit in this stone cellar, life outside is going on almost as before.

> It cannot be that in this moment
> The green forest murmurs and the fields rustle!
> That the Volga gleams in joyful freedom
> Like a blue satin ribbon . . .

> It cannot be . . .
> The iron grating on the window,
> The door with a peephole—
> Here these are the boundaries of the world.
> The hearts of people are fearful, lonely . . .

> I am dying, I cannot breathe . . .
> Oh God, how painful is my journey.

Fortunately I remembered freedom and my former life more and more rarely.

The instinct for self-preservation did not allow me to think or torment myself. I tried to create some sort of illusory prison existence.

Zina Stanitsyna, my cellmate from Solovki, ended up in the cell with me. She taught us algebra and geometry, and she made up arithmetic problems—somehow time passed.

In a whisper I would tell stories from French novels.

Things were much harder for Olga Ivanovna Nikitina, an old weaver. She had worked in the mill for thirty-five years, and like all weavers she was deaf. She couldn't hear whispering, and speaking in a loud voice was not permitted. Her eyesight was bad; she could not read in the prison darkness. She was an old member of the Party, one of those Ivanovo weavers who had fought at the front in the Civil War with Furmanov. She had received a ten-year sentence because she had spoken at a meeting and, with her peculiar rough directness, had asked:

"You say they are all traitors. Had Lenin himself lost his eyesight? Couldn't he see the people who surrounded him?"

And here she sat and whispered to herself all day long—trying to prove that she had spoken the truth.

Olga Ivanovna had a daughter living in freedom, a fifteen-year-old called Nata. This foolish girl did not know that letters sent to prison are censored. She wrote her mother that she wanted to join the Komsomol and start her studies. In order to be accepted she had hidden the fact that her mother was in prison. "I write everywhere that you are dead; otherwise no one will take me. If you don't deceive *them,* you won't be able to survive."

Her mother, unable to tell her that her letters were being censored, wrote back:

"You should be as honest as your mother was always honest toward her homeland. You should always write the truth."

And Nata answered her: "Look, you were always honest and you ended up in prison, and the sly ones live happily in freedom." So she didn't understand anything and continued to write letters that tore poor Olga Ivanovna's heart apart with fear for her daughter.

Everything was agonizing that reminded us of freedom.

One time I noticed that the guard on duty was carrying home a package of children's toys. To me this seemed unbelievable: within half an hour he would be seeing his children! My heart broke.

From time to time, approximately once every ten days, about five women guards from inspection would burst into the cell, strip off all our clothing, and conduct a search. The search was unbelievably humiliating. They searched our hair, our mouths, and even worse. Dirty fingers touched our bodies. They threw our linen on the filthy floor, and the director of the prison building answered our complaints by saying, "If your head is cut off, you won't cry about your hair."

What could they possibly find? A scrap of a letter not handed in the day after it had been received, as required by prison regulations; a hidden photograph of your mother or children; a little figure made of bread—all that was considered criminal and received the heaviest punishments: deprivation of books, deprivation of walks, deprivation of correspondence, detention, solitary confinement. Of course the prison administration knew they wouldn't find anything criminal on us. The search was conducted only to frighten and humiliate us.

And here we sat, six terrorized, dim-witted women on our little stools, and time flowed slowly and pressed against the heart like a stone. In the end we fell into apathy, and we didn't even want anything to happen that would lead us out of this situation.

> I live as if in a dream,
> Around me and within me
> This dim diffused light without shade.
> Many days, many days, many days.
>
> I hear a noise of careful steps beyond the wall,
> And the strangled whisper of deep voices,
> And still sometimes the noise of locks,
> And the rustling of the accursed peephole.
>
> I live as if in a dream.
> And it appears dimly to me,
> That I am lying on the silted river bottom
> Under cold, heavy, green water,
> And the boats go by above me.
>
> High above, waves gut the riverbank,
> The summer sun burns, the winter snows fall,
> The wind whirls furiously over the waves . . .
> But quietness reigns in the deep.
>
> High above, my poor mother
> Keeps calling to me.

Her strong voice reaches the very bottom of the river
Where I lie helplessly alone.

Mama, don't make your daughter languish, don't torment her,
Mama, quiet your poor heart,
I cannot awake, here one cannot breathe,
Do not torment yourself, poor mother!

I live as if in a dream.
Around me and within me
This dim diffused light without shade,
Many days, many days, many days . . .

One event shook me out of this heavy lethargy. Maria Danielian, my neighbor in the cell, had lived a very full and interesting life. She told me a lot about the Baku underground where she had worked during the first years of the Revolution. I envied that she had lived such an active life, while I had vegetated with routine daily tasks. I looked up to Maria, although from fear of being overheard, we never talked about the catastrophe of the 1930s, but I wanted very much to know how she would explain it, how she would make sense of things in a way I never could. Maria, by the way, was a historian by profession.

One day Maria said:

"If I ever leave here someday, I will start living again as if nothing had ever happened. Never will I tell anyone what I've lived through, and I myself will forget everything."

I was indignant:

"Only a hypocrite could talk like that. We certainly could not have imagined that this dark underside of life existed, but it did exist. It existed even back then when we were walking around freely and believed in justice. Even then there were these terrible interrogations, these prison basements where people were beaten mercilessly, where they forced people to sign lies. How can I forget that, if somehow I get my freedom back again? I do not want to forget, I want to understand."

To expand on this theme was dangerous. Maria stopped talking with me and declared that I was sliding into the opposition. And I realized that since she did not want to slide down herself, she had completely stopped thinking.

She wrote endless letters to Stalin, assuring him that she had never criticized the decisions and actions of the Party.

But I did not want to stop thinking.

A deep repulsion for this voluntary slavery, this slavery of thought, enveloped me. I shall think, I shall remember everything. I must survive and tell people everything I have seen. I cannot understand everything now, but I do see that what is being done is evil.

I shall bear witness.

This decision had grown in me, and it brought new purpose to my life. I tried to understand every detail of every story I heard, to remember everything I saw around me.

My life took on meaning.

Liza

It was Saturday, the day for writing letters. On the preceding day we had received such obligatory, warm, and conventional letters from our relatives. What could they write us every two weeks when letters had to go through ten prison censors? Everyone is healthy, the children are smart and beautiful, be brave, keep yourself healthy, we need you. I know they certainly won't write me that the children are sick, they won't write that my mother can't sleep at night, and that grief is killing her. I calm myself, I soak up every loving written mark of Mama's clumsy handwriting. I kiss my son's block letters and the outline of my daughter's hand that grows bigger and bigger, and now it is already the same size as my palm, though it was once so tiny. These letters live with us for one night. Tomorrow I must return them. They will also take back our photographs, and I must impress them in my heart. Mama, Papa, and the children are in the photo. The girl's hair is all cut off. But it is winter right now. That means she has been sick, maybe with scarlatina, maybe with diphtheria. I don't know anything, but I do know that a week ago she was alive and her hand was drawn in outline, and I kiss the imprint of her fingers. I am a happy woman. I receive letters every two weeks—this bundle of love and caring warms my heart and brings with it the will to live.

But Liza, my neighbor in the cell, hasn't received a letter in two months. She left two daughters behind, six and twelve years old, still living in freedom. The older girl, Zoia, wrote her regularly, reporting that the younger one, Lialia, wouldn't obey and tore her new dress. Now she braids her hair in pigtails, and they are already twenty centimeters long. She sent a photo.

It showed two blond girls, smoothly combed with slanted parts in their hair. The older one certainly had braids, but they weren't quite twenty centimeters long and were really quite small and funny. She evidently tried to show them in the picture. They probably made her proud. Liza amazingly manages to hide this photo from the cell search and it has lived with her for two months from the day she received the last letter. This is a great crime and you could end up in solitary confinement for it. Liza was nervous and decided to give up the photo, since she could have heart failure from the anxiety of keeping it.

Liza is the most hypochondriacal of us all and is forever worrying about her health. She is a strong but homely woman. She tells us that she sings well, but we unfortunately cannot verify this, since we are only permitted to speak in whispers and singing is absolutely forbidden. Liza loves to tell about her great success with men, but I don't believe this at all, looking at her homely face and her strong, coarse figure. I don't relate very closely to Liza in general. She doesn't like to philosophize; she talks a lot about food, the dresses she used to have, and the furniture she left in her apartment. She does not belong to the intelligentsia, and she is irritated by our ruminations as we search for a first cause.

But yesterday, after we all received letters and she was again left without a letter, she cried for a long time and at night told me her story in a whisper.

"You all lived the good life, but I lived badly as a kid. We were beggars. We didn't have a father, there never was one. The man of the house where our mother worked knocked her up and fathered my sister and me." Liza was ashamed of this and had never told us about it before. I realized why she had never liked our stories of childhood, how we had been taught music, how we had Christmas trees, and how my father used to spoil me. "And my mother, my sister, and I had good voices, and we sang in the courtyards, and they gave us a lot of money. We could have lived well, but my mother drank. And her voice was like Nezhdanova's. She used to get drunk and sing and cry. She sang well and was a good person but drank from grief. I always envied children whose mothers took them to school, but if I saw children with their father, dressed up, clean, I felt like throwing mud at them.

"We lived in the corner of a basement. And suddenly when I was fourteen, the Revolution began. People came to us and said they were moving us from the cellar to an apartment on the second floor. Some rich family had lived there. They had thrown everything over and run abroad, and the apartment was given to us with everything left there, with all the stuff in it. There was a piano, there were dresses, dishes. Mother dressed up and she dressed us up. They gave us three rooms. We lived in one because it was cold, but the other rooms we kept in order and dusted. And then it got warm, and we began to live in the whole apartment. My mother worked as the building manager, and my sister and I worked at the factory. So we fell into heaven. At the factory everyone loved us because we always sang—at work and in the evening. We dressed really well because the rich folks had left a sewing machine and many dresses, and our mother sewed all the time and altered the dresses. She even stopped drinking.

"In the evenings friends would come to our place. It was like a club. We would eat whatever there was (my mother was a cook for a government worker, and she cooked well), we'd drink out of brandy glasses, and we'd sing and sing. Then our mother died, she had TB. But at least she was happy in her last years. And my sister and I got married. I married the chairman of the factory committee, and she married a foreman. They were Party members and so we joined too. We lived really well. The greatest sadness was when Ilych died. I joined the Party as a Lenin recruit. My husband made me study the way Lenin had told us to.

"I had two daughters. I dressed them up like little dolls. The oldest already started to study the piano. She did well and also loved to sing. She had a high pure little voice, like a little bell. Our daughter used to sing at a children's matinee at the factory, and she would be wearing a silk dress with a Young Pioneer necktie, and my husband would say to me, 'There isn't a girl in the world who's better than our Zoia. She'll be a People's Artist.' And I would remember how I used to stand in the courtyard and envy children who had a father, and I loved our Soviet government so much that I would have given my life for it."

Liza cried through the whole night. It was the first time she had told me everything, and I was ashamed that I had thought her coarse and stupid because she was always reminiscing about the apartment and the furniture.

And after dinner they gave us paper so we could write letters. Liza also wrote, advising her daughters to take care of themselves and study hard.

Suddenly the peephole in the cell door opened and Liza was given a letter. But it was not the usual kind of letter at all.

"Dear Mama," wrote Zoia. "I am fifteen years old and I am getting ready to join the Komsomol. I need to know whether you are guilty or not. I keep wondering how you could betray our Soviet country. After all, everything was so fine for us. You and Papa were workers. I remember how well we lived. You sewed silk dresses for me and bought candies. Could you really have taken money from *them*? It would have been better if we had worn simple calico dresses.

"But maybe you aren't guilty? Then I won't join the Komsomol. I will never forgive them for what they have done to you. But if you are guilty, then I won't write you anymore, because I love our Soviet power, and I will hate our enemies, and I will hate you, Mama. Please write me the truth. I would rather that you are not guilty and then I will not join the Komsomol. Your unhappy daughter, Zoia."

Liza froze.

Of the four short sheets of paper they had given us for letters, she had already written on three. She sat as still as a stone. Then on the fourth page she wrote in big letters:

"ZOIA, YOU ARE RIGHT. I AM GUILTY. JOIN THE KOMSOMOL. THIS IS THE LAST TIME I WILL WRITE YOU. BE HAPPY, YOU AND LIALIA. MOTHER."

She handed me Zoia's letter and her answer and beat her head on the table, choking with tears.

"Better if they hate me . . . How will she be able to live without the Komsomol? She would be an outcast if she started hating the Soviet government. Better if she hates me."

She sent off the letter, gave up her photograph, never again spoke of her daughters and never again received a letter.

Poor Liza!

Suzdal

After a ten-month incarceration in the Kazan prison, all of us, and I in particular, had turned into half cripples, oppressed, dying from scurvy and spiritual depression. My head hurt constantly. Rarely, rarely I awoke without my head hurting, but on those happy days I couldn't keep a clear head for long. When the door creaked open unexpectedly or a book fell on the floor, it was enough to start me on a migraine attack. The others were not in much better condition.

But meanwhile Kolyma needed working hands, and it was already decided to transfer us to work in the camps. It was clear that we were incapable of work, and they decided to give us some rest under somewhat better conditions before sending us to the camps.

We didn't know all this and therefore when they put us in vans and took us to the train on May 10, 1939, it disturbed us frightfully. A change in the rhythm of life, a meeting with neighbors from the next cell, a meeting with old acquaintances—all that became an unbearable burden for me.

I lay on the bunk in the train compartment with an insane headache and constant vomiting brought on by the least movement.

All around me everyone was enthusiastically talking nonstop, trying to tell one another about everything they had gone through for the past year.

As if in a fog, I saw Zhenia Goltsman near me. She was changing wet rags on my head. I took her by the hand and squeezed it. She answered me. So we made peace with each other. Zhenia sat near me the whole night, and whenever I opened my eyes, I met her tender glance and felt the touch of her cool hand on my burning forehead. Then we sat for a long time on a siding, but I lay there unmoving, tortured by pain.

The next day we arrived at Vladimir prison. There I also saw and felt nothing except my lacerating pain. I was half delirious, and my memory of this trip floats to the surface in fragments. I remember myself in an open truck in which they were transporting us to Suzdal. To this day I don't understand why they took us through the crowded streets of Vladimir in broad daylight in an open truck and not like other loads with a closed tarpaulin over them. And most astonishing is that in the middle of a large lively street our truck broke down—we had a flat tire. While the driver changed the tire, a crowd of people gazed at us in horror. I remember the face of an old Jewish man. He raised both hands and loudly prayed in Hebrew, and tears coursed down his cheeks through his gray beard. Probably someone from his family was in prison. Seeing his face distorted in horror, I glanced back at my neighbors. Certainly we presented a terrible spectacle: prison uniforms, brown with gray stripes, dim eyes, fearful greenish-white faces . . . and around us the futile, frightened guards, chasing away the crowd.

They fixed the truck and we drove on.

We arrived in Suzdal. The wooden houses and the churches immediately astonished us. It was strange to walk on dirt streets, strange that the floors in the prison's entryway were not stone but were cleanly washed wood. There was a smell of fresh-baked bread, manure, hay, and other good things.

But the most amazing thing awaited us along the way to the bathhouse where they took us directly upon arrival. The bathhouse stood in a flowering cherry orchard!

Remember that for three years we had not seen trees, sky, moon, or rain! On walks they had taken us into the fenced asphalt prison courtyard. While walking we were required to look at the ground. Everywhere and always we had been enveloped in a disgusting prison smell—disinfectant, slop buckets, boots, cheap tobacco, dirty sick bodies. And suddenly we had landed in a flowering cherry orchard!

The moon shone and reflected on the shining leaves. Every branch was speckled with sweet-smelling cherry blossoms that rustled in the light wind . . .

A crazy agitation took hold of us. We breathed in this smell of earth, flowers, and trees. We pulled off sprigs and chewed them, and the bittersweet taste penetrated to the heart. Oh how I wanted to throw myself on the earth and drink in its fresh aroma with my whole body!

We took turns washing. Because I was sick, I was put last in line so that I could stay longer in this splendid garden.

We returned to the prison at dawn. An hour went by before they distributed us back into our cells.

I ended up in a cell for two with Lida Dmitrieva, whom I had already lived with in the Solovki prison. I had dreamed of falling in with some interesting new people. I wanted to talk and exchange thoughts. But when I arrived in the cell, I was consoled right away—it was a monastic cell made all of wood, with wooden beds and hay mattresses that smelled good. In the middle of the room stood a simple wooden table and two stools. The furniture was not screwed to the floor, and the cell was reminiscent of a normal room. But the greatest wonder was the window: only half of it was covered with a screen, and through it you could see churches and the bare springtime woods flashing with a thousand ravens and crows. One flowering apple tree was even visible!

Above everything stretched the pale straw-yellow morning sky with rosy clouds. Sky! Do you know how beautiful it is? If people didn't see it every day and every hour, they would be astonished and would go to the world's end to gaze at it, as they now go to gaze at the sea and a few other rare sights like waterfalls and caverns. I could not gaze enough at the sky, and for hours I sat by the window, not taking my eyes from it. Our window faced west. How beautiful the sunsets were! Never did a single work of art shake my soul like the beauty of that window through which I could see the sky and the silhouette of a graceful bell tower.

Here is a poem I wrote about that view:

> On the golden silk of the sky
> Dark violet storm clouds swirl.
> The web of branches spreads
> The bare wood of springtime.
>
> The brocade skyline glows!
> In the light of the fading golden sunset
> The huge hulk of the ancient convent
> Darkens.
>
> The air is still. The silhouettes
> Of ravens and crows gleam.

Strangely it reminds me of an
Old forgotten dream.

For four centuries in this cell
The days went slowly by for hermit sisters,
As they watched the golden sunset
From this same window.

These very same bell towers
Blackened against the pale gold sky,
And their hearts beat with the same pain,
And in the same way they longed for miracles.

And I, living in the country of the Soviets,
Imprisoned in a convent,
Gaze at the same silhouettes
Against the fading sunset glow.

The hours run by . . . I gaze from the window
Putting poetry together in a simple way.
If all of it were not so sad,
Perhaps it even would be funny.

Four days after our arrival in Suzdal I awoke to the sound of an ax chopping wood outside the window. Lida also could not sleep.

"Could they be chopping down our orchard?"

It was highly probable. In Solovki we had already lived through the time when they cut down all the trees in the courtyard where we took our walks. They tore up the grass and uprooted every shrub. We had lived through it painfully back then, but now after three years in prison, we had responded to the cherry orchard as to the most splendid beauty . . . Yes, it certainly was the most splendid beauty!

The garden was visible from the courtyard where we walked, and we gazed at it and dreamed of Saturday, when they would take us back to the bathhouse, and we would breathe in its aroma, its incomparable charm.

And now suddenly they were chopping down our orchard. We listened all night and when we heard the blows of the ax, it seemed to us that the blows were beating against our own bodies.

Could it be that tomorrow they will board up the window and we will be robbed of the sky again? We are completely under the power of our torturers!

Lida and I cried all night and got up in the morning feeling crushed. We didn't want to eat or read. With fear we went out on our walk and saw our splendid cherry orchard rustling in the wind, untouched.

We had been mistaken. They had not been chopping it down—they were repairing the fence.

From the two-month stay in Suzdal an impression remains of golden sunsets and a sweet-smelling cherry orchard.

How much and how little a person needs!

How much—because besides bread a person still needs beauty. And how little—because we only saw the sky through a window and we only walked through the garden once a week. I have seen much beauty in my life—more than once I have heard Chaliapin and Rachmaninov. I have seen beautiful paintings, I have read wonderful books, but the most beautiful thing I have ever experienced was the Suzdal sky and the Suzdal cherry orchard.

Transport

Early on the morning of July 10, 1939, after a two-month stay in Suzdal, we realized that something unusual was happening. People walked up and down the corridor noisily, ceaselessly, unlocking cell after cell. We heard voices shouting commands and, most astonishingly, the voices of prisoners. Finally they came to us:

"Get your things ready."

And within half an hour:

"Come on out."

They led us into the courtyard. About thirty or forty women were already standing there. The greenish pallor of their faces and their strange expressions again amazed me. Several of the women had shaved heads. Among those with whom I had been imprisoned were Maria Danielian, Nina Verestova, and Liza Tsvetkova, the same one to whom her daughter had stopped writing. Zhenia Goltsman was not there. I asked Nina about her, and she told me that Zhenia had died. (This turned out not to be true.)

Olga Ivanovna Nikitina wasn't there. She lay paralyzed in the prison hospital.

Someone called to me:

"Which one of you here is Olga Sliozberg?"

I answered. Olga Radovich came up to me, a twenty-six-year-old girl, neatly put together, with a crown of golden braids on her head and a sort of white collar on her prison dress. Her ineradicable Ukrainian blush broke through even the prison pallor.

"I've always dreamed of sharing a cell with you," said Olga. "We would probably have many interests in common. I have heard of you. But I always ended up with uninteresting people and no one to talk to."

I had also heard of Olga. She was an art historian, and in addition to that she gave dramatic readings. We of course had much in common, but basically we were never close: Olga was amazed at my tortured search for reasons, my thirst for justice. For her it was clear that we had fallen into the clutches of bandits, and we had to adapt ourselves and survive these terrible years, not turn into hysterical women and decay morally.

I stood next to Olga and we decided to stay together in the future if possible.

After several roll calls and checks, they put us into the hands of the convoy, we got into closed trucks, and we were driven back to Vladimir.

We gazed at the cherry orchard, the bell towers, and the silhouette of the monastery for the last time. A new, terrible, unknown life awaited us.

In Vladimir we spent the night, and the next day we were loaded onto heated freight cars and taken east.

In our freight car there were seventy people. We talked unceasingly. Exchanges with such a mass of people were intoxicating after three or four years of prison isolation. At last it was possible to speak out loud. We shouted and sang. If you stood on the bunks, you could look out a low, narrow crack that ran like a window along the whole side of the freight train.

During the transit, I finally heard how Liza sang. She really had an unusual voice. The timbre was pure gold. She sang without any strain, like an overflowing river. Sometimes she sang the romances of Glinka and Tchaikovsky, and she sang them the way she had learned them in an amateur singing class. But when she sang folk songs—"Faraway, faraway the steppe stretched beyond the Volga," or "There in the steppes at night the coachman froze to death," or "Ah, my garden, my garden"—I never heard a better performance in my life.

Askhab, a Tatar woman from Kazan, traveled with us. This was an almost illiterate woman, the mother of six children. Why she was imprisoned I do not know; she never spoke of it. She was very active, arranged an isolated and comfortable little place for herself, and was immediately ready for business. She pulled thread out of an old blanket, procured two sticks from which she made knitting needles, and began to knit a jacket. When I asked her whom she was knitting it for, she answered, "Are you stupid or what? When we get to the camps, I'll trade it for bread or sugar."

And I hadn't thought it would be possible to trade things for bread or sugar. Askhab knew how to get along.

When everyone had quieted down, this busy Askhab sometimes sang songs from the Far East in a sweet high voice, songs full of such sadness and charm that one wanted to cry.

Among us there were many storytellers. Galia Ivanova knew many poems of Pushkin by heart, all of *Eugene Onegin, Woe from Wit* by Griboedov, and "Lieutenant Schmidt" by Pasternak.

Olga Radovich recited splendidly. Natasha Onufrieva recited *The Idiot* by Dostoevsky word for word. She told it over three days.

Once at a stopping point, while Galia Ivanova recited *Woe from Wit*, the commander of the convoy and three soldiers came into our freight car. They apparently had been listening, quickly opened the door, and wanted to confiscate the book. (Books were not permitted.) We said there was no book. The commander grinned and answered that with his own ears he had heard someone reading. They began a search. They turned over the whole car, but there wasn't a single book. Galia proposed that she would read to the commander without a book and began to recite: "My uncle—high ideals inspire him . . ." The commander stood there for ten minutes carefully looking around to see if someone wasn't showing her a book. Then he gave up, shrugged, turned, and went out. All the same it seemed to him that we had tricked him.

So we kept busy—with literature and singing. No one spoke about our cases or about politics. Everyone was glad that they had removed us from prison and that we were going to a camp. But we were frightened and repulsed by any word that might be construed as political.

One evening during some long stage of our trip, the lock to the doors of the freight car that separated us from the whole wide world flew off because of the jolting. It was sunset. The vast steppe lay there in full blossom. Into the stinking, suffocating air of the overcrowded carriage poured the broad breath of the steppes with its aroma of grass and flowers. We stood stock still. And suddenly a hysterical voice sounded out: "Guards, guards, close the door!" The train was moving and nobody heard. The voice sounded again: "We must rouse the guards. They will think that we did this ourselves, that we wanted to run."

Not one person wanted to run. People could run who were connected with the criminal world or with political organizations. But what, for example, could I do if I were given freedom but no passport? My dreams went no further than the apartment on Petrovka Street in Moscow, and anyway they would take me from Petrovka the next day and return me to prison with a doubled sentence.

And so we stood silent and gazed at *freedom* lying there just beyond our outstretched hands.

At a small station nearby, the door was shut and our vision of freedom disappeared.

I don't remember if it was in Sverdlovsk or Irkutsk that we stood on a siding for a day, and they led us into a disinfection station. It was a beautifully equipped establishment. We undressed downstairs and were ready to go upstairs when we saw that the guards were standing along the staircase from bottom to top. We crowded together.

Almost all of us stood there, eyes lowered, with red spots on our faces. I looked up and met the eyes of an officer, the head of the guards. He looked at me with a frown and said:

"Well, come on, come on, don't hang back!"

And suddenly I felt relieved. It even seemed funny to me.

"I spit on them. For me they are no more men than Vaska, the ox, whom I was afraid of as a child," I thought and, impudently looking into the eyes of the guard, I was the first to go forward. Behind me came all the rest.

And so we passed along the line of guards. Later we discovered they had done the same thing that day with four other groups of women from our train.

Above on the landing there was a mirror covering the whole wall. We hadn't seen ourselves in more than three years. All the same we were women. Seeing the mirror, we ran to it in a crowd. I ran up to the mirror and, standing in the crowd, I could not figure out where I was.

And suddenly I saw the tired sad eyes of my mother, her hair streaked with gray, the familiar sad lines of her mouth . . .

It was I. I stood there, my mouth wide open, and could not believe that I was no longer the young woman to whom people on the street would turn and call out *Miss*, but this sad old woman who looked about fifty . . .

The chief of the guards shouted:

"Come on, come on. Your group has twenty minutes to wash!"

We ran into the bathhouse and began to take wash basins for ourselves, secretly laundering some rags, starting, in other words, all the usual scramble of prisoners on a transport.

But for a long time I remembered the sad, tired face, the gray head, the eyes that gazed at me from the mirror, and tried to accept the thought that it was I.

This stage of the journey lasted thirty-four days. During this period they gave us very little water: there weren't enough containers, and the distance between stations was long. I didn't suffer too much from thirst, but there was a woman with us in the carriage who was seriously diabetic. She was a doctor named Zavalishina. She was dying from thirst. We gave her two and three times the ration from our own water, but for her that was like one swallow.

I usually saved a half glass from my portion in order to wash. One day she saw how I cleaned my teeth and washed myself and said, "What cruelty! Washing yourself with water when someone wants to drink!" I felt terribly badly, and even today I cannot remember her eyes, like those of an exhausted horse, without feeling a stab in my heart.

She died on the thirtieth day of the transport.

On August 14, 1939, we arrived at the transit station in Vladivostok.

KOLYMA

Kolyma, Kolyma
Strange planet!
Twelve months of winter,
And the rest is summer.
—A LOCAL JINGLE

Magadan, My First Camp

We arrived at the camp in Magadan after four years in prison, in which the major punishment and debasement of our human dignity was being deprived of work. They received us well. We were drastically different from the camp inmates: we had pale green faces, frightened eyes, and complete incompetence. The first three days we didn't work. We rested and for whole days we discussed the advantages of camp life over prison life. We could see people and talk with them.

The population of the camp (around a thousand people) seemed enormous to us: so many people, so much conversation, so many possibilities for finding friends!

Nature. We walked around inside the barbed wire of the camp zone and looked at the sky, gazed at the distant hills, and walked up to the stunted trees and stroked them with our hands. We breathed the moist sea air, felt the freezing rain on our faces, sat on the damp grass, and touched the earth with our hands. We had lived without all that for four years only to

76

discover that it was completely essential; without it one cannot feel oneself to be a normal person.

Work. We had been dreaming of work and speaking of it in words that seemed high-flown, stupid, and insincere to the camp inmates who detested the painful forced labor.

And then came the third day of camp life, when they told us that those who felt strong enough could go out to work. (Within a week going to work would be required.)

The night before we were as excited as if it had been before a holiday. Eighteen people, including me, decided to go to work. We so much wanted to go out of the camp zone, walk in the street, leave the barbed wire area, see the forest and the sea.

"Choose a brigade leader," said the head of the guards.

The brigade chose me. I had already taken a solicitous look at my brigade. Intellectual faces, gray heads. Two professors, one writer, two pianists, one ballerina, about six Party workers. All city people. Everyone's muscles were atrophied from four years of inactivity. All of my brigade members dream of showing through labor how honest they are, how eager to work, how really Soviet they are. The guards lead us out of the zone, and we walk through the construction area of the town.

We come to a large empty lot on the outskirts of the city. On a small hill stands an almost finished hospital building, where ruddy cheerful young women clean the windows, converse among themselves, and flirt with the guards and the male construction workers.

A Kolyma drizzle is falling, but we enjoy it. It seems to us that we are almost free.

The foreman, Kolmogorsky, comes up to us. He is a slender man of about forty, stylish in our eyes, dressed in a tall hat of Persian lamb's wool and shining boots, with a padded jacket, tightly gathered by a broad belt. With a warm smile, he turns to me and explains our task:

"You will dig out the ditch. It has been started and is one meter deep. It needs to be deepened to three meters. The work norm is nine cubic meters of earth a day per person. You personally don't have to work, since they don't have a norm for the team leader. The length of a working day in the summer is fifteen hours. There is a one-hour break for lunch. Work begins at six in the morning and ends at nine at night. They'll bring lunch at one o'clock."

After this he gives out heavy rusty shovels, and we start to work. We don't understand what nine cubic meters are. We vaguely understand what a fifteen-hour workday means. We are full of enthusiasm.

I post my squad with three meters between each person and take my own place. We begin to work. I have announced that I'll signal a smoking break for ten minutes every hour.

The rain is drizzling. The ground is clay. It turns out that the shovel digs into the ground very badly, and we get hold of the wet clay with only the tip. The clay is terribly heavy and tends to fall off the shovel while we lift it very slowly up to the edge of the ditch. We don't have the strength to throw it with a jerk. All the same we take on the work bravely. I don't have a watch, but I clearly feel that a terribly long amount of time has passed. I am utterly exhausted.

"Smoking break!" I announce.

My brave brigade protests:

"What do you mean? Not more than twenty minutes has gone by!"

Of course it may have been only twenty minutes, but I don't have anymore strength and neither do the others. We lay down our shovels and sit on the handles.

"Smoking break is over!" I command, and again we begin to dig.

Before lunch we take probably thirty smoking breaks, and it becomes harder and harder to give the command to go back to work, to dig the rusty, uncomfortable, clay-covered shovels into the ground and throw an offensively small bit of clay onto the edge of the ditch.

They bring us a lunch that seems sumptuous from our point of view. Fish soup with fresh Siberian salmon, pieces of roasted salmon, and even *kisel.* No matter how tired we are, we eat with satisfaction. (At that time we didn't yet know that during the first week everyone gets very filling food because the amount of food you receive doesn't depend on how much you work. Hunger will begin later when we fail to fulfill the norms.)

It seems as though the bell for getting back to work rings improbably quickly. We take our places and begin to dig. A courageous young woman, Raia Ginzburg, stands beside me. I see how sweat pours from her brow in an unnatural way. She works, biting her lip, but every time I get ready to call a smoking break, she pleads with me: "Just ten more shovelfuls." After our breaks she also pushes me: "Give the signal for going back to work."

I look at her with respect. She has small soft hands and a delicate little figure. She has heart disease. She has never worked physically. She is much weaker than I but more steadfast. I admire her and try to keep up with her.

The day drags out unbelievably slowly. Kolmogorsky comes up. I try to read in his expression how much we have done, but I don't understand.

In one of our breaks, young women from the floor-washing brigade come up to us and laugh:

"Well, Kolmogorsky really found something for you. This sure is hard work!"

"And do you fulfill the norm? Do you succeed?" I ask.

"Us? We do three times the norm and then we embroider handkerchiefs. We are used to it. We've been in the camp five to seven years already."

I look at them with respect.

"And what kind of a person is Kolmogorsky?"

"He's finishing his sentence. He's been in the camps since 1930. He's a Cossack. A smart cookie, sets things up for himself, has more than enough girls."

We dig. Quitting time will probably never come. I've lost count of the smoking breaks, and by the end of the day even Raia does not protest when I announce a break.

We dig and the rain drizzles. Our heavy padded jackets are soaked through, and the clay plasters our boots. We dig. Finally the bell rings. Quitting time. The return trip seems unbelievably long.

The first day we pass the dining room and go to the barracks to wash before dinner. But it turns out that going back to the dining room is unthinkable; we don't have the strength. We collapse on our bunks, instantly fall asleep, and very quickly the bell rings for wake-up time. In the future we go right from work to eat dinner, though we're dirty and plastered with clay, and then we go off to the barracks.

We dig for three days. We vaguely, anxiously realize that the ditch is not getting any deeper, that nothing like nine cubic meters a day per person is to be mentioned. But all the same I somehow hope that we've done quite a lot. We certainly have tried so hard!

At the end of the third day Kolmogorsky comes up with a measuring stick and measures. Then he grins strangely and invites me to come into the office. I enter and see a sumptuous table. On it there is a tablecloth of clean burlap, cheap grain alcohol, condensed milk, salted salmon, green onions, and pig fat. To me it seems like a fairy tale. He invites me to the table and I sit down. He offers me grain alcohol and announces that I cannot refuse—"otherwise *blat* won't work."

I bravely drink some of the grain alcohol for the first time in my life. It is really disgusting, but I realize I have to be on good terms with him.

My legs feel weak from the alcohol, but my head is still clear. I [want to] switch to a diplomatic conversation.

[He says,] "Bad, very bad. You did three percent of the norm. Probably your girls were fooling around with the men in the bushes."

"What do you mean! We have such a fine brigade! All of them are upstanding women. Almost all are former Party members. They try with all their might! But this work is hard for us. We are older women from the city who've spent four years in prison . . . Give us different work like washing floors and windows, and we'll show how conscientiously we can work . . ."

"Stop it! Well, if you'd done half the norm instead of just this three percent. You have to agree that it's not very much. Tell me honestly—are your women running after the men?"

"No, no! Can't you see what kind of people they are? They are trying with all their might. These are cultured people, former Party members."

And suddenly I see that the mask of gracious conversation has left Kolmogorsky's face.

"Ah, former Party members? If you were prostitutes, I would let you wash windows and you would do three times the norm. When these Party members dekulakized me in 1929 and were driving me out of my home with my six children, I said to them, 'But the kids—what are they guilty of?' And they answered: 'This is Soviet law.' So now please observe Soviet law and dig out nine cubic meters of dirt!" He laughed loudly. "Follow Soviet law!"

I turned and went out.

"Wait, lady! I know you weren't a Party member, I saw your case. I'll be frank with you. I like you a lot. I wouldn't mind having an upstanding woman. I'm sick of these prostitutes. And with hard work and hunger you'll perish. I'll switch you to brigadier of the house girls. I'll look after you."

Before my eyes stood the faces of Raia, Rosa Borova, and the other women. They were all waiting for me, hoping.

"I don't agree," I answered. "However it goes, that's the way it goes! I want to be with my own people."

"Whatever, you can do as you like," said Kolmogorsky.

I returned to my brigade. I was with my own people.

Altunin

Unfortunately I have forgotten the first name of this extraordinary person. His last name was Altunin, and he was from the Voronezh region. At first I think he was a leather worker and then he transferred to Party work. He was a handsome man, about forty years old, with a reddish beard, a pure Russian type. Before he had apparently been very strong, broad shouldered, and large. In 1938 and 1939 he had been in the mines and there, as they say, went downhill and lost his health. He grew weak and coughed, spitting up his lungs. He was wonderfully skillful with his hands, and they sent him to do tool repair in the women's brigade at the construction site in Magadan.

Here is the story he told me.

"This is how it began in 1937: this one's an enemy, that one's an enemy. We throw them out of the Party, we raise our hands—put our comrades to death.

"At the beginning I said I was sick. I didn't go to Party gatherings so I wouldn't have to raise my hand, and then I see you have to do something. You can't do nothing. We're destroying the Party, we're destroying good honest people. I didn't believe they were all traitors. I knew these people well.

"I sat down one evening and wrote a statement in three copies: one to my Party organization, one personally to Stalin, and one to the Party's Central Control Commission. I wrote that we were destroying the Revolution. Maybe it was just local activity, a local crime against the Party. In this case it's a local catastrophe, but if it's happening all over Russia—then that's counterrevolution.

"I wrote—poured out my whole soul. I showed it to my wife. She says, 'You're killing yourself. If you send this statement, they'll arrest you the very next day.'

"And I say, let them arrest me, better to be arrested than to raise your hand and put your comrades to death.

"And it happened just the way she said it would. I sent out the statement and within three days they arrested me. They processed it quickly. Ten years—and then to Kolyma."

"And you never regretted doing that?"

"No, one time I did regret it. There was a terrible frost and they sent us to dig up stumps in the forest. The tools were rusty axes—no crowbars or picks. We suffered over those stumps, just barely dragged out four of them. Then we say, to hell with them, and we built a bonfire and burned the stumps. In the evening the foreman comes, and we haven't done any work.

"Straight from the woods to detention. And the cell is three square meters and a window with no glass. There's no stove. I ran and ran around this cell, and suddenly I was so upset: the others were put in prison, but I put myself there. And what had come of what I had written? Everything was the same as before. Soltz might be ashamed, but for Big Whiskers it's all the same, you can't get through to him. I could be sitting right now with my wife, kids, in a warm room with a samovar. As I thought of that, I began to hit my head against the wall so that these thoughts wouldn't get to me anymore. So I ran around the cell all night and swore at myself with my last words for missing my peaceful life."

Altunin worked with us through one winter. In the spring of 1940 he died in the camp hospital of tuberculosis.

Igor Adrianovich Khorin

At the end of December 1939 they transferred our brigade to "easy" work. We sawed and chopped firewood in the courtyard of a five-story building; then we distributed the firewood to each floor. We took turns distributing the firewood so we could warm ourselves up a bit, and then we would saw and chop again from eight in the morning until six in the evening, and the temperature was about fifty degrees below zero.

The workers of the NKVD and the contractors lived in these warm and well-built apartments. Almost always there was the smell of tasty food and sometimes perfume. Children ran around, and now and then you could hear music playing on the radio. And for us in the barracks, there was the smell of foot wrappings and felt boots drying on the stove. You could hear the voices of tired, hungry people, and occasionally you heard the terrible cursing of a criminal who had wandered into the barracks of the politicals. The residents of the comfortable apartments were as afraid to talk with us as if we had the plague. I don't remember a single instance when I was invited to sit down and warm myself or when they gave me something to eat.

And suddenly I had unheard-of good luck. The clerk who kept track of the amount of time prisoners worked and wrote down payments for the duty roster got sick. The head of the office came up to me and asked if I could keep track of the workers' salaries. (My case file indicated that I was a labor economist.) In general it was completely illegal; there was a rule for politicals: OHPW—Only Hard Physical Work. But the salaries were going to waste, and occasionally they had to put a *zek* to work, even one with a tough political sentence.

With great pleasure I went to an office, a warm lit room, and sat down at a table. In the office cleanly dressed, well-fed nonpolitical women prisoners worked. Each of them had a husband in the camp leadership. They ran out for lunch in the middle of the work day to the apartments where free people lived, walked around without a guard, began work at nine o'clock in the morning, and finished whenever. The only man in the office was a draftsman. His name was Igor Adrianovich Khorin. He was an ill-tempered person of about thirty-five who seemed to have tuberculosis.

I had an unbelievable amount of work to do. I had to reconcile and figure out a pile of about two weeks of orders, so I didn't really notice much of what was being done around me and worked without raising my head. I very much wanted to prolong working in the office, to have a rest from the frost, from the sawing and chopping of wood, and from making the rounds of the floors with that impossible weight. I paid attention to Khorin in connection with the following episode: A girl asked him to lend her a ruble. He went out and within fifteen minutes gave her a paper ruble. The girl ran to the buffet but quickly returned laughing: the ruble seemed to be simply a piece of paper, artistically drawn like a ruble. Everyone passed it around and was enchanted with the artistry. Igor proudly smiled and said:

"It's just a trifle of what I can do!"

I was told that he had been a famous counterfeiter and changed the winning numbers on government bonds. In addition he was a remarkable chess player, gave demonstrations of games on thirty boards at the same time, and beat the best chess players in Magadan.

I enjoyed my work and prayed to God that the bookkeeper would have a prolonged illness. My life was only spoiled by the fact that I finished work very late, and it was really frightening to walk alone at night through Magadan's very dark streets filled with deep snow.

I need to explain that there were few women in Kolyma. Criminals who had finished their sentences and those men who were unguarded (economic criminals and prisoners with light sentences) and had lived without women for years would simply throw themselves on a woman walking alone, like wolves on their prey. Once a drunken cook from a steamship frightened me, threatening me with a knife to make me go with him. I began to cry out and the patrol grabbed him. I was deathly afraid and every evening I lived through the same tortures. So one time when I left work at the same time as Khorin I asked him:

"Let's walk together. I am terribly afraid."

"You aren't a little girl. Go along," he answered and quickly walked ahead.

After that naturally I didn't want to talk with him.

One day I got hold of a little volume of Lermontov, and in the lunch break I was reading it. I noticed Khorin's sharp glance; he was looking at the book. I locked it in the drawer and went to talk with the foremen. When I returned, I couldn't find the book, although the drawer had been locked. Very upset (books in the camps are extremely valuable), I didn't even want to talk about my loss, knowing that you don't fight with a master thief. At the end of work, however, the book reappeared in the drawer and in the book was a note: "I very much apologize for my rudeness. I must speak with you. I will wait for you at the exit. Khorin." Amazed and happy at finding the book, I went out after work. Khorin was waiting for me. It turned out that he hadn't known about the existence of Lermontov, and that day he had been reading much of the book and even memorizing it. His abilities were remarkable.

"Tell me about Lermontov, when he lived, who he was," he asked me. When I told him that he was killed at the age of twenty-seven, Khorin almost cried.

From that day on we walked home together, and all our conversations were about literature. I recited the poems of Blok, Tiutchev, Pushkin, and Akhmatova to him—those that my memory retained. I even retold whole novels by Turgenev, Tolstoy, and Dostoevsky. He drank in everything, as the parched earth soaks up blessed moisture.

The life he had lived was terrible. He was the son of an officer, the oldest of six children. He hated his father because his father's wild brutality made life hell, not only for the orderlies who reported to him but also for his wife and children.

As a ten-year-old boy, he was sent to a military school for the sons of the nobility in another city. In spite of the strict regimentation that oppressed the nervous, freedom-loving boy, he didn't want to go home to Kazan for the holidays. In 1917 his father was literally torn apart by his soldiers who detested him. His mother went abroad with the five younger children, his military school dispersed, and Igor became a street waif. Hatred for his father and a grudge against his mother who had thrown him into the arms of fate—these feelings were transformed into a love for the Revolution. He joined some sort of military group. Short and thin, he looked like a ten-year-old at the age of twelve or thirteen. Unusual observation skills, memory, and cleverness all made him an indispensable scout. He fought through the whole Civil War and then got typhoid and spent half a year in the hospital. Another patient in a neighboring bed in the hospital was an educated person. He noticed the unusual capability of the boy and began to prepare him for the university. In a half year they finished math and physics at the high school level, but then Igor's teacher died. Before his death he gave Igor a letter to his colleague, a teacher at the university. After coming out of the hospital, Igor went to the addressee, and that person helped him enter the university in the department of physics and mathematics.

At first he took great pleasure in his studies, his friends, and the whole arrangement of his life. He even applied to become a Party member, but some member of the commission who had heard about his father voted against letting the son of an *officer* into the Party. Furious, Igor (who never had much self-control) threw a stool at the man. After that he was expelled from the university. So his academic career, which had lasted several months in all, came to an end.

And a new phase of life began for Igor: the criminal world welcomed him with open arms. He drew the winning numbers for government bonds, sold fake diamonds—he showed the real ones first, and then, using sleight of hand, instantly switched them. He still had some of the manners of a young man from good society, and they helped him deceive people. He knew how to comport himself, dressed well, and sometimes even threw a French phrase into his speech with an excellent accent, having picked this up from his mother, who had been educated at the Smolny Institute.

But in spite of all his talents, his criminal activities didn't last long. The authorities arrested him and sent him to the White Sea Canal. He spoke little of his camp life, but I know that thanks to his fortunate status and capabilities, he created a life that wasn't too bad, working as a draftsman and topographer. He was sharp-eyed, however, and saw much cruelty, injustice, and suffering. After he was released, he went to the theater and saw *Aristocrats* by Pogodin. I can't forget the rage with which he spoke of Pogodin.

"How sorry I am that I never met Pogodin! I would punch him in the snout so he wouldn't get rich on human pain and wouldn't tell such lies!"

At the White Sea Canal he got together with a girl who was a student. He lived with her but only for a short while. Like me, she talked about literature and read poetry to him. Sometimes they managed to get hold of some sort of book. Once they got a volume of Mayakovsky, and Igor learned it all by heart. He left the camp with the profession of draftsman and a strong determination to pull out of the criminal world and become a writer.

He took up residence at a dacha outside Leningrad. For whole days he read and wrote *Stories of My Life*. He never worked legally anywhere but earned money doing drafting work for others. This sounded very suspicious. His solitary life with books and notebooks did not fit with his criminal past, and Igor was arrested as a parasite. If he considered that his first arrest was deserved, his second arrest outraged him to the depths of his soul. He told the investigators that he had decided to become an educated person and a writer, but they pinned some fantastic criminal charge on him. In addition, the engineer who had given him work was arrested as an enemy of the people. All this happened in Leningrad in the atmosphere of suspicion after Kirov's murder. In short, he was sentenced to ten years, according to the CA (criminal activity) statute, and was sent to Kolyma. Along with bitterness and cynicism, there was in him a certain childish naïveté. Not knowing another life besides that of the camps and of thieves, not knowing women besides prostitutes (his short love affair on the White Sea Canal remained only a fleeting trace in his soul), he exaggerated the noble character and high morality of the intelligentsia. He sometimes asked me how we sat at the table. Did the mother and father sit at the head of the table? Did their daughters serve them? How did my husband propose to me? Was I engaged for long? And so forth. He looked at me from below to on high, as if looking at some sort of special higher being. I remember one comical situation. Somehow in a burst of self-deprecation, Igor said he didn't even have the right to stand close to a woman like me.

"But what are you doing comparing yourself to me?" I answered. "I was born in a fine and successful family surrounded by love and tenderness. Any number of books, museums, and theaters were available to me. If I had had a life like yours, I too would have become a thief."

He: "No, you never could have become a thief."

I: "But why not? I certainly could have become one!"

He (with irritation): "Yes, and you certainly would have been caught on the first day!"

Well, it's true. Thievery requires carefulness, sharp eyes, observation, and many other qualities that are completely absent in me.

Not knowing how one must converse with a decent woman, Igor behaved with prim and proper old-fashioned courtesy toward me. He never took me by the arm and never led the conversation into intimate themes. Only once he talked with me as a man to a woman. They sent me ten kilometers from Magadan to the village of Marchekan to finalize the workers' orders. I was frightened to go alone, and I asked Igor to think of some assignment in Marchekan and take me there. On the road he was gloomy and silent. But the day was beautiful. The March sun shone clearly, and the sky was radiant. I said:

"No guards, no dogs, no one is shouting out: 'Step right, step left—I'll shoot.' We are walking along like normal people . . ."

He was silent. It seemed as though he hadn't heard me, so busy was he with his thoughts. But suddenly with shining eyes he said:

"And why aren't you afraid of me? After all I'm a man too!"

I answered with full conviction:

"Not only am I not afraid of you, but if I had to send my daughter on this trip, I would ask you to accompany and protect her."

He grabbed my hand and kissed it. I thought tears were shining in his eyes.

I became really true friends with Igor. This was the only bright page in my camp life. Our friendship was infused with a warm poetic love of literature. I did everything in my power to introduce him to literature. Much more gifted than I, he instantly felt what was precious in what I managed to tell him. Once I recited a poem to him, "The Dying Swan" by Balmont, which had stuck in my memory from my younger days. He wrinkled up his face like a music lover who hears a wrong note and said:

"Better to recite something else from Nekrasov or Blok. This is just candied fruit."

So Igor and I were friends for three whole months. And then suddenly everything collapsed. Our group of prisoners was dispatched to the taiga to cut down trees on April 4, 1940. Unexpectedly they announced at night that tomorrow no one would go to work. They were dispatching us on a transport.

Such is camp life.

That night I was awakened by a knock on the window above my head. It was Igor. He had made an opening in the frame so I could speak with him. He asked what he could do for me. I was amazed at how he could get into the women's camp, find out where I slept, and make a hole in the window frame. Only a person from the camps would understand how difficult that could be. Apparently he had used all his connections, money (he made money winning at chess), and cleverness, in order to say good-bye to me. I asked him to communicate with my relatives that I wouldn't be able to write for a long time because of having to move. He did this for me.

I never saw Igor again, but within a year I received a letter from him. He was in the hospital in the last stages of tuberculosis.

"I am dying," he wrote, "and I want to tell you that I think about you all the time. You were the last ray of light in my life. Remember the day when you said, 'We are walking along like normal people'? And I raged with fury in my soul. That which is so accessible to normal people is as unattainable for us as the moon in the sky . . ." Then came lines of poetry.

This letter was confiscated from me during a routine search. From his poem I remember only the last stanza:

> I also call you my friend of the heart,
> Because the summer of our lives ends in
> The twilight of the Arctic Circle,
> Because my song and yours have ended.

His friend had added a note to the letter: "Igor Adrianovich Khorin died on May 5, 1941." He was thirty-six years old.

Mama

Those who have not waited cannot understand
That your waiting for me
In the middle of a fire
Was what saved me.
—K. SIMONOV

I had a toothache. In the evening after work I went to the boss and asked him to let me go to the hospital. The boss looked at me attentively and stated:

"There is no need to go. It will get better by itself."

To argue would have been useless. I sat down near the stove and began to endure it. The pain was colossal. I cried from helplessness, from pain, from resentment. Toward morning the pain began to subside, but a huge gumboil had swollen up on my cheek. At the morning roll call, the boss looked at me again and stated:

"Now you may go."

I went. The frost wasn't too strong, the temperature was minus thirty-five, the sun was shining, and it was a ten-kilometer walk. The pain had abated. I was hot and very tired from the sleepless night, from pain, from tears, from my whole life.

I decided to take a rest and I lay down in a snowdrift. Right away a sweet torpor seized me and I fell asleep. And I saw my mother's face in a feverish dream, red from stress and rage.

"Stand up this minute!" said Mama.

"Mamochka, please don't wake me up. I feel so happy, things are so good with me! It is wonderful to die this way and not to suffer anymore. Mamochka, let me die!"

"You will die, you will be resting, and what about me? I will have to live with the thought that I'll never see you again, that you died in a snowdrift? I have no right to die. I have your children on my hands!"

I stood up and went on. Everything floated in front of my eyes. Within a half hour, completely exhausted, I lay down again in a snowdrift, and again I saw my mother's face and again got up and trudged on. It took me five hours to walk those ten kilometers. Several times I lay down in snowdrifts and got up because I kept seeing my mother's face.

In the hospital I collapsed unconscious with a temperature of 40.5 degrees and lay there for a week. The doctor was amazed that I had been able to walk ten kilometers in such condition.

Galia

I worked at logging with Galia Prozorovskaia as a teammate. At the beginning she was stronger and more skillful than I, but gradually she began to lose strength. She worked more and more slowly, and we began finishing our general norm (eight cubic meters a day for two people) later and later. Everyone was going home, but our stack wasn't yet collected, and we didn't have the strength to move faster.

I was always the first to give up.

"Let's stop, Galia. We'll finish tomorrow, I can't do anymore."

Galia looked at me with the eyes of an exhausted horse and said:

"And the norm? Can you get along on four hundred grams?"

(If you fulfilled the norm, you got six hundred grams of bread a day, and if not, you got four hundred grams. This two-hundred-gram difference determined whether we lived or died because one could not live and work at fifty degrees below zero on four hundred grams of bread a day.)

"Oh yes, of course . . . The norms! Well, let's try and make one more effort." We stacked up the firewood, with me cheating unscrupulously, sticking snow and branches inside the pile. Galia pleaded with me:

"Please don't. What if they find out? How shameful! We, former Party members, are burying snow in the wood pile."

Somehow or other eight cubic meters get stacked, and it's already completely dark, but we have to walk five kilometers to get home. And here we are trudging along the return road. The frost freezes your spine, hands, and face. It takes the fullest exertion of will to walk for an hour and a half or two along an empty forest road when each foot weighs a ton, when your knees shake from weakness and hunger, when the kerchief covering your face turns into an icy shield and makes breathing difficult.

But ahead are the warm barracks, hot soup, and two hundred grams of heavy, damp, but tasty bread. Ahead is a rest on our bunks, friendly faces, a warm stove with a fire burning in it. And so we walk.

Every day we leave our work later and later, and the road home gets longer because the clearing where we cut wood is farther and farther from the barracks.

One day Galia and I were walking in silence, hardly able to drag our feet. It was deathly cold. The moon was shining and reflected on the snow, lighting our way. We were already getting close to the camp when suddenly Galia fell flat on her back and lay there without moving.

"Galia, Galia," I tugged at her. I didn't know if she was dead or unconscious.

Galia lay there lifelessly. There was no question of my lifting her because I didn't have enough strength for that. I tugged at her and pushed her but got no answer. I took my hand out of my mitten in order to feel her pulse and instantly froze my hand. I stuck it inside the front of my jacket, but it wouldn't warm up. It had no feeling. Gradually it began to hurt—and that meant it was alive. But I hadn't found out whether Galia had died or fainted.

"If she has died, they may just as well pick her up tomorrow, but now I must keep going or otherwise I too will freeze. But if she is alive? Within an hour she'll turn into a piece of ice." I can do no more and I decide to walk on, rather than for both of us to freeze.

I decisively take several steps on the road, then turn back.

"Galia, Galia!"

No answer. What am I to do? I shrug and again start walking in the direction of home, and again turn back.

"Galochka, Galia!"

No answer. And suddenly I hear the squeak of a sleigh and the clattering of a horse on a parallel road, about two hundred meters from ours. I run, I scream, I stumble across, I fall, out of breath from the frost, from screaming, from running.

Finally I get close to the driver who is hauling manure in his wagon.

"For God's sake, help, a woman is freezing!"

He is very unwilling. He too is freezing, tired, and dreaming of the warm stove, soup, and two hundred grams of evening bread ration.

I plead with him, I cry, I cling with my arms to his padded jacket when he wants to drive away. Swearing he turns toward our road, and together we load Galia onto the manure. We go by foot because the poor horse is also barely alive. In about fifteen minutes we reach the barracks, sit by the stove, and share our soup with our savior. He turns out to be a singer from Leningrad. We talk about the theater, about music, and Galia, regaining consciousness, lies on the bunk, warms up, and tears stream unceasingly from her eyes.

Bread

If we fulfilled the norms, once a month they gave us an additional kilogram of bread.

We long dreamed of this bread. How tasty this bread was! Usually I received the bread, but one month things did not work out so well. Several times I fell short of the norm, and the monthly bonus didn't happen.

For a long time I had had a premonition in my heart, but when we arrived back from work the day before our day off, we rushed to the list, and I didn't find my name on it. I felt great bitterness. I had hoped I might have been listed for that kilogram of bread all the same.

Those who were on the list ran off joyfully to receive their bread, and those who were not made indifferent faces and pretended not to notice how the others were feasting.

The day off was spoiled. True, my neighbor did give me a little piece of her bread, but this was certainly not the same as a whole kilogram.

When we returned from work the next day, the woman on guard duty met me with an exclamation:

"Run to the barracks, look at what's lying under your pillow!"

My heart pounded. I thought that probably they had given me bread after all!

I ran to the bed and threw off the pillow. Under it lay three letters from home, three letters! For half a year I had not received a single letter.

The first feeling I experienced was sharp disappointment: it was not bread, it was letters!

But following that reaction came horror.

What had I been reduced to, if a piece of bread was dearer to me than letters from Mama, Papa, and the children!

I tore open the envelopes.

Photographs fell out. My daughter glanced at me with her blue eyes. My son had knitted his brows and was thinking of something.

I forgot about the bread and I cried.

Basia

Basia was nineteen years old. For Zionism she had received a sentence of five years of hard labor in the camps.

She and her fiancé, a twenty-year-old student, were arrested together. Basia looked like a typical angel, if one can express it that way. Golden locks, blue eyes, clear rosy cheeks, a hundred and fifty centimeters tall, lips like cherries. But rarely can appearances be so deceptive. Basia was far from an angel. She was a girl with a very strong character. And even more of a voice. Basia's voice was incredibly piercing and high. She meddled in everything, stood up for truth. If she was in the barracks, you could hear it.

One day at roll call, the guard who gave out the work assignments came up to her:

"You go to the place where the guard on duty sits, and you'll wash the floors."

Washing the floors was considered soft work: it was warm and it was women's work, not like carrying firewood with oxen or hacking the earth with a pickax. Basia eagerly agreed, but when we returned from work, we saw her in the barracks bitterly crying, and in her piercing voice she recounted how the guard had treated her to sausage and lard at the beginning and then began to approach her. She had hit him with a wet rag, and he got angry and said:

"Tomorrow you go carry logs with the oxen."

Basia was terribly afraid of oxen, and they didn't listen to her. They were used to rough voices and dirty language, but Basia ran around them, called them disgusting animals, and cried. They would lie down and pay no more attention to her than they would to a fly. Two or three days went by. The guard who gave out work would again tell her to wash the floors, and the work would again end up with the oxen. Finally the guard had had enough, and he decided on extreme measures.

"We're getting no work out of you," he announced at roll call. "You fuss around all day, you keep the oxen busy, and nothing comes of it. Tomorrow you join Prokhorov. You'll carry logs together as a team."

Prokhorov was one of the few men in our camp. He repaired harnesses, fixed tools, and carried the heaviest logs. He was a man of about fifty with a terrible expression, huge shoulders that looked like a chest of drawers, and long arms reaching almost to his knees. They said that during collectivization he had killed three people. We had never heard such an unparalleled virtuoso of filthy language. He seemed terribly frightening to Basia. She sobbed and said she would not go with Prokhorov. A solitary prison cell would be better. Suddenly Prokhorov entered the barracks.

"What are you bawling about?" he asked Basia. "Afraid of Prokhorov, are you? Don't be afraid of Prokhorov, be afraid of the bosses! Prokhorov won't harm you." He turned around and went out. Puzzled, Basia calmed down and the next day went to work with Prokhorov and two yokes of oxen. From that day on a strange friendship developed between the huge gorilla-like Prokhorov and the angelic Basia. He fed her and worked for her. Our Basia got plump and told us that Prokhorov was a very good person.

Once the whole barracks was laughing at a story Prokhorov was telling, but Basia kept stamping her foot at him and crying out:

"Shut up, shut up!"

Prokhorov, paying no attention to her, said:

"I load the cart, look around, and my Baska isn't there. I look this way, that way, she is standing behind a tree crying, her hands frozen, and she can't button up her pants. I did up her buttons, tied her belt, made a little fire, warmed her hands, my little Baska. I sat her on a log and she came back safe and sound. That's Prokhorov for you!"

Basia worked with Prokhorov for two years, and he protected her like a devoted dog.

When she was released, Basia went to join her young fiancé who was serving his sentence in one of the distant men's camps. Her fiancé was apparently a pushy guy who had succeeded in gaining his boss's confidence, and when he was freed, he stayed on working for the camp supply department. When Basia arrived he had prepared a room with a year's worth of food that was sumptuous from the camp point of view. But in the camp people were dying of hunger. It wasn't hard to guess where these supplies had come from.

Clever Basia understood the whole situation at first glance. She had seen camp life, and she herself had gone hungry because of the bosses' thievery.

After pouring out the whole truth of what she had seen straight to her disheartened fiancé's face, Basia got into a passing car without taking even a taste of the prepared treats and returned. In Yagodny she got a job in a dining hall and within a year married the best shoemaker in Yagodny, Monia Lourye. Monia had been a student at the Literary Institute, but luckily for him, his shoemaker father sometimes had made his studious son help him at work. This saved Monia's life. Throughout his whole sentence, he patched the camp people's boots that were heavy and thick with dust and repaired their felt boots that had been burned. Sometimes he sewed elegant slippers for the wives of the bosses. And when he was freed, he set himself up nicely in Yagodny. Basia gave birth to a charming angel, Mishenka. She turned out to be a very good mother and wife. Their room was big, and Basia's home became a refuge for all those who were freed but hadn't yet managed to get settled. I myself lived with them for a week or two. I liked Monia and little Misha too. The head of the family was, of course, Basia. This was the first real family I had seen in eight years.

Monia used to say to me:

"I've seen many miracles, but I never would have believed that someone could possibly survive the Kolyma camps and remain a virgin."

Gold

We were going to the meadow to mow. We stopped for a rest and cooked kasha. And then I went to the brook to wash the dishes. I scooped up a bowl of water, sloshed it around, poured it out, and grains of gold remained on the bottom of the bowl. This made an amazingly strong impression on me. Gold . . . What would I need it for in the camp? But there is something magic in this dust. Grains of gold had gathered in a crack of the tin bowl and were sparkling in the sun.

"Gold, gold!" I cried.

All the women gathered around me to gaze at it. Prokhorov came up.

"You call that gold! It just looks like it. It's a fake," he said positively and poured the dust on the ground.

Everyone quieted down, got busy with her tasks, and forgot about the gold.

We walked on farther. Prokhorov was leading a horse ahead of us. I somehow found myself beside him. After a long silence he said:

"Well, you certainly are a fool. Educated, but a fool. What would you do with gold? We're living here quietly and raking hay. But if they find gold, do you know how many people would be hurt? Have you ever seen how they work in the mines? Isn't your man there? You don't know? Maybe he's been lying in a mine shaft because of this gold for a long time. A person can dig for gold for just one season and then—it's all over. Aren't you a fool?"

"So it was gold?"

"Of course. What else?"

Polina Lvovna Gertzenberg

For some time my neighbor on the bunks was Dr. Polina Lvovna Gerzenberg, a Polish Jew, a Communist, and member of the Sejm.

Doctors had the right to excuse sick people from work. Those who had anything to trade were willing to give away a lot for the possibility of being excused from hard labor. Several doctors improved their lives by taking these voluntary gifts. Polina Lvovna was completely impractical. She suffered from hunger like the rest of us, and she didn't even want to write herself a prescription for cod liver oil, which they gave to the most exhausted. She dressed in handmade bark shoes and fourth-hand trousers patched with sackcloth.

During the winter of 1941, or the beginning of 1942, an announcement appeared on the board describing the Russian-Polish negotiations according to which all Poles arrested on Polish territory after 1939 were to be released.

They really did free the Poles, but the Poles couldn't return from Kolyma until the ocean was navigable. They didn't work and could go out of the zone, but they lived as before with us in the barracks.

Suddenly the camp leadership became agitated: an order had come by plane to dispatch six members of the Polish Sejm to the mainland. Among that number was Polina Lvovna. In order to dispatch these six people, a chief public prosecutor from Dalstroi arrived. His first directive was to dress up those being dispatched. They called Polina Lvovna to the storehouse, and the boss of the camp triumphantly presented her with a surprise: a silk dress, suede shoes, and a sealskin coat. Great was his amazement when

Polina Lvovna said she was going to fly in the clothes she had been wearing for two years. No matter how they talked with her, no matter what they offered her, she would not take off her padded trousers patched with sackcloth and her padded felt boots. And forcing her to change was forbidden. Looking this way she went to her farewell interview with the public prosecutor. He was very upset when he saw her, but he pretended not to pay attention to her apparel. He reported on the negotiations with Poland and ended his speech with these words:

"Our countries are fighting now against a common enemy—German Fascism. I hope that when you return you will spread no slander about the Soviet Union."

"I can give you my word," said Polina Lvovna, "that I will spread no slander about the Soviet Union. On the contrary, after victory I will speak the truth, only the truth, and the whole truth in the Sejm, in the press, everywhere."

They could not object, and she went out, the bosses shooting dark glances and we shooting admiring glances at her.

Labor

As I recall, when I was the leader of an agricultural brigade we culti-
vated cabbage. Cabbage in these places saved the whole camp population
from scurvy. Under conditions of permafrost, we fussed about our cabbage as if it were a baby. Several times in the summer we fertilized and fed
it, sheltered it from the mist coming off the frozen ground, and endlessly
watered it. How happy we were when, in spite of the drought and the evening frost, in spite of the June snowfalls, they grew white tops! We were
very hungry, but we never permitted ourselves to eat unripened cabbage
heads in the fields. We tore off the outer leaves and cooked gray cabbage
soup. One day when I was walking into the field, I noticed that a whole
row of cabbages had no hearts in the middle leaves from which the head
of the cabbage grows. At first I thought this was some ordinary pest who
had eaten them and that we had to begin to fight it quickly. And suddenly
I saw how one of the workers from our brigade, a convict called Valia, was
calmly tearing out the hearts and nibbling them like sunflower seeds.

"Look, why are you doing that? You are killing the whole harvest!"

She smiled blankly and answered:

"What the hell do we need it for? It's all the same when they are fed to
the bosses."

I almost hit her and anger flashed from my eyes, but she innocently
smiled.

"What are you going so crazy about?"

Labor was the only human activity left to us. We didn't have families,
there were no books, we lived in filth, stench, and darkness, and in the

women's barracks there was terrible cursing. We endured humiliation from any supervisor who could enter the barracks at night, make the half-dressed women stand up, and with the excuse of a search, rummage in our beds and our underwear, read our letters and diaries. In the baths for some reason men assisted us, and when we protested, the bosses laughed and answered, "When your head is cut off, you won't cry about your hair." Labor was human and clean. We did peasant's work that millions and millions of women had done before us.

Life showed us that by overcoming incompetence and physical weakness, by gaining work skills, and above all by having a different attitude about work, we worked better than demoralized criminals, although the mass of them were younger and stronger than we were, and the majority came from uneducated families where they had acquired the habit of physical labor from childhood. The dekulakized peasants, of course, worked best of all, but the brigadiers (former kulaks) fought for the politicals, in spite of the fact that it was easier to talk with the thieves, and with us the brigadiers had to stop all cursing. They knew we would work hard and systematically. The criminals would work away very fast for an hour, so it was impossible to keep up with them, but when the brigade leaders left, they would lie down and sleep, not caring if the seedlings withered and the frost killed the young growth.

Heavy peasant labor in the outdoors, far from the guards, distant from strange, evil people, remained one of the only bright memories in the darkness of camp life.

Often we would walk into a far field with our team of six people. Three of us would cut the hay with scythes and three would gather. You walk along the field with your scythe. The bright expanse of the poor Kolyma land lies before you. A splendid aroma seeps from the fading field. A pale transparent sky. Thoughts flow freely. You remember everything beautiful there used to be in life. And you begin to believe that this perennial labor, these fields and sky—this is reality. It has been, it shall be, and all the unnatural horror that has happened to us will go away, just as the Tatar horde went out of ancient Rus.

It was painful when labor, in which we had invested everything human that remained to us, turned out to be a mockery, senseless and punishing.

We hacked ditches out of the frozen ground so that melting water could flow through them.

We worked at fifty degrees below zero with heavy pickaxes. We tried to fulfill our norms. If snow covered our unfinished ditch overnight, we cleaned it out and deepened it exactly to the norm. Probably no one would have noticed that it was ten to fifteen centimeters short, but it was a question of honor—and certainly water wouldn't otherwise flow from the field as it needed to.

It was very heavy work. The ground was like cement. Our breath froze in the air. Our shoulders and lower backs hurt from the exertion. But we worked and reasoned that without this heavy work, without our bloody calluses and frozen feet, the land of Kolyma could not be conquered.

The criminals swore at us with their last words because we showed that it was possible to do ten times more than they did. And in the spring when the ground thawed out, a tractor was brought in with a ditch-digging attachment, and in an hour it dug a ditch that it had taken a team of six people two months to dig.

"Why aren't all the ditches dug that way," I naively asked the leader of the team.

"And then what will you do? Lie around on your side and get fat? No, my dear, they sent you to the camp to work!"

I was terribly ashamed of my high-level thoughts and speech. God, what a disgrace! They punished us with meaningless work, and we fulfilled our punishments with enthusiasm! What slaves we were! I swore not to invest my soul in work anymore and to get around it wherever I could. I didn't succeed in this. I couldn't change my nature and work the way the common criminals did, but my enthusiasm diminished.

Yet all the same, work saved us. Among the politicals there were categories of people who refused to work. Many women were afraid of heavy labor. Some discovered that they had hundreds of illnesses, preferred to receive nourishment at a lower norm, and didn't overexert themselves at work. Others (much more rarely) had affairs with the bosses, who arranged easy work for them. Almost all who avoided work died. Those who went into prostitution lost their inner core, their perseverance, self-discipline, and pride. With their very first failure, they had to fall back into regular work and died under its weight. Those who didn't work because of their alleged weakness and illness died from hunger and also from spiritual disorder. They were challenged by the absence of a powerful diversion—labor— which requires the exertion of all one's physical and emotional strength. There were situations in which even those who worked did die, but those situations were much more rare. That's the way it was with the women.

With the men, the healthiest of them turned into invalids after one or two seasons of panning for gold.

Men naturally couldn't love the work that destroyed them, and they spoke with horror of the mines.

Devil's Wheel

A small camp section that we called Devil's Wheel consisted of two temporary huts for workers, some little huts where the guards lived, and huts for the brigade leaders. The population of Devil's Wheel was forty-five people. There were forty prisoners, of whom thirty-three lived in a *political* hut and seven in a *jolly* hut.

In our political workers' hut there were bunks. Almost nobody had actual personal possessions. The beds were covered with army blankets, and the pillows were stuffed with straw. No one stayed there during the day except the old woman who kept the stoves going.

In the evening we went to bed early, exhausted from hard work. Once in a while a book ended up in the hut, and someone would read aloud by the light of a homemade wick lamp.

We gathered in groups on the bunks and talked softly in order not to disturb the sleep of the exhausted women.

In the jolly hut the picture was completely different. Seven wooden beds stood there, covered with rosy, gaudy, blue-flowered blankets. The pillows had embroidered pillowcases. On the pillowcases were pictures of pretty girls with huge eyes taking up half the face, doves, flowers, and embroidered sayings like "Dream about me, dear one, I am sick with love for you" or "Day and night I can't get along without you." Above the beds hung handmade rugs of sackcloth with embroidered cats, swans, flowers, and Japanese women. On the table stood an object of our envy—a real kerosene lamp with a glass shade.

Girls from the jolly hut worked separately from us and came home from work much earlier, at two or three o'clock in the afternoon. They often got sick and received permission not to go out to work. In the hut they entertained themselves far beyond midnight. The accordion squealed, the drunken voices of girls shrieked, and the hoarse voices of men wheezed.

The organizer of the entertainment was a foreman named Sashka Sokolov, a swindler from Odessa, smart and clever as the devil. He launched a rather successful venture, inviting guests from neighboring gold mines, treating them to alcohol, pleasant conversation, and the society of girls. Sashka also didn't get along badly with us. He had to arrange things so that we didn't complain and so that we worked. In order for us not to complain, he organized a kind of quarantine. For a year while we lived there, they didn't let us leave the village, and no one came to us from headquarters. We had to work because if we didn't, they wouldn't feed us. Otherwise Sashka didn't bother us, and we loved him to a certain extent because he never interfered with us about anything and didn't steal food from us. He didn't need to steal. He was commercially minded and knew how to receive a solid income from the guests visiting his jolly hut.

We set ourselves up formally according to our sentences. The nonpolitical prisoners were in the jolly hut, and the politicals were in the work hut. In our political hut there were several old peasants with minor sentences. Sashka did not object. What would he need these old women for? But once a young girl, Alla Shvander, came up to the bunk where I slept and rather politely asked, "Will you take me in with you? I don't want to be in that hut." We took her in. She was a tall, pretty, twenty-year-old girl who spoke in an educated way. She had ended up in the camp as the lookout for a gang of swindlers. Her parents, people from the intelligentsia, didn't notice that seventeen-year-old Alla had become friends with a young man at the skating rink and that she had become his lover. He turned out to be the head of a gang. Alla was a good girl but very weak willed and suggestible. She herself knew this was her weakness and naively told us, "I still have one year to go." (Her sentence was three years.) "Don't let me go to that hut or I will be ruined there."

We took Alla under our protection. Sashka came after her several times, demanding that she move back to the jolly hut, but we made such an outcry that he simply covered his ears, and seemed to give in to us.

Alla worked with us, loved to hear readings or stories, and dreamed that when her sentence was over she would get married and become a decent woman.

A suitor appeared—Kostia, a carpenter from a neighboring sawmill, a good fellow who gazed at Alla with worshipful eyes. He came to us in the hut like a real suitor, bringing treats to the mothers-in-law, as he called Raia and me, and for hours at a time he would stand with Alla in fifty-degrees-below-zero weather, hugging her and covering her with his sheepskin coat. He planned to wait a year for her and then get married. This was young love, blossoming so wonderfully in the midst of the filthy, dirty camp life. He admired Alla, her beauty, and her education. He himself was a simple working fellow from Siberia. Alla bathed in the waves of his adoration and liked his honesty, directness, and strength.

We watched the growth of this romance with delight, and we protected it from everything. Sashka also knew about Kostia and, it seemed, didn't even try to hurt the young pair.

One day he sent Alla to carry wood to a forest hut.

"Konstantin is waiting for you there," he whispered to Alla, and she rushed to the unexpected meeting on a sled, rosy, graceful, tightly belted, sitting behind the horses with radiant eyes, urging them on with joyful cries.

She went away and did not return for the evening roll call.

This was a serious breach of discipline for which you could get into enormous trouble.

Alla did not return for two more days.

And on the third evening she came into the barracks exhausted, with an earthy gray face and a distracted gaze. She fell heavily onto the bunk and wailed from pain, grief, and shame.

. . . she was going to a meeting with Kostia. She saw from far away that the stove was warm in the hut. That meant he was waiting. With joy she opened the door and fell into the arms of six bandits who were waiting for her.

Sashka had arranged this.

He had received a thousand rubles from these bandits.

Everyone was in shock. We created unrealistic plans to avenge Alla. We cursed Sashka.

A boss of the guards came into the barracks.

"Where were you for three days?"

"Ask Sashka," began Alla.

"I define your outrageous behavior as an attempted escape," the boss stated and sat down to write the protocol.

We began to explain, but he yelled at us and threatened to write us down as accomplices to the escape.

The protocol for escape was a doubled sentence for three years, and for accomplices too. We were quiet. Alla cried, and we had bad consciences because we hadn't known how to stand up for her.

The next day Sashka called Alla to him and said that he could put a stop to the case if she would agree to go back to the jolly hut. How could the poor girl argue with him? She felt she was under his power and was afraid of the sentence. She realized that everything with Kostia was finished. Sullenly she came into our hut and gathered her things. I timidly reached out to her, and in response I heard terrible cursing.

Unexpectedly, about three days after this incident, they called me to the town of Elgen, where the camp headquarters were and where it might be possible to seek justice against Sashka.

I was called in because of a letter from my mother who, it turned out, had not received any correspondence from me in a year. My mother had written to the chief supervisor of the camp, a fat, uneducated old woman, who was cantankerous but sometimes good-natured, if she happened to be in a good mood.

This fat woman with a swollen face and a military uniform sat in the office where I first entered.

"Why aren't you writing your mother? Have you no conscience?"

"I do write, Citizen Supervisor, but obviously my letters aren't being sent."

"Yes, there are many swine here. You write a letter and give it to me. I'll send it."

This beginning encouraged me, and I made a decision:

"Citizen Supervisor, I would like to speak to you about something, but if our foreman Sashka finds out, I will certainly die. If you don't want to get involved in this affair, please God don't tell him that I told you."

I was terrified. It wouldn't cost him anything to do to me what he had done to Alla. It would be simpler to kill me.

I told her the story of Alla.

"What scoundrels, what swine! He does it with the leader of the guards. And does the head of the guards take part in their drunken orgies?"

"He does."

"Well, you go away and be quiet. I'll deal with him."

She did not deal with him, and everything remained as it had been before. To give her credit I must say that Sashka never found out about my denunciation. I didn't sleep at night for a long time, however, cursing myself for being a Don Quixote and imagining what Sashka would do with me, if he found out.

Alla lived in the jolly hut and became the most dissolute of the inhabitants. She drank heavily and cursed from morning to evening. She never visited us and looked at us with a kind of evilness and contempt.

Within a year she got her freedom, and within the next eight months after that she was caught with a gang in a nasty affair—they had killed and robbed a whole family.

Sashka's attitude toward us was rather complicated: He never dared to enter our hut in his underwear, as he did with his girls' hut. He didn't dare to swear at us and even addressed us using the formal *vy*. We were very interesting to him; this was the first time in his life that he had encountered educated and decent women. Our impracticality annoyed him. I remember this situation: They didn't give us dynamite, and we dug out the ditches by hand with pickaxes. A demolition expert from a road team lost his heart to one of our women. He proposed blowing up our ditches from underneath, and then we would only have to throw out the dirt. But receiving no response to his love and feeling offended, the demolition expert left. Enraged, Sashka stormed into our hut and, finding out how things stood, waved his hand and said bitterly: "With you Socialism will never be built."

He sometimes launched into conversations with us and was very happy when he caught us in a lack of knowledge about things that were simple from his point of view. He very much wanted to show us that, although he hadn't attended a university, he was smarter than educated people. (He certainly had a better understanding than we did of practical matters and of human relationships.) But he was even happier when he could demean us and show that even though we were politicals, we were not better than the next guy and wouldn't turn down sweets. He very much wanted to involve our women in the nightly drinking sprees and invited one or another to "have some fun," but invariably he was turned down.

There was a beautiful Cossack woman among us, Ania Orlova. At forty-two, she had retained a stately bearing, a hot glance in her black eyes, and the low voice of a violoncello. She was the brigade leader's assistant.

Regardless of her physical strength, skillfulness, and familiarity with village work, Ania very much valued her position, not having to work ten hours a day in the bitter frost of Kolyma and not straining herself with heavy pickaxes. Sashka played on this vulnerability. At first Ania casually told us, as if it didn't mean anything, that Sashka had asked her to sing Ukrainian songs some evening.

She looked at us and met indirectly critical glances. Then one time she said, "I'm so bored—maybe I'll go to Sashka's sometime and listen to the accordion . . ." Again silence.

And then when Sashka gave her an ultimatum, "Either you stop avoiding our company or you go to work with all the others," she decided to go to the jolly hut for an evening. We saw how, with deliberate calmness, she took out her only formal outfit—an embroidered Ukrainian blouse—put on lipstick, pulled a white shawl over her shoulders, and walked between the bunks past a row of critical eyes. Then we heard the accordion, Ania's low chesty voice singing Ukrainian songs, the rumble of approval, applause, and again Ania's voice.

Ania came back before morning, and the next day Sashka impudently slapped her on the shoulder, saying that Ania was "one of his crowd, but all the rest of you are from the lousy intelligentsia—you are black nuns."

Ania went around with an impudent look, as if she could care less. But from time to time she would throw out a comment like, "Well, are we going to die like this in this convent? No matter what they are, still they are people, there are songs . . ."

Everyone was silent.

And within three days Sashka walked around our hut and consoled his friend, the famous swindler, Volodya:

"Volodechka, don't be upset. I will introduce you to whatever girl you want."

And Volodya answered in a languorous voice:

"No, you deceived me. You promised me a girl, but in the morning when I woke up there was an old granny with me, and she thought she was the greatest."

"Volodechka, don't get upset. You'll sleep with the intelligentsia at night"— he expressed it more colorfully—"but during the day we'll chase them off to work. And if you don't like this, I'll bring you a twenty-year-old today."

Sashka was pleased with himself. He acted like a buffoon, laughed, and again repeated:

"We'll sleep with them at night, but during the daytime we'll chase them off to work!"

I have to give him credit; he didn't fire Ania from her brigade leader's job. He couldn't help having the satisfaction of hitting her on the shoulder and encouraging her: "Don't get flustered, he's a fool, Volodka doesn't understand anything about girls. You are still a hot number . . ."

Ania didn't go to the jolly hut anymore, and Sashka didn't insist on it. His goal had been achieved. Through Ania's face he had lowered the standing of the whole intelligentsia, and he was very satisfied.

At Devil's Wheel for the first time I got to know women who were sentenced for their religion. They brought five women to us who had been arrested for refusing to work at the collective farm on holidays. Sashka fully realized that, although they were young, they weren't a good fit for the jolly hut. They called one another sisters, slept, ate, worked, prayed together, and almost every Sunday or church holiday sat together in the isolation cell. The thing was that they gave us three days off a month, so that meant we had to work one Sunday. In addition to that, if the working days were cancelled because of bad weather (a blizzard or frost with temperatures less than fifty degrees below zero), these days were counted as days off, and then we worked not one but two or three Sundays. The religious women refused to work and were put in the isolation cell. They peacefully gathered in the cell, although there was little there that was good: in the winter the stove hardly gave out any heat; in the summer clouds of mosquitoes flew in through the broken window.

However, the religious women worked more diligently than anyone else, since they were used to peasant labor. No matter how hard we tried, we could not catch up with them in our work.

One of the religious women, Grania, sometimes received packages from her husband, who was serving a sentence at a stable a thousand kilometers from us and was soon to be released. Grania was arrested half a year after him, and she correspondingly awaited the end of her sentence several months later.

One day Sashka came to us and announced that tomorrow, Sunday, was a working day. Then he said to Grania:

"Your husband has sent you a smoked fish. Go out to work, even if you don't do anything, and I'll give you the package. If you don't go—don't be insulted, but I won't give it to you."

"Whatever you wish," said Grania. "We are not going to work."

Her sisters eagerly supported her. And they wanted so much to eat that smoked fish! We were certainly all starving!

One time the girlfriends of two hardened criminals came running up to us—Sonka, who was Sashka's girl, and Liubka, who lived with the head of the guards. They always knew all the news. And today the news was considerable.

First of all, the following Sunday—Easter Sunday—we didn't have to work. It was a day off. And more importantly they had permitted Grania's husband, Ivan, who had already been released, to visit his wife. He was arriving on Sunday at noon. (At eleven o'clock the bus arrived at the nearest station, which was about an hour's walk from our camp. At four o'clock he had to leave because at five the return bus would depart.)

The next day at half past eleven all of us were already gathered at the gate of the zone. Liubka and Sonka, who could cross the forbidden line, ran out of the zone, watching for Ivan's arrival.

Finally Sonka ran back with the cry, "He's coming!" We were afraid to miss the very moment of this meeting and the expressions on Grania's and Ivan's faces.

On the road a man appeared. From the camp point of view, he was dressed very well: high boots polished to a shine, a new blue cotton shirt . . . His beard was clipped. His cheeks, shaven.

Grania wanted to run to meet him, but she was unsteady on her feet. Two sisters supported her under her arms. She was pale and only her eyes were burning. About ten steps before he got to her, Ivan went down on his knees and bowed to the earth before her.

Grania also went down on her knees and bowed to the earth before him. Then he came up, held her, and they kissed each other three times. Ivan also kissed the sisters three times and gave them presents: cotton head-shawls and painted eggs. Then he gave them a bundle with gifts. There was smoked fish, a piece of pork, *kulich,* and even an Easter cheese cake, and he invited them to prepare the meal.

He bowed to us. He went up to Sashka, gave him something, and Sashka said, "Of course, of course, take your wife and go for a walk in the forest."

Ivan took Grania by the hand, and they walked out of the zone.

Sonka and Liubka ran after them to see what they would do. Sonka returned completely astonished: they were sitting on stumps at the edge of the forest, talking with each other.

"Just think," said Sonka, "Five years they didn't see each other and they're sitting on stumps, talking. In his place Sashka would gobble me up! And these guys just talk! He told her he's building an *izba.* When she gets her freedom, the *izba* will be ready."

Within fifteen minutes Liubka appeared.

"They're still talking! He said the boss promised to write for their sons! He also told her about the horses, they're better, they don't fall down dead, some of them even had foals."

In other words, we learned all about Grania and Ivan's behavior and conversation.

At about three o'clock they were called to dinner. We all went out of the barracks in order not to disturb them. The table was sumptuously covered, and the smell of boiled pork and smoked fish turned our heads.

But still they didn't sit down at the table right away. They prayed for a long time and sang Christ Has Risen from the Dead. Then they ate, laughed, and talked.

At four o'clock Ivan left.

Later Grania told me how Ivan had gotten work in a stable. The roof collapsed, rain poured in, and the horses got sick and died. The criminal prisoners working in the stable (this work was privileged because it was warm) absolutely could not and did not wish to care for the horses. The hay was half rotten, they were too lazy to bring enough water from the river, and the horses could hardly stand. They didn't shovel the manure regularly. The criminals stole oats that were ordered for the mares in foal and cooked an oatmeal pudding for themselves.

The horses began to die and the authorities began to speak of sabotage. The boss, who also understood very little about horses, became afraid. The only thing he did was to send the carpenters who worked in the gold mines to fix the roof of the stable. In this way Ivan ended up working in the stable and saw how the others had been abusing the horses.

One day when the director of the mines arrived to see how the work was going, he came to the stable and saw Ivan cleaning out the infected foot of a young horse. It hurt her and she was trembling all over, but Ivan spoke to her tenderly:

"Now stand still, silly girl, this will do you good."

He wiped iodine on her foot, wrapped it in some sort of rag, patted the horse's muzzle, and kept talking to her:

"Well, is it better?"

The boss came up to him.

"Do you love horses?" he asked.

"Yes, I can't help pitying them when they aren't cared for. They're starving and aren't even given enough water."

"Would you like to be a stableman?"

"I would like that."

In short, Ivan became the senior stableman. He even found hay that they had forgotten and that was covered with snow. He had the roof repaired and the manure cleaned up. The horses drank their fill and ate as much as it was possible to feed them. They revived and the boss took hold of Ivan and arranged things so that he wouldn't leave the stable when he got his freedom.

Ivan built the *izba* himself. When Grania was freed, he came for her.

She also began to work in the stable. Their sons, who were already fourteen and fifteen years old, arrived and entered a boarding school.

Within a year Grania had twin girls.

This was the rarest case of a happy life in Kolyma. And it gave me such joy to receive short letters from Grania about her family, children, husband, and horses, which she loved with all her soul.

Sliozberg in the early 1930s

Sliozberg with her husband and children in 1933

Sliozberg with her children in 1935,
less than a year before her arrest

Y. R. Zakgeim in the early 1930s

Y. R. Zakgeim's prison photographs, 1936

Sliozberg's children with their grandparents in 1937

Sliozberg meeting with her children in 1946

Sliozberg at the dacha with her grandchildren in 1960

Sliozberg on her eightieth birthday in 1982

Sliozberg with her great-grandchildren

Hatred

In 1942 I got frostbite in my feet. They put me in the barracks for the goners. They really should have put us in a hospital and treated us, but we were happy that they didn't push us to work, that we were fed, and that the stoves were warm. The majority of those lying in the barracks were in a state of alimentary dystrophy, and therefore, for whole days the conversation was about how to bake a pie, what sauces one could prepare for a turkey, and how tasty a buckwheat kasha could be. With the help of my neighbor on the bunk, Mirra Kizilshtein, a good soul, my feet slowly recovered, although they had been planning to cut off my toes and heels. Mirra gave me manganese baths and rubbed my feet with cod liver oil. I gradually pulled through. We had been living that way for two weeks when they brought a new group of sick people in from the sixth kilometer. Terrible rumors had long ago reached us about that company. Their boss was a certain Liza Keshve. I had met her at a transit camp. She was a gray-haired, forty-year-old woman with impudent, dissolute eyes. One time a literary argument started up between us. Liza was a literary critic, and her head was tightly crammed with literary information, dates, and names. I said that for two hours of conversation with Romain Rolland I would gladly pay with a year of prison. I had so much been wanting a way to entrust my whole experience to a great writer so that he could report to people everything that was buried in the prison walls, that was bursting out of my soul, that had to be told to people. With reverence I called out the names of writers who were the conscience of the world: Tolstoy, Chekhov, Veresaev, Garshin, Korolenko, and the only one of all the living writers who was worthy of this constellation—Romain Rolland. Liza called me sentimental and began to talk about Lev Tolstoy's sanctimoniousness, Mayakovsky's depravity, and Nekrasov's flagrant dishonesty with money. In her opinion, the moral tenor of a writer and the character of his creative work were not interdependent, and a bad person, even a stupid person, could be a great writer.

I don't know what other meaning literature had for me if it was not that through literature I could interact with fine and good souls, with wise people who helped me think about life.

Liza, however, loved literature as she loved exquisite jewelry, elegant moves on a chess board, or collections of interesting jokes. In other words, we did not agree.

Camp life also divided us. I was a manual laborer, while Liza was a brigade leader in charge of a small temporary work group, where thirty women were cutting down trees. They brought the surviving women (many had died) to the barracks for the goners, and they told me terrible things about Liza, this lover of belles lettres.

Liza was involved with the commander of the guards, a dull and insolent man with whom she got drunk. They robbed unhappy women who had fallen under their power. Terrible things happened in this temporary work group. Liza insisted that young girls give themselves to her lover and the other guards. Orgies took place in the guards' quarters. There was one room where wild debauchery of every sort took place publicly to the brutal laughter of the group. They stuffed themselves and drank at the expense of the women prisoners from whom they had stolen half the rations. The women there were terribly starved and, at the least attempt to resist or file a complaint, they were beaten half to death. Those who refused to go to work hungry were tied to a sled and pulled through the snow into the forest. I remember the way Masha Mino's eyes widened in horror. She was one of Liza's victims. She talked to me in whispers, looking around every minute, afraid that someone might tell Liza. "I tell her, 'I don't have the strength to work, I'm starving, I want bread, don't you understand?' And half drunk, with gray disheveled hair, hands on her hips, red and insolent, Liza says: 'So you want bread? And I want a young guy, but there's no one—I have to be patient!' And she chuckles: 'I want a young guy, get it?'"

Finally, in spite of beatings and force, people stopped working. They didn't get off their plank bunks and quietly died. Wood from the temporary work group stopped arriving. A commission was sent. The people were in such bad condition that they had to put them in the barracks for the goners and relieve them from work for the whole winter. The commander received a sentence of three years for the death rate, and Liza was demoted to general laborer.

In the barracks for the goners I made friends with three women.

The first was Mirra Kizilshtein. She was a biologist, the daughter of a doctor, and very interested in medicine. In our barracks for the goners she treated everyone with the most traditional means, and this got people back on their feet. Of course they were all young healthy organisms, only exhausted from hunger and backbreaking labor, and they responded quickly to any help and simple rest. For example, for a sick stomach she gave people manganese to drink, and strangely enough this helped. She treated my feet and gave a massage to someone else. We called her our doctor.

The second friend of mine, Nina Gagen-Torn, came from a very cultured family. Blok used to visit their home. In the barracks Nina wrote a story about her childhood called *Swan Song* and read it to me.

After rehabilitation, she lived in Leningrad and became a famous ethnographer. But we didn't get together there.

The third friend was Masha Mino. Her mother was the illegitimate daughter of the famous Petipa. Petipa always cared for his daughter and gave her an education. When Masha was about sixteen, Petipa went on tour with his ballet troupe to Siberia where Masha's family lived. Masha saw a charming, brilliant dancer and fell in love with him. It turned out that he was her grandfather. "No one else ever had a first love like mine," laughed Masha.

Before the Revolution Masha had joined the Bolshevik Party. I remember she told me how, with the censor's permission, they printed a loyal book about the anointed sovereign Nikolai II, in which fragments of many of his speeches were printed (with references to newspaper publications). They all ended in the same way: "So, let's drink to it, gentlemen!"

Masha was arrested in 1930 for a sharp speech against dekulakization. At that time her father and her four children remained free. They lived in their own home outside Moscow in Ilinskoye, where her father had worked as a country doctor before the Revolution. In 1956 after a quarter of a century, Masha returned to Moscow. Her father was already gone. Her sons met her warmly and lovingly. A spiritual connection, however, did not develop—there was too much difference in their interests.

Masha received a miniscule pension because after the camp, while in exile, she had lived and worked on a collective farm. One day a friend from the factory, a member of the Party Committee, visited her son's house.

Having learned about Masha's past, he began to talk with her about being restored to the Party: "As a member of our Party since 1916, you will receive a special pension with many privileges." Masha kept quiet and then answered, "No, I was not in your Party. I was in a completely different one."

I recovered and, leaving for work with a heavy heart, said good-bye to the poor goners who were so sick.

They sent Mirra and me to do light work—to hack peat out of the ground and spread it on the field. The work really wasn't very difficult, but the cold at that time was about forty-eight to fifty degrees below zero, and we had to work about ten hours a day. True, some of the time we were in a heated freight car where we went three times a day for ten minutes in order to warm up.

The first person I met at the place where work was distributed was Liza Keshve, who greeted me joyfully.

"Ah, my literary opponent! Let's work as a pair so we can talk about something different from bread and meeting the norms! Man does not live by bread alone, does he?"

I looked with horror at the quietly impudent face of Liza, and the words of farewell rang in my ears from when I had said good-bye to my poor fellow sufferers, dying in the barracks of the goners.

I said nothing about them to Liza. You ask me why? I was afraid of her in the most vile way and didn't want to have her as my enemy. I understood that her downfall was a temporary thing and that she would show her real self again someday. The only thing I could do out of a sense of social responsibility was to mutter something about working with my bunk partner, Mirra. We started working together in the section that was farthest from Liza and went to get warm in the heated freight car only when Liza came out of it, so we never ran into her.

One time I went into the heated freight car to get warm, sat down, stretched out my frozen feet to the fire, and began to drink hot water, delighting in the warmth and rest. Suddenly the door swung open widely and Liza came swaying in, took a few steps, and fell on the floor with a groan. She had had a heart attack. I crouched there but didn't move from my place. Liza was gasping and wanted to tell me something but could not. Through the open door the fifty-degrees-below-zero frost flowed in. I stood up to close the door and took a step in Liza's direction. She thought I was going to help her and cried out, "Water!" But I closed the door and returned to my place near the stove. I didn't want to help her. I couldn't touch her, just as I wouldn't have been able to touch a rat that had fallen into a trap. I sat there near the stove, frozen like a stone, and Liza gasped and beat her head on the ground. In my heart I raged with hatred for her and wished she would die.

The door opened and Mirra came in. She threw herself on Liza and began to unfasten her clothing and untie her scarf, uncovering her face.

"Olga, come, help me carry her to the bench."

"I will not come."

"You've gone out of your mind, she's dying!"

"Let her die, I will not care for her."

Liza's face was twisted, one eye popping out. She looked at me with horror.

"Quiet," cried Mirra. "She can hear and understand, you've gone out of your mind!"

"Let her hear. Why should she have a good death? Let her suffer."

Mirra was beside herself. Her soul was outraged. I sat by the stove and was amazed by the strength of the hatred that flooded my heart.

"I will tell people of your behavior! She's dying. Help me this minute to lift her!" screamed Mirra.

"I will not touch her. Let her die," I said, stepping across Liza's feet and leaving the freight car.

Liza did not die. Mirra reported my behavior with outrage, but in spite of that we stayed friends. Several people criticized me, others supported me, and the situation was painful for me.

It was painful for me, and I hated with a fierce hatred those who had led me to the point where I would not give water to a dying person, but I hated Liza the most intensely of all those I met in the camps because she was the most despicable.

Skeleton in the Closet

A relative of mine, a good and kind woman, once said to me:

"You know the very best time in our lives was our first year in Leningrad." I figured out that it was 1939. "We were so happy in those days, we danced every day, and it was such a nice group of people . . ."

She got along well with me, even loved me. But [in 1939] I had already been in prison for three years. Of course she didn't need to go into mourning. I was not insulted, but I remember a dream I had that year.

I dreamed I was running in the snow, and dogs were chasing me, hunting me. I was a peasant woman, and my master was hunting me with dogs. I ran without hope, without strength. Around me was a dead snowfield. In the distance the dark forest loomed. On my right stood a viewing platform, and my master and his guests were watching the hunt. Among the guests I saw two of my brothers. They were sorrowful but decently quiet.

One brother showed the other his watch, and I realized he was saying, "She'll hold up for another half hour."

There is a story by Dickens in which an innocent woman was tortured to death in a castle, and her skeleton was walled up in a closet. No one knew anything about this clearly because they were afraid of the evil master who could take brutal revenge if one word came out about his criminal action.

But there was a rumor that occasionally in the quiet of the night you could hear groaning and knocking on the wall, as if someone were languishing, gasping, wanting to get out into the air, and could not.

Years went by. Life went on in the castle. People fell in love, got married, had children, sowed wheat, went hunting, wrote poetry, and feasted. But everything gave the impression of something being wrong. There was no joy in this castle, there was no true love, friends didn't trust each other, children didn't respect their parents, people drank wine but did not really enjoy themselves, they filled themselves with bread and meat, but it did not taste good. Even the birds did not sing near this castle . . .

Because in the closet was the skeleton of an innocent woman who had been tortured to death.

I don't blame you, my brothers and sisters! You are not to blame that they have made you believe that you may not do, speak, or think anything, that you believe these events are outside the limits of understanding for normal people, outside the categories of justice or pity. You have locked up this chamber of your brain. You danced, lived, worked, gave speeches. You forgot about the *skeleton in the closet*, but it sat inside you; its noxious breath permeated your soul. And when I saw you again after ten years, the first thing that hit me in the eye was the trail of noxious breath from the skeleton in the closet.

You tried to forget it, but it was there, and you stopped believing in justice, stopped believing the words and speeches you had heard and had expressed yourself.

The skeleton in the closet existed, and you knew about it.

Mirage

*Steel is tempered when you heat it until it is red hot
and then plunge it into icy water.*

Many asked for a review of their cases; they wrote appeals to the prosecutor general of the USSR and letters to Stalin.

I didn't write even once, not out of pride but because of a deep conviction that nothing would come of it.

And one more thing: I understood that to be able to endure, I had to grit my teeth, not weaken my soul with impossible dreams.

But my mother lived on hope. As if it were a job, every day for the first four years after my arrest she went around to all the big shots. Beginning with the prosecutor general for the USSR and all the way up to the office of Kalinin and Peshkova, there wasn't an office where she hadn't stood in endless lines, hadn't asked for a review of my case, hadn't cried, trying to move hearts with the fact (unbelievable to her) that her daughter, the mother of two children, had been imprisoned for no reason at all. She wrote me too that she was going to all the high-level officials and tried to reassure me with the promises of various authorities, but I gave her hopes not the slightest significance. I believed it was good for her to be doing something; it would comfort her, but nothing would come of it.

But miracles do happen! She succeeded in getting a review of my case!

Actually the case had been cooked up very sloppily, but the main thing was that there was some kind of temporary softening of the regime, my case was reviewed, and on June 3, 1940, I was totally acquitted of the accusation of terrorist activity against Kaganovich.

During the summer of 1940, we lived on Bird Island at the confluence of two mountainous rivers. On this island there was a large forest in which we were cutting down trees, and there was lots of driftwood that we had to gather and tie into rafts. Our brigade leader was a good man from Siberia, Sasha, who had been dispossessed as a kulak. On the riverbank stood big unclaimed piles of driftwood, and we could always act as if we had collected them. So we worked peacefully, Sasha didn't oppress us, and the results were always good enough to qualify us for the first category of nourishment. In addition, the men who tied the rafts together were, like Sasha, former kulaks from Siberia, and they caught fish and treated us to dinner. Yes, and there were many birds' nests on the island, and often we found duck eggs. This was the easiest summer of my whole sentence.

One morning they brought the mail from the person in charge at Elgen. There was a telegram for me: "The Supreme Court of the USSR [according to some number] has completely rehabilitated you, as of June 3, 1940. So happy." The whole family had signed.

And then it began! I walked around as if drunk on dreams. I mentally caressed my children, mother, and father and told them everything I had lived through, imagined every detail of my return, starting with our meeting at the Kazan station and right up to that blessed moment when I laid my head on my mother's knee.

Letters began to arrive. Mama told me in detail how she had talked with high-level officials, how everyone had tried to dissuade her and even frighten her by saying that she and the family could be sent away from Moscow, but she never diverted her attention, and truth prevailed. How on the day of the review she sat in the rain on the street in front of the courthouse from early in the morning until five o'clock at night, and then a man in an MGB uniform came out and said to her:

"Well, Mother, I congratulate you. They've released your daughter." And the man had tears in his eyes.

Mama wrote me that the whole time she had hidden from the children that I had been arrested, telling them I was on a business trip, but now she had told them everything because my son was already ten years old and my daughter was eight and they could understand.

But time went by and nobody confirmed the review of my case. Summer passed and winter began.

Like a dream, our easy life on Bird Island came to an end. We were sent back to ditch digging. The Kolyma winter raged on with its usual frost, fifty degrees below zero.

And then one day our [assistant] brigade leader, Ania Orlova, came to the ditch where we were working and stood near me. She was quiet for a long time and then said:

"Be strong, Olga!" and she handed me a telegram. There it read, "The prosecutor general of the USSR protested the decision of the Supreme Court. Under a second review of your case, you have eight years of deprivation of freedom because you did not denounce your husband (article 58, section 12). Be brave. Mama."

I passed my telegram around silently. They read it and no one said anything.

Ania glanced at me sympathetically.

"You might want to go to the barracks and lie down."

"No, I don't want to." I began to hack away with my pickax. To stay in the barracks alone right now with nothing to do was unthinkable.

At night, covering up my head, I repeated like an incantation: "I will endure. Three years and four months more. I will endure. Forty months. I will endure. I give you my word, Mama. You can wait for me. I will endure."

And then letters came that had been sent before the telegram, and in them Mama wrote of how truth had prevailed, how my children were waiting for me, how everyone was so happy.

> No, a human is stronger than steel.
> What is steel!
> To walk, crawl, shuffle, drag yourself,
> To bury your face in your mother's lap,
> To bury your face and cry.
> Or perhaps to pray?
> One thing in the world can comfort me,
> Brings relief from pain—
> Burying my face in your lap,
> And crying the way children cry.
> The dead have no shame,
> And to a dying soul there is one consolation—
> To whisper into your lap
> The sacred name of Mama!

The Goner

The winter of 1943 was very hard. The bread ration was reduced from six hundred grams to five hundred. And besides bread they gave us cabbage soup made from rotten cabbage with herring heads (the soup served in a half-liter scoop consisted of two or three leaves of cabbage with one herring head) and three tablespoons of thin gruel made from cooked grain with a half teaspoon of vegetable oil. For supper a herring tail the size of a finger, and we had worked for ten hours in fifty-degrees-below-zero weather. People began to fail.

At first I worked with Galia Prozorovskaia, but after she fell in the forest they transferred her to repair work.

Then my work partner was Raia Ginzburg. We worked together in a friendly way, although we could just barely walk—she was covered with boils and abscesses. Each of my feet weighed a ton, and my knees buckled as if they were made of cotton. So we dragged ourselves about until March, and then a group was sent to an agricultural storage center in Elgen. There they were beginning spring work, removing the snow from the farmland and preparing the seedlings for planting in a greenhouse. Our brigade leader, of course, tried to send away the weakest people. Raia fell into this category, and I was left alone.

To be finished with cutting down trees was of course a great joy. In Elgen it certainly was easier—you didn't have to go into the forest but could go instead to the more habitable agricultural center with places to warm up, and once a month it was even possible to get a loaf of bread for fifty rubles. (We earned about fifty rubles a month.) But Raia very much did not want to go away without me. We loved each other and, once parted, we might never run into each other again, since the twenty kilometers between us would be like the distance from Moscow to New York in normal life.

She was getting ready for her trip and left me her poor housekeeping things. I poured the remaining straw from her mattress into mine so that it was a little softer for sleeping; she left me her wick lamp (in Elgen there was electricity), she gave me a knife—but a search lay ahead, and I would have to throw the knife away anyway.

Earlier I had been considered strong, and many wanted to work as partners with me, but now almost all my friends had been sent away. Several pairs had not broken up, and the remaining singles were much younger and stronger and had joined each other. For the first time I realized that I was almost a goner, and people weren't very eager to work with me. I didn't feel offended by this. I myself was afraid to partner with very weak people; a pair had to meet the norms of two people—eight cubic meters, out of which I would have to do five or six with a weak partner, and at this point I didn't have the strength to do it. I decided to work alone. I already had the skill, and I could cut a large tree down at the roots with a two-hand saw one meter long, saw it into three meter pieces, and pile it into four-cubic-meter stacks. It was possible for one person to work with a two-handed saw because in the snow the saw moved smoothly in a narrow groove. I fulfilled my norm and somehow or other was able to stay in the first category. (In other words I got five hundred grams of bread a day.) But it was very depressing to spend the whole day alone in the woods. Depressing and terrible because I have a bad sense of direction. Finishing my work when almost everyone else had gone home, I never was sure how to find the road, and getting lost meant death. Time went slowly, and it seemed as though winter would never end. But within a month and a half they transported an additional group to the agricultural center, and I was part of it.

We walked twenty kilometers from early morning until night, and it seemed to me that I could not make it—my legs were terribly weak, and each one felt as though it weighed a ton.

We arrived late in the evening, and I immediately ran into Raia. She had prepared hot water for me and some sugar. She had gathered a whole bundle of straw for a mattress and gave me a place on the plank bunk near her. Oh, how warm friendship is! We talked together for a long time. She had been lucky. She had been sent to a monthlong course in vegetable gardening and completed it very well. A place at the agricultural center was almost guaranteed for her. This agricultural center seemed like salvation—working in one place with much easier work than in the woods. In the summer it was always possible to sneak vegetables; in the winter we worked indoors—in the greenhouses. Raia had already spoken with the boss of the agricultural center, Onishchenko, telling him how well I worked and that I was resourceful and strong, and she was sure they would also take me. I wasn't sure of it. I already knew how weak I had become, and there were these weak legs. They could not move at all. But all the same I hoped I could rest, get a little stronger, and that then they would take me there.

The next day we went out to work. We had to remove the snow from the fields of the agricultural center. We carried it on sleds and were tied together like a pair of horses.

Several times I caught an anxious glance from Raia, and she tried to pull more strongly because I could hardly walk.

"It's hard for you to work with me," I said. "I have grown very weak."

"It's not at all difficult, only don't have such an unhappy expression, walk vigorously because Onishchenko is watching. He doesn't like goners."

Onishchenko stood at the gate of the agricultural center, and every time we dragged out the snow, he watched us carefully. He had to choose permanent workers, and he studied us carefully. Every time we went past him, Raia anxiously watched me and implored me:

"You have such an unhappy face, can't you walk vigorously for just a few meters? Smile, please!"

I saw myself as if from the outside: how my neck and chin were stretched, how I had fallen forward with my whole body, and my cursed feet wouldn't walk at all and were dragging behind somehow. Smile? Oh, how hard it is! I managed the crazy grin of a cadaver.

No, I didn't deceive Onishchenko. He didn't choose me. After clearing the snow, I was sent back to the forest.

> They fly, they fly south,
> But I have remained,
> A wounded bird on the ground.
> I see my youth in a haze . . .
> In the blue southland, in the distant south,
> They swim in life-giving fire
> My winged friends,
> What cold snow . . .

The Chief of the Guards

It was a very difficult day—I woke up with a terrible migraine. With horror I wondered how I would be able to work. I didn't have a temperature. I had nothing to give our medical assistant, Valka, the thief. I had already given her the last pair of stockings from my package a month ago for a migraine. Without that she wouldn't give me a release. I looked out of the barracks. It was so cold that I calmed down a bit. Probably it was colder than fifty below zero and they'd have to write it off. I lay down on the bunk, got warm, and dozed off. Alas! A metal rail was struck and rang out—time to get up. We heard a voice:

"The air is hissing! That means it is colder than fifty below!"

And the brigade leader's answer:

"No, it's forty-eight."

Well, there's nothing to be done about it. We must go to the forest.

During this period I was working alone because my partner, Galia Prozorovskaia, had fallen sick. I had to cut down trees, get rid of the branches, cut the trees into three-meter lengths, and stack them into a four-cubic-meter pile.

Work was practically impossible; the cold permeated one's bones. All the same by four o'clock my pile was built. But with horror I realized it didn't have four cubic meters in it. I had to cut down just one more tree, cut it up and pile it. But I absolutely did not have the strength to do it.

I decided to take a risk. Maybe they wouldn't notice. I walked toward the camp. Just as I got out on the road, I saw the chief of the guards. This was a man about thirty years old, healthy, good looking, dressed in a fur jacket, a gray Karakulian hat, and felt boots to his knees. His face was freshly shaven, rosy, and tranquil. He smelled of vodka and eau de cologne.

"Have you already met your norm?"

"Yes, there is my pile."

He walked over to it and immediately saw that it was not four cubic meters.

"You did not fulfill your norm. Cut up this one tree and then you can go to the camp."

"My head hurts. I am very cold. I cannot work anymore."

"I don't find it very cold. The weather is calm. Be patient." He sat down on a stump and began to smoke.

I had to work another hour. He smoked and from time to time observed: "Norms are norms. One must work honestly."

I collected logs three meters long and then literally strained myself with their weight, but he continued to smoke.

Hatred for him boiled in my heart. Going home I thought of all the misfortunes that I wished would befall him. He could get caught under a falling tree and I would laugh and not help . . . He would die and I would be happy. But alas! All that was completely unreal; he was a healthy thirty-year-old fellow, stuffed with food, warmly dressed, and tranquil.

This scene took place at the beginning of March 1944, and on April 27 I completed my sentence and gained my freedom.

By November I had rested and put on a little weight. On November 7, they arranged a celebration in the dining hall. For dinner there was added sweet food, and they were selling wine. I sat at a table alone. Suddenly a man came in and turned toward me. It was he, the chief of the guards, on whom I had wished all sorts of evil.

"May I sit down?" I nodded. He looked at me and recognized me. His face began to shine, as if he had met a friend. "For heaven's sake, it is you, Sliozberg! How you have changed, how beautiful you have become! How are you? Are you married?"

"No, I live alone."

"And how have you settled? Where do you work? Do you have a room?"

"I have a room. I work in the office."

"Oh, how delightful it is to run into you! I really don't know anyone here. What luck for me! But how beautiful you look, so well dressed." Instead of my camp rags, I was wearing my only nice article of clothing—a white blouse! "I have a favor to ask you. Invite me to your place! It would be so pleasant to talk with a woman!"

I answered him in a rather playful tone:

"And do you like me?"

"I like you very very much. Don't think that I ever compared you to the prostitutes. I always knew what kind of person you were."

"So. That means you like me now and you have always liked me?"

"Yes, yes, of course!"

His eyes were shining; he caressed my hand.

"Well, I have never liked you, and now I like you even less!"

His face expressed deep insult.

"Ah, so? Well, in that case, good-bye."

He walked away with an air of unappreciated virtue. I went home. I didn't hate him anymore. He wasn't worth it. He was simply a fool.

Nadezhda Vasilevna Grankina

Nadezhda Vasilevna Grankina and I were in the same freight car on the way to Kolyma, and in Magadan we lived in the same barracks.

This was Barracks 7, the very worst, with seventy people in double bunks.

There were so many people that I knew many of them only by their last names and by sight, but we never uttered a word to each other. That's the way it was with Nadia and me.

One white night they sent us to water the potatoes. A horse was carrying water, and a small colt ran after her. Sometimes he ran after his mother along the riverbank, sometimes he dashed between us, jumped around, and played. But once when the colt wasn't running after his mother, the water carrier started to take the water to another area. Discovering that his mother had disappeared, the colt began to call her, rush about, cry out—in general he was desperate. And suddenly I saw that Nadia had turned pale, trembled, and wept.

"What's wrong with you?" I asked. I had never seen Nadia cry.

"Look, that is probably the way my Kinusia rushes about searching for me and crying."

Nadia told me she had left her daughter with her mother, a severe old woman barely subsisting on a small pension. Nadia's mother very much blamed her daughter and son-in-law, assuming they had done something wrong and that was why they had been sent to prison, and had dumped her granddaughter on her. The girl was weak, lame from polio, afraid of her grandmother, and too intensely tied to her mother. Nadia asked me about my children. I was ashamed to complain. My children lived with my parents who idolized them. My sisters and brother helped them.

From that day on Nadia and I were never separated. We slept next to each other and at work we tried to be together.

We of course told each other about our lives. I must say that Nadia's fate was determined from the day of her birth because of church law. Her father, a widowed priest, could not marry her mother who was his house-keeper. The two children, Nadia and her brother, were illegitimate. This was a terrible disgrace. They concealed the children, hid them, and finally gave them away to the childless brother of their mother, who served as deacon in the church at Tsarskoe Celo. The uncle and aunt were good people and raised the children as if they were their own. The peacefulness was only disturbed from time to time when their mother appeared and fought with her brother and sister-in-law about the right way to raise the children, criticizing the way they ate, the way they entered the room, and so forth.

Before she entered school Nadia did not know that she was an illegiti-mate child. In school the girls were from the nobility and even from the court. Many mothers forbade their daughters to have contact with Nadia. This hurt her deeply.

Nadia took to the Revolution wholeheartedly. She even wanted to join a young Communist organization. (The Komsomol didn't exist at that time.) When she applied, she was asked why she wanted to be a member of the organization. Nadia answered that Communists were followers of Christ, wanting to help poor and deprived people. Loving Christ, she wanted to be with them. Naturally she was not accepted.

In 1919 her mother took her from starving Petrograd to Lugansk, where she began to work as the manager of linens for a hospital, and Na-dia, who was already turning sixteen, worked as a medical assistant. She again applied to join the Komsomol, and this time they accepted her. She was happy. But someone found out that Nadia was the daughter of a priest, and they threw her out.

She started to work as a librarian in a military unit. She was enthusiastic about her work.

In 1922, she met her hero—Ephim Grankin. He had fought through the whole Civil War, lived only for the Revolution, and, like Nadia, paid little attention to how he lived. They married. A daughter was soon born. They named her Kina—a nickname for Kommunist International!

But after 1925 big troubles began: her husband fell sick (the conse-quence of a war wound), and he was demobilized from the army. And in

1927 they threw Grankin out of the Party for being a Trotskyite. Nadia had little understanding of politics; she was sure her husband was a pure Leninist-Communist. Grankin got a small pension; all day long he read Lenin and Marx and tried to demonstrate that he was correct. He only wanted to work in the field of political education, where of course a career was closed to him. Although he came from a peasant background and could do anything with his hands, he wanted no other work but politics. Nadia had to support the family. There was no work in Lugansk. They had to go back to Leningrad. They settled in with her mother in a small communal apartment. Her mother hated her son-in-law, and Nadia lived between a hammer and an anvil. She began to work in a library. She left her daughter sometimes with the grandmother who didn't want to care for her and sometimes with her husband, who considered it beneath his dignity to do housework and child care. When her daughter turned ten, she got polio and became lame.

In 1936 they arrested Grankin and sent Nadia to Samara, allegedly so that she could look after her sick husband, who could not take care of himself. She had to take her daughter with her, since the grandmother did not agree to have her left there.

Grankin didn't turn up in Samara. They transferred Nadia to Orenburg. Her husband wasn't there either. During this time he was in the prison hospital in Leningrad, where he soon died. Without money and without an apartment, Nadia had a very hard time with her sick daughter on her hands in Orenburg. Finally she put together some kind of work and found an apartment. But it was 1937 by then. They arrested Nadia, gave her a ten-year prison sentence, and sent her daughter back to Leningrad to the grandmother. For two years Nadia was tossed from one prison to another, and in 1939 they sent her to Kolyma in the same transport that was taking me there.

I have already written about how we became friends in Kolyma. We tried to stay together, but in the camps you don't always get to arrange things for yourself.

In 1943, when we were cutting down trees in the forest, an amazing event occurred. At one time in her life in search of work, Nadia had enrolled in some courses in machine embroidery and finished them. In her file there was a diploma for finishing the program. Unexpectedly they called her to Elgen to a prisoners' workshop, and she was able to work there for the rest of her sentence, almost four years. This was great good luck—work in a warm place, women's work, and sometimes one could do a few jobs on the side and never go hungry.

I found out about Nadia's further fate after I got my freedom.

The whole time Nadia tried to make a connection with Leningrad, where her daughter and mother had remained. Her heart broke from fear for them. Finally in 1945, Nadia received news that they had both died in 1943. Later Nadia told me she felt consoled that they weren't suffering anymore.

What bitter consolation!

One way or another Nadia survived this sorrow and continued to live. She held onto one dream—to go free. The camp was so disgusting to her that she could think of nothing else but ending her sentence. And she still had about a year and a half to go.

During this time embroidery became more and more popular. There were many ladies (the wives of the bosses) in Elgen, and Nadia had only two hands. So they had to create a waiting list. Fighting broke out among the grandes dames. "Why did she make five curtains for M. N., and N. N. only got two?" "Why does the waiting list never get to my blouse?" V. Y. cried. "I was the first to order a tablecloth," complained N. N. In short, by the end of 1946 she had accumulated a pile of uncompleted work. The ladies rushed to the boss of the camp, saying, "How can you liberate her and leave us without our embroiderer?" The boss tried to quiet down his ladies, promising somehow to detain Nadia. At this time news came to Elgen that the authorities were doing something with Tsilia Kogan in Magadan. Tsilia completed her sentence in 1946 and, of course, dreamed of freedom. They liberated her, and to celebrate the event she put on an entertainment for her friends who remained in the camp. In her farewell, Tsilia said, "Finally I am through with this slave labor. I wish the same for all of you." Alas! These words were passed on to the boss. A new investigation began, and poor Tsilia received a second sentence for making an anti-Soviet statement. It turned out that the expression *slave labor* was forbidden in the camp. We were all shocked, and Nadia of course was also. It was not surprising that, when Nadia learned they had called several lady clients and asked them what Nadia had ever said on this or that occasion, she looked deathly pale. It was absolutely clear that they were preparing a second sentence for her too.

In the meantime, hearing that a relatively young *political* woman was going to be released, a crowd of potential bridegrooms crowded to the camp gate. They were as a rule not political prisoners. (Their crimes were negligence, embezzlement, abuse of passport regulations, etc.) They didn't want to marry real criminals and were searching for an *upstanding* woman. One of these men, a certain Boris, managed to find his way into the workshop.

He proposed the following to Nadia: he would arrange for her release and she would marry him. How he was planning to do this, Nadia did not know. Out of her mind with fear, she agreed. He seemed less terrible to her than a new sentence.

They released Nadia right on the scheduled day, and Boris took her to a distant gold mine where he worked as a supply person and where there wasn't a single other person with whom Nadia could even have a conversation, not to speak of having a friend. Within just a few days Nadia began to feel physical and moral repugnance for her husband. She dreamed of leaving. But how? He talked all the time about how much she cost him, how much he had spent on her freedom, clothing, and even her nourishment. Nadia didn't have a kopeck; Boris had taken all her documents, including her bread ration card. They began to fight day and night. And so they lived in a state of war in one room for two months.

During this time an accountant-inspector, Vikenti Yakovlevich Tulitski, came to their mine from Magadan. He was sent to the camps because of a relationship with the wife of a big boss, for whom it hadn't been difficult to dispose of a rival by means of a fictitious accusation. The article in the Constitution called for a light sentence, and Tulitski, after gaining his freedom, worked in Magadan and earned a good salary.

Tulitski stayed in the barracks where Nadia and Boris were living. The sound of their voices traveled clearly, and he quickly figured out what was going on. He dropped in to visit Boris. Sometimes Nadia treated him to dinner; occasionally Vikenti and Boris drank a small glass or two. One day he arrived during a family scene, and he proposed to Boris that he pay Boris's expenses for Nadia. To her he said:

"I can't insist that you marry me, although I would be happy to have you as my wife. I'll take you to Yagodny or Magadan, and there you can live as you please. If you are able, you'll pay me back the debt."

Nadia agreed to go away with him, and on the long trip she assessed his thoughtfulness and unobtrusiveness. In short, they registered their marriage in Magadan and began to live together in a friendly way. Incidentally, Tulitski, out of a sense of "gentrified" honor (he was Polish), did not permit Nadia to work: "I can earn money for both myself and my wife." And Nadia also did not want to work. She did the housework in their eight-square-meter room; her home became a refuge for all the newly freed politicals. (It was 1948, and all who had survived after 1937 were allowed to go free.)

Tulitski was flattered that former writers, artists, Party workers, doctors of science, and directors of factories came to his home, and they all honored him as the host of the house. So they lived for eight years until the end of 1956. For the first time in her life, Nadia lived quietly and safely.

At this time everyone had left for the mainland in order to be rehabilitated. Nadia too was drawn to her beloved Leningrad. On the mainland Tulitski went to visit his relatives in the provinces, and Nadia went alone to Leningrad. From the railroad station she went to her brother who had become a very high-ranking military person. He opened the door to Nadia and, without greeting her, asked, "You have been rehabilitated?" Recognizing that it hadn't happened yet, he said, "In my position I cannot take you in. After rehabilitation, you'll be welcome." And he slammed the door. Nadia stood on the street, not knowing where to go. Fortunately she remembered the telephone number of her coworker at the library, Sima Aronovna Sulkina. She tried calling her. The reaction was the complete opposite of her brother's. Sima recognized her voice. "Nadia," she cried out, "You have returned? Come here immediately. I've been thinking about you constantly!" Sima met her like a sister. Tulitski soon arrived, and they spent almost a whole year together in Sima's winter dacha in Roshchino.

Within a year Nadia was rehabilitated, and they gave her a room in a communal apartment. Tulitski started work as a landscape gardener in Leningrad. He wasn't yet old; he was around fifty and bursting with energy. One must not forget that he had gone through Kolyma—that is, through fire and water. He acquired new friends; got involved in business, where he found easy money; and met women of dubious behavior, in whom Tulitski had always been very interested.

His relationship with Nadia began to deteriorate. He valued her as a good, upstanding person and an excellent housekeeper; he delighted in her pirogi and shashlik. He wished that she, like he, could live happily and not think about the past. He condemned her desire to write her memoirs and even feared them. In part, she wanted to visit the home where she had lived with her husband and Kina until 1936. The building was at the other end of Leningrad, and transportation there was very bad. Nadia was afraid to go by herself; she feared the rush of memories. She asked Tulitski to come with her. He promised to go but kept postponing it. Once on returning home, he said to her:

"I went to your old address. Your building was destroyed in the war. Now they are building nine-story prefab-paneled buildings there. There is no reason to go."

So Nadia's intention remained unrealized. What did she have to offer in contrast to his happy life? Visiting museums and theaters? Reading books? Was this what he sought?

My relationship with Nadia was very close. She used to stay with me in Moscow, and I visited her in Leningrad. I could tell that her relationship with Tulitski was going to end in divorce. But in the middle of the 1960s, he became ill with lung cancer. Nadia forgot all his offenses and for a year and a half carefully looked after him. It was especially hard when, about three weeks before his death, he became paralyzed. He lay in bed at home. Caring for him was terribly difficult, but Nadia selflessly did not stir from his side day and night.

After Tulitski's death it became clear that he had left some debts and not a kopek of money. And Nadia, who hadn't been employed in the North, received a miserable pension, thirty-five rubles a month, and of course it was impossible to live on this. She began working in the cloakroom at a school. The advantages of this work were the long summer vacation and the winter holidays. After Tulitski's death Nadia and I got together a lot. She came to visit me every summer at the dacha outside Moscow, and I went to her for the winter holidays. We felt especially close to each other because we were both writing our memoirs.

Because of my character, I talked a lot with my relatives and acquaintances about the prisons, the camps, and the purges. This subject had not yet opened up. People eagerly came to me with questions: why were people imprisoned, why did they sign . . . ?

Having told the stories several times, I could write the story smoothly; it was easy for me. Not so for Nadia. She was afraid to describe what she had lived through and even hid her past life from new acquaintances. She often tried to make me afraid, saying I would have to answer for my stories. Everything could change; it was important not to forget that we had signed a "nondisclosure" document when we were liberated . . . In addition to that Nadia didn't have even a middle-school education. She wrote every page over and over again three or four times. Possessing a brilliant memory and being unusually conscientious, Nadia created a serious piece of work that in the opinion of historians will be very useful for research. In this work there is an enormous number of names of prisoners, investigators, directors of prisons, and those who managed the daily routines of prisons. Part of her memoirs is published in the collection *Till My Tale Is Told*. The rest will be archived at Memorial.

Life brought one more blow to this honest, good, infinitely patient person. Remembering Tulitski, Nadia suddenly had doubts that he really had gone to her old apartment. Something didn't ring true about his story. And so Nadia gathered her strength and went to her previous address. To her amazement the three-story prerevolutionary building stood there in the same old place. With trepidation she rang the bell at her former apartment. A heavy sixty-year-old woman opened the door, and with difficulty Nadia saw a resemblance to the twenty-year-old Verochka, her former neighbor. Nadia explained who she was. Vera Ivanovna remembered Nadia, received her warmly, and invited her to come in. The old communal apartment had changed into a modern single one where Vera Ivanovna's large family, her children, and her grandchildren lived.

Vera Ivanovna told her the following about Kina:

"After the death of her grandmother at the beginning of 1943, Kina stayed on alone. She sat in her icy room where everything had been burned. She bundled herself in rags and went out of the house for bread only once a day. She could hardly walk, but all the same she got bread. Once Kina came home—she looked so pale and lost. She wanted to say something, but I wasn't paying attention to her. This was the time when my mother was dying. Kina kept quiet, went to her room, and closed the door. Only the next day I went for her. The girl was dead; on her face was the mark of a blow, her bread card wasn't there, and I realized that someone had taken it."

"I can't, I can't," cried Nadia. "And the murderer is alive and walking in the street. I would strangle him with my own hands! No, just think," said Nadia. "This was in 1943. I was young, strong. I could have warmed, fed, saved her! But for ten hours a day I was sewing blouses for those vile ladies! I can't, I can't bear this!"

Nadia did not recover from that blow. She soon had a stroke, and at the beginning of 1983 she died.

Freedom

Let's go back to the Kolyma story.

In 1941 they should have released Nadia Fedorovich, who had been arrested in 1936 and given a five-year sentence.

She had left a nine-year-old son in freedom, an irritable, proud boy. At the beginning he lived with his grandmother, and when his grandmother died in 1938, he had to wander around among his relatives, who felt burdened by him. After supporting him for a year or a year and a half or so, they tried to send him on to another uncle or aunt. He wrote his mother complaining about his relatives: "They give bread with butter to their own children, but to me they give margarine, I wear only old clothes from Lenka and Sashka, they never buy me anything new." And more: "The boys say my mother and father are convicts."

Nadia counted the days until she would be released and dreamed of taking back her son.

For the day of her liberation, June 25, 1941, we prepared a whole trousseau for Nadia. Someone gave her a skirt, someone a slip, someone a blouse. Nadia was the first to complete her sentence. We didn't know that the war had just begun. (They didn't give us newspapers.) But something in the air felt anxious, Nadia was nervous, and although preparing herself for freedom, didn't believe that it would come.

June 25 did come. It came and went. An agonizing month went by. Finally Nadia was called to the office of the camp director at noon.

In the morning we went to work as always. Nadia stayed in the barracks. Before the break I went up to her.

"Maybe this will be the last time I see you. Your agony is coming to an end."

"I don't know," answered Nadia. "I feel something painful in my heart."

In the evening we returned. Nadia was sitting by the stove smoking.

The man on duty warned us in a whisper: "Don't go up to her, she is going crazy, they didn't release her."

Nadia had been made to sign an order that she would stay in the camp *until there was a special directive.*

And her son certainly had known that Nadia was supposed to be released on June 25. She had kept begging him not to fight with his relatives and to be patient a little longer. She thought with horror of how her son would perceive her letter in which she told him that their meeting had to be postponed until an uncertain future time. But her son did not receive the letter. The censor did not permit that criminal communication telling him her sentence was completed but that she had been left there until there was a special directive.

Nadia did not know her letter had been censored and not sent. She waited for an answer and did not receive one. Suddenly in the winter of 1942, a letter arrived from an unknown person who had found Boris with pneumonia at a small way station near Irkutsk, took him in, and cured him. He reproached Nadia for forgetting her son when she was released. She was a bad mother, had probably gotten married, and was living well for herself while her fourteen-year-old boy, having traveled from Riazan to Irkutsk without a ticket, was dying of hunger.

By then we knew about the war and knew that letters were not getting through. Nadia ran to the director of the camp, she wrote an application to the prosecutor, rushed about like a lioness in a cage, but everywhere she was met with a cold answer: "Correspondence is forbidden until the special directive is received."

And so she didn't find out what had happened to her son and where he was. Her son, by then a homeless stray, had fallen in with a gang and in 1947 turned up with a five-year sentence in a camp for criminals in Kolyma.

The time for release arrived for several more women, but all of them who had been convicted of serious political crimes had to remain, pending the special directive. A whole assemblage of people, *overstayers*, developed. In truth, misery loves company. Others, the ones more prepared for the fact that they had to remain, didn't take this as a tragedy, as Nadia did, but all the same there were several suicides. People couldn't bear the thought that the freedom for which they had waited and counted the weeks and days had been moved into the indefinite future.

In the camp things became worse and worse. Agonizing and unending hunger, fierce discipline, and widespread despondency. In this atmosphere on April 27, 1944, my release date arrived.

Judging by the letters from my relatives, it appeared that the Supreme Court had changed my crime from article 58, point 8 (committing terrorism), to article 58, point 12 (failure to denounce my husband). This was the lightest of the political statutes, and with it they released people on time. But for four years they hadn't sent me official notice of the change in statute, and I didn't know if there had been such a decree in reality or if they had deceived my mother, and everything remained as before. I was weary from waiting. The winter of 1943–44 was the most terrible for me. I think I went a little crazy, couldn't focus on anything else, and spent the whole time guessing and speculating about whether they would release me. I went to work and speculated: If I get back to the barracks at five o'clock they will release me, and if I get there later they won't. If it is a hundred steps to that pine tree, they will release me, and if it is more, they won't, and so forth.

Finally on the first of April 1944, they called me in and confirmed that on November 21, 1940, they had changed my criminal status to article 58, point 12.

Freedom became a reality.

I lived the final weeks as if in a fog. Camp interests became strange to me, I feared thinking of freedom, and I didn't know what else to think about. People said I wouldn't be allowed to see my relatives in Russia.

I dreamed that I would come back from work to my room, lock the door (one must lock the door), lie down on my bed, and under a real electric lamp, read a book from the library.

I dreamed that I would eat my fill, that in the terrible frost of Kolyma I wouldn't go out to work in the forest; I would settle myself somewhere in an office, in the warmth. I dreamed that there would be no roll call, profanity, and cursing, that I would not live with prostitutes and pickpockets. I dreamed that on a summer Sunday I would go for a walk for the whole day. I would walk along the road only as far as I wished, and no one would forbid me, no one would yell: "Stop where you are! A step to the right or a step to the left and I'll shoot." But I dared not dream of more than that. I was afraid of disappointment.

On April 27, 1944, they released me precisely on time. Of our whole group they released only me. The rest had to stay there until 1947. My mother's efforts had saved three years of life for me.

Everyone thought I was a lucky woman. But I cried the whole time. I didn't know how I would live alone, without family, without the friends to whom I had become so close in the camps.

I immediately put in an application requesting permission to go to the mainland, but I received the answer that I would have to stay forever in Kolyma.

Forever. How many times I was forced to sign that forever!

Forever in Kolyma, eternally in Karaganda, forever forbidden to go to Moscow.

This eternity turned out to last twelve years until the Twentieth Party Congress, but how those twelve years stretched out!

Nikolai Vasilevich Adamov

By 1944 I knew that the sentence given my husband—ten years without the right to correspondence—meant that he had been executed and that I was a widow.

And then a friend appeared, offering a foothold in life. I married Nikolai Vasilevich Adamov.

He was the complete opposite of my first husband. Zakgeim was a refined intellectual, encyclopedically educated. He knew the natural sciences deeply, had defended his dissertation on the natural sciences of the eighteenth century, and had a profound understanding of music and art. You couldn't imagine that he would curse or shove anyone.

Nikolai was a miner's son from the Donbass. He was the oldest of four children. Finishing a state technical school, he went to work in a candy factory at age thirteen. In 1918 when Nikolai was sixteen, the Whites took the Donbass. In order not to give them the coal, the miners flooded the mine in which Nikolai's father worked. The Whites grabbed him and hanged him. Nikolai was the oldest in the family and became the breadwinner. It was hard to give up caring for his mother and younger sisters, but the pull to go to the front and the wish to avenge his father were even stronger. He left home, joined the Red Army, and spent the whole Civil War at the front.

In 1927 Nikolai graduated from a veterinary institute. And again they drafted him into the army as a Commissar in the Special Far East Regiment.

In 1935 he was arrested for making anti-Stalinist statements. The investigator began to question him about his wife. Realizing that they might take her too, Nikolai observed that he wanted to give important testimony privately to an authorized representative of the NKVD. When they were alone, Nikolai said, "Keep in mind that if my wife is arrested, I will bear witness against you so that you will get a more severe sentence than I." They didn't touch his wife, but she was so frightened that she left Nikolai.

Nikolai received a sentence of five years, and the authorities sent him to Magadan in the spring of 1937. After he arrived there, a Colonel Garanin started going on a rampage. This was one name that filled the prisoners with terror. For many he added a new sentence of ten more years *for sabotage*. In the camps he shot people with his own hand. At this time the most terrible place was a penal camp called Serpantinka. That's where Nikolai ended up.

The barracks there were so packed that prisoners took turns sitting on the ground, leaving the rest standing. In the morning the door would open, and they would call out ten or twelve people by their last names. No one would respond. Then they would grab the nearest ones and take them out to be shot. One time Nikolai himself fell into this group of ten, although they had called the last names of completely different people. They herded them into a covered truck and took them away. All the guards were drunk. In a corner of the truck there were some rolled up sacks. Nikolai crawled under the sacks. They arrived at the place and took the prisoners out of the truck. Within several minutes they were shot. The guards returned alone and went back to the camp. Nikolai managed to get out from under the sacks in the evening and joined the prisoners sawing wood.

One day the door opened and they called for Adamov. He of course did not respond. They went away. Then again they came back and asked, "Which of you is Adamov, the veterinarian, since our pigs are falling sick." "Ah, so," said Nikolai. "Then I am Adamov." They took him to the pigsty where the pigs stood, barely alive and up to their knees in the mud. He washed them off, removed the manure, cleaned their legs with iodine, and the pigs survived.

The authorities valued him, and Nikolai settled into taking care of the pigs. Then Garanin disappeared somewhere, leaving the living prisoners to be returned to a normal camp, and those who had completed their sentences were freed, among them Nikolai.

As a free man Nikolai began to work in the supply house in Yagodny and then became its director. It happened that after I was released, I too had started working at the same supply house as a bookkeeper.

Members of the NKVD often came to the supply house. I was terribly afraid of them. I felt that they could arrest me again for any little thing. I tried to answer all their questions as fast as possible, to be polite with them. Nikolai observed me with a grin. "Why are you afraid of them? Just think what they are and who you are! Spit on them! They are used to slurping up free booze, but they won't get it from me."

Nikolai often came to the accounting office where I worked. It gave me great pleasure to talk with him. He had a sharp, observant mind. He had seen a great deal, both at the front and in prison. He confided in me and I in him. And the times then were dangerous, the war hadn't ended, and you could be sentenced for one wrong word.

Associating with Nikolai became a necessity. We spent every evening together. But to my sorrow, he was suddenly transferred to another supply station at the Burkhala gold mine, sixty kilometers from Yagodny. He began to come to see me every Sunday. Without Nikolai, work at the supply house became so boring that I got very depressed.

During this time I had unexpectedly gotten to know Alexander Alexandrovich (I don't remember his last name), the director of a school. He belonged to the gentry. An extraordinarily well-educated person, he had finished the university and knew literature and many languages. He was not wealthy, and even before the Revolution he had been working as a literature teacher in a provincial gymnasium. The Revolution, of course, affected him. He was arrested, then exiled. He wandered about Russia and finally ended up in Kolyma. After serving out his sentence, he began to teach in his special field in a local school, and then they assigned him the task of organizing a school for adults. But where could you find teachers in Yagodny? I had talked with him about literature, and he proposed that I teach literature in his school.

At first I refused. I didn't have training in literature, and I didn't know how to teach.

"If you only knew the kind of teachers I have! Wives of NKVD workers!" exclaimed Alexander Alexandrovich. "And look, what if I arrange an examination for all of you?"

He gathered all the teaching candidates together and dictated two pages to us. I made two mistakes (with commas, though) and was very embarrassed. But the director was very enthusiastic: "Don't be upset. Compared to them you are a star! Do you know how many mistakes the history teacher made? Twenty-eight on two short pages!"

So I became a teacher of literature. I had no experience nor a program nor a literary method nor any books. A. A. gave me little books of Pushkin, Lermontov, Gogol, and Krylov. He and I decided that I would start with biographies of the writers, read some of their works aloud, and then perhaps we would find textbooks and a program.

My students were all NKVD workers. I had never even suspected that in Russia grown people could be so illiterate. They had never read anything and had only vaguely heard that Pushkin, Lermontov, and Gogol were great writers. I told them their biographies, read *Stories of Belkin, Dubrovsky*, "Borodino," short stories by Gogol, and fables by Krylov.

At first everything was very successful. They listened closely. They especially took in Gogol. They laughed, asking to have it read again. In general, the job did not go badly. But one day I made an irreparable mistake. I said that Marx and Engels were very interested in Russian literature and greatly appreciated Pushkin. One of my students stood up and asked me:

"And why are you giving us the opinions of these Germans?"

Shocked by this question, I said:

"I was speaking of Marx and Engels. They are our teachers!"

The next day A. A. called me into his office:

"Why did you have to talk about politics? You were denounced for suggesting we could learn from the Germans! (And this was actually in 1944.) In addition to that, they summoned me in too and asked about you. When they found out that you had been in prison for a serious political crime, they reprimanded me for inviting you to do pedagogical work without getting prior approval. In short it's clear to me that you may be arrested again. Quickly get away from Yagodny in any direction. Run!"

Completely crushed, I ran home. Nikolai was sitting at my house, having arrived for a visit. After listening to my story, he said:

"Get your things together immediately. I'm taking you to Burkhala. You'll be my wife. We will get the marriage registered and you'll be Adamova. I myself will settle your problem with the school."

I went with him and later we joked that it was Karl Marx who had arranged our marriage.

Nikolai was a great craftsman in every way. He obtained a half-demolished little apartment consisting of a bedroom and kitchen, put it in order himself with the help of some friends, and built a brick oven in which the wood caught fire with one match and which stayed warm for a whole twenty-four-hour period. Somewhere he found a broken kerosene lamp, repaired it, made a good lampshade, and we had regular light at a time when the majority of people suffered with little wick lamps. I also enjoyed organizing our life. I embroidered pretty curtains for the window and a beautiful big tablecloth for the table. Friends came to visit, and I happily prepared refreshments.

My life began to appear to be somewhat normal, human. I realized that I had to resign myself. I had to give up any dream of seeing my children.

Many women envied me. I had a good, caring husband, a comfortable life—what else could one need?

And suddenly everything abruptly changed. I received a letter from home in which I was informed that the director of Far East Construction, Nikishov (in fact the *master* of the whole Kolyma region), was in Moscow for an advisory meeting at the Council of Ministers. My brother, Mikhail Lvovich Sliozberg, was friends with the deputy minister of defense, Vladimir Nikolaevich Novikov. They decided that Novikov would ask Nikishov to give me permission to leave Kolyma. He did so and Nikishov promised to take action.

In those years people tried not to remember their connections with enemies of the people, and even more so not to ask favors for them. So the actions of Novikov as well as those of my brother Misha were extraordinarily bold.

The following day my sisters and my brother's wife went to Nikishov's secretary. They brought her a big package of foreign cosmetics and a box of chocolates. The secretary received them with great friendliness and said that within a month Nikishov would be in Magadan. He would have a permit for the mainland as well as a steamship ticket for me.

All the charm of life in Burkhala faded away. I dreamed only of my children. Nikolai did not want to part with me at all, but he did everything he could to help. He collected bread ration cards for me, got money and food, and made arrangements with the driver of a freight truck. It was early spring and there was still a pretty deep frost. I was going to have to ride more than five hundred kilometers. They constructed a warm little cab out of plywood in the back of the truck. Nikolai made some sort of gasoline heater and got three American woolen blankets. I set off for Magadan. It turned out right away that my little cab was cold, smelled of gas, and shook unbelievably. The whole three days of the trip I was utterly exhausted by seasickness. But all that was trivial because I was going to the children!

In Magadan a blow awaited me. Nikishov wasn't in the city; he had gone off to the gold mines somewhere. I settled myself at the transit prison, lived on bread alone, and every day tried to find out when Nikishov would arrive. They said that he could be traveling around the gold mines for as long as four months; it wasn't possible to predict.

There was nothing to eat—my bread ration cards were used up. I had no hope of a quick meeting with Nikishov. In short, I had to gather myself together and go back to my own mine.

I don't even remember how long we drove. I was really sick when we arrived. "It means this is not my fate!" I repeated to myself. I tried not to show Nikolai how hard this was for me. And he was happy that I had returned. He tried to create some contentment for me and was tender and patient with me. And so we lived for a couple of months. Once we went to the movies and saw *Guilty Without Guilt,* with Alla Tarasova.

Even today I remember this movie down to the last small detail. The yearning of the mother for her lost son, her meeting with him—all of it affected me so much that I began to cry desperately. Tears flooded through my hands. Nikolai took me home, talking to me as if to a child, and quieted me. I lay in bed, turned toward the wall, and tried to hide from Nikolai that I was still crying. He walked around the room, sometimes coming up to me and putting a dry towel under me so that I wasn't lying in a puddle. He lay down very late, but he too didn't fall asleep for a long time, feeling my cheeks with his hand to see if they were wet. I couldn't stop my tears until morning.

Probably I had a kind of psychic illness. Nothing could make me happy. I tried to hide my sufferings from Nikolai, but he felt them very subtly.

Suddenly a friend of Nikolai ran into our room and cried out:

"Run to the mine director's home. Nikishov arrived not long ago; you can speak with him!"

I ran. The mine director lived in a separate house located in a fenced-in section. Not far from the entrance shrubs were growing. I decided to hide myself in them, and when Nikishov came out, turn myself over to him. He had been described to me—he was short with red-striped riding britches.

I waited for an hour or two. Suddenly the door opened and Nikishov appeared, surrounded by guards. I immediately recognized him from the description. He started toward an automobile. Afraid that I would lose him, I jumped from the shrubs with a cry:

"Comrade Nikishov! My name is Sliozberg. You promised Novikov in Moscow that you would release me from Kolyma!"

The reaction was very funny. Nikishov apparently thought I was going to kill him. He covered his face with his hands and cried out:

"Grab her!"

I was immediately surrounded by soldiers. I continued to cry out:

"I am Sliozberg, you promised Novikov to release me from Kolyma!"

Realizing what I was talking about, Nikishov grandly pronounced:

"She may go." Then he got into the car and rolled off.

Again we began to search for transport to Magadan. Soon Nikolai found out from a driver who had come from Magadan that Nikishov was in Magadan. The next day the car was going there and they could take me.

Nikolai asked:

"You aren't afraid of the trip? You won't get sick again?"

Could I be afraid? I would walk those five hundred kilometers on foot!

Driving was easier than in the winter. There was no frost, and I sat in the fresh air instead of in the little cab. I don't remember if I was seasick. I absolutely don't remember how I got there.

At our farewell Nikolai said to me:

"Wait for me. I will definitely come to you."

At that time I did not believe his words at all and did not think of them. But his promise came true, though not right away.

Nikishov's secretary welcomed me very courteously, remembering my sisters and sister-in-law, and took me to a waiting room.

Within a half hour I had the permission in my hands to leave Kolyma for a fourteen-day stay in Moscow.

Verochka

I waited for the embarkation of the steamship that would take me back to real life after seven years in Kolyma.

Two women with daughters came up to me. These women were from Elgen. One, Sophia Mikhailovna, had been our doctor; the other I recognized only by sight. Sophia Mikhailovna had two daughters who had remained free, and she had managed to send them packages and money even from the camp, and then when she was released, she set herself up very well, since she was well known as an excellent pediatrician and treated the children of all the bosses. She worked in three different locations, had a private practice, and sent all she earned to her children.

In 1945 her daughters, thirteen and twenty years old, came to live with her, and now in July 1946 the older of the two, Verochka, was returning to the mainland. Sophia Mikhailovna's face was covered with red spots, and in her eyes there were traces of tears. Verochka, a slim dark-eyed girl, was morosely silent.

While Sophia Mikhailovna was well dressed and walked like a lady, her fellow traveler, dressed in boots and a padded jacket with her hands damaged by rough work, was recognizable as a camp inmate. She was openly bewildered and kept saying to her daughter:

"Nadia, give me your word that you'll study and stop your silliness. Give me your word, Nadia. Otherwise you might ruin yourself!"

At this Nadia kissed her and said:

"Now, I already said I'll study, Mama! And putting red on my lips and dancing is—well—I won't do it, if it's so unpleasant for you. Calm down."

Sophia Mikhailovna came to me requesting that I look after her daughter who was traveling to the mainland in order to bring her grandmother, Sophia Mikhailovna's mother, to Magadan. I promised to look after her. At this moment the steamship began to embark. We ended up together in the hold of the ship, on the top level of a triple bunk.

I lay on my bunk all day and thought about how I would be meeting with my almost-adult children. How would I explain to them the way in which their mother and father had become enemies of the people? With these thoughts I could hardly sleep at night, but during the day, listening to the conversations of others, I was distracted and sometimes slept.

One day having just woken up, I heard a conversation between Vera and Nadia. They were going through Vera's suitcase and looking at what Sophia Mikhailovna had given her daughter. Apparently the things were good because Nadia said:

"All the same you have a good mother. She doesn't have an easy life working in three different places, and still she managed to buy so many things for you. What a mother!"

To this Vera answered with what was to me astonishing bitterness:

"It would have been better if she were a worse mother and a better human being."

"Well, my mother is certainly a good human being," said Nadia, "Everyone says so. But what of it? She doesn't understand me! She begins her usual, 'We struggled, we fought, we argued all night! And you're only interested in dresses and dancing!' I said, 'Look what you fought for—you certainly got it!' And then she turned pale, trembled, I was even afraid for her. 'Don't you dare speak of what you do not understand!' So in point of fact, arguing isn't allowed either. And she is so impractical! With her education she only works as a ticket-taker in a bathhouse. For a whole year we were barely able to scrape together enough for my boat ticket, not to speak of things for me to wear!"

Nadia very quickly found a boyfriend and spent days and even nights with him on deck. Their love bloomed. When I tried to talk with her, she answered that she was an adult, this was a very good guy, and probably she would marry him. I couldn't object.

Vera lay silent for whole days; sometimes she read letters and sometimes she cried. We traveled for a whole month; gradually we got closer, and she told me her story.

In 1937 when she was twelve years old, Vera's childhood ended with the ruin of her family. Memories of her earlier family life seemed to her unbelievably resplendent.

Vera's father was the most well-known surgeon in the small southern city where they lived. Verochka loved to visit him in the hospital, loved the general admiration of her father's mastery, his authoritative directives, his gentleness, kindness and happy fatigue after work. He always said to her, "You'll be a doctor. You are cut out to be a doctor. Everyone in our family is a doctor—your grandfather and your mother and your father are doctors."

Her father and mother's work was the most important preoccupation in the life of the whole family. Her father's writing table was a sacred place to which Vera was only permitted to come to clean, but it never would have occurred to her to move a piece of paper or a test tube.

Her father's university friend, Nikolai, an old Bolshevik and the director of the health department for the whole city, came to call on him. He had had some kind of unpleasantness. He discussed something with her father very intensely. Verochka heard the words: "Degeneration . . . Thermidor . . ." One day her father arrived home very upset and said to her mother: "They have arrested Nikolai." Her mother was terrified: "Where is the truth, if they consider someone like Nikolai an enemy? Probably he is right—it's degeneration." And her father answered: "I can't understand anything. I only know one thing. When they bring a person to me with a broken skull, and I make him back into a whole human being, I am right. Ours is good work. A doctor, if he's an honest doctor, is always right."

When they came to arrest her mother and father, Verochka looked at her father with horror as he sat gloomily and silently, watching how they dug into his desk and leafed through his books and letters. Once when some soldier smashed a test tube, he made an involuntary movement, rushing toward the desk. The command rang out: "Sit down!" Her father turned from the desk, and the rest of the time he sat bent over and kept silent for two hours while they conducted the search.

When they were led away, her mother, sobbing, turned to Vera and said:

"Verochka, take care of Julia. She is young, she'll even forget her family name. I won't be able to find her. Take care of her, Vera."

Her father put his hand on Verochka's head and said:

"Be strong, Vera, and take care of yourself. You already are a strong person. Take care of yourself and Julia."

Verochka was left alone in a frightening and disordered apartment with her five-year-old weeping sister Julia. Within half an hour a car arrived, and the children were taken to two different orphanages. They put Vera in one in their city, but Julia was taken to an orphanage near Gorky.

Twelve-year-old Verochka had a single life goal. She would search for her mother, father, and Julia. She caught up with her little sister rather quickly. They gave her the address of the orphanage and, in answer to her beseeching letter, one of the caretakers, Olga Arsenevna, began to write to her, taking the poor orphans under her wing. (Later Verochka found out by chance that Olga Arsenevna's brother had been arrested.)

It was more difficult with her parents. She simply learned her father's sentence: ten years without the right to correspondence. Her mother she found in Kolyma two years later.

I well remember when Sophia Mikhailovna received her first letter from Verochka in 1939. I was in the barracks. Someone came running from the CED (Cultural Education Department) and said there was a letter for Sophia Mikhailovna. Before that time she had endlessly inquired about her daughters' address, but they didn't answer her. She thought this letter would have some information about the children from the MGB. Throwing on a shawl, pale-faced, she ran to the CED, and within a half hour, crying, she came back to the barracks with the letter from Verochka and her photo. Of course she passed the letter around. Everyone cried and looked with admiration at the thin girl with the shaven head and dark-blue eyes. Everyone read her dear brave words, written in half-childish handwriting. She comforted her mother, gave her Julia's address, told her about her father's sentence, wrote that she was studying hard, would definitely become a doctor, and that Julia had a very good caretaker.

Sophia Mikhailovna came back to life. She had a goal for her life: to survive and to be reunited with her daughters again. She tried in every way she could to gather money in order to send it to her daughters. She treated the bosses' children, performed abortions, did not shrink from the gifts of patients, with all the consequences that stemmed from that. There were situations when, for money, she released criminals from work. That was, of course, against our interest because she could grant only a limited number of releases from work, and often even very ill people were not permitted time off, while some Sonka Kozyr or Mashka Torgsin spent her time lying in the barracks. Many judged Sophia Mikhailovna harshly for this, but she did try to lighten our life just a little bit. For this one she wrote a prescription for cod liver oil or some sort of vitamin; for that one she arranged a transfer to much lighter work, and to this one she gave a day of rest.

The children's home where Verochka ended up was bad. The director shamelessly took pots of milk for her own children from the kitchen, and the staff followed her example. The teachers had their favorites among the older children who went to their homes to help with the housework and the vegetable garden, and for that they received privileges. Nourishment was naturally bad and the building was a dirty mess. The children were outraged and cursed the director and those who sucked up to her.

Once at an official gathering for the November 7 celebration in 1939, after the director's report on the government's care for children, fifteen-year-old Alik Andreev stood up, independent of the regular program, and said:

"Maybe the government does care for us, but our teachers only think about how they can steal our food. Even the rug we got for the recreation room is spread out in the manager's room."

And then what mayhem broke out! The chairman rang a bell and called out that it wasn't Alik's turn to speak, but the children yelled, "It's true. And chocolate that we were given for a holiday, the teachers took half of it, and in our rooms the heat is bad, but in their bedrooms it's like a hot-house." Several of the children who were the teachers' favorites also yelled, "Be quiet, you little sons of Fascists!"

Then Alik jumped up on a chair and cried out, "No, I am not the son of a Fascist. If the director were as good a Communist as my father, we wouldn't be starving. He was a real Communist, and that is why he was put in prison."

Several times Verochka tried to shout and support Alik, but the care-taker sitting next to her squeezed her hand and whispered, "Be quiet, you'll get in trouble yourself." And Verochka kept quiet.

After Alik's outcry, everyone fell silent, and an empty space formed around him. He came down from the chair, realizing that he would not be forgiven, that they would use this episode to destroy him.

And later, remembering Alik's eyes and that she had kept quiet, Vera groaned at night and cried and turned red, hiding her head under the covers. Alik was arrested and sentenced to five years in a reform colony for underage criminals, according to article 58, point 10 (agitation against the Soviet government). He was charged with discrediting the Soviet court. The caretaker then said to Vera, "You see, it's good that I stopped you."

In 1940 the children's home where Vera lived was moved beyond Tash-kent to the east. To her delight, it so happened that Julia's orphanage moved to a village fifty kilometers away from Vera's, and Verochka dreamed of somehow seeing Julia. One day a driver who knew Olga Arsenevna and Julia arrived from Julia's orphanage.

"Your little sister is very sick with dysentery," he said. "She is as thin as a blade of grass and is covered with spots. Of course there should be nour-ishment for her, but what kind of nourishment do they have there!"

Shortly before that Verochka had received her first package from their mother. In it was sugar, powdered eggs, three chocolate bars, a package of vitamins, a blouse, and a knitted scarf. She decided that with such riches, she would go to Julia and save her. And so at night the girl ran away from the children's home and went to Julia. She feared they would find her, as she was afraid of stray dogs and evil people.

She walked for five nights and during the day she slept in the bushes. On the sixth day she arrived. She really did find Julia, pale and thin as a blade of grass, all covered with some kind of eczema. The sisters threw themselves into each other's arms and held onto each other, afraid that something would separate them. Olga Arsenevna brought them to her room and decided to request that Vera stay in their children's home. She succeeded and Vera really helped Julia recover. She gave her own ration of sugar and oil to her, sometimes got fruit from work on the collective farm, and exchanged things sent by their mother for eggs and white bread.

When Verochka turned sixteen, she left the children's home and became an apprentice lathe turner at a factory. By this time the war had started, and adolescents were taking the place of workers who had been sent to the front. Verochka became qualified as a lathe turner and sometime afterward took Julia from the children's home to stay with her on her bunk in a dormitory. This little mother raised Julia very strictly, seeing to it that she studied hard. Sophia Mikhailovna regularly sent packages, and the girls somehow survived.

In 1945 Sophia Mikhailovna was already working in Magadan as a free doctor. With her high-level connections, she was able to get permission for the girls to come to Kolyma to their mother. How happy they were when the steamship brought them into Nogaev Bay on a rainy day in August 1945!

They met their mother, who was less changed after eight years than they had expected. The same long shining brown hair, the same soft hands, the same kind eyes!

Their mother had a good room where everything was prepared for them, starting with the beds with new nightshirts under the pillows and ending with perfumes on the little toilet table and embroidered Ukrainian blouses. Their mother cooked them Ukrainian borscht (the way they'd had it at home) and dumplings filled with cream, caressed them, and couldn't stop talking with them. A month went by in blissful tumult, memories of childhood, stories of the eight years of separation, and reacquaintance. On the first of September, Julia went to school, and there was the question of what Vera would do. She tried to say that she was qualified as a metal lathe operator and could work at the auto repair factory, but her mother covered her ears in horror.

"Enough—you and I went through hell. Now everything will be different. I will arrange for you to do light work—as a secretary for the Dalstroi administration—and you will enter the tenth grade in the school for working youth. (Verochka had finished only nine grades.) And then we'll see. You certainly want to study to become a doctor. This is my goal—to give you an education, as your father wished."

So Verochka began to work as a secretary in the Dalstroi office. In her new job Vera encountered the customs that were particular to Kolyma. There were two categories of workers: former prisoners and contractors. The former prisoners usually worked in the areas that required really hard work—bookkeepers, typists, estimators. They were called *hard workers*. Contractors were very often people without any qualifications but with handsome résumés. They took on work as directors of departments, secretaries, and so forth. It happened that the chief accountant was a contractor, but his assistant was a former prisoner. The assistant worked but received a salary that was a quarter of what his boss received.

The wife of the boss of the personnel department led the planning office. She not only did not understand anything about her work but didn't consider it necessary to even sit through an eight-hour day. Often during work hours she could be seen in stores, or one could find her at home where, under her supervision, an old orderly (the bosses' orderlies came from among the prisoners) papered the walls or did general chores. But planning work didn't suffer from this, since a former economist from Gosplan worked in the planning office. This was a quiet, timid person, ready to sit in the office day and night, doing the work of two or three.

Verochka was taken up by the contractors as one of their own, but the former prisoners, intimidated by their experiences in the camps, talked very little with her. Her new acquaintances' interests were alien to Vera, being nothing more than romance and clothing. She was irritated by their scornful attitudes toward the former prisoners, whom Vera saw as the same kind of people as her parents.

Vera worked in the same office as the accountants. The assistant to the main accountant, Andrei Petrovich Shelest, supervised the accounting business. He was good looking, of remarkable stature, and a person with a broad open nature. He had been imprisoned for embezzlement, not for a political crime. The nonpoliticals thought that they should have far more rights than the enemies of the people.

Opposite Andrei Petrovich sat two bookkeepers behind two small narrowly placed tables. Simochka, a beautiful young woman, was the wife of an engineer-contractor; and Olga Ivanovna, a woman of about fifty who had recently been released from the camps, was pale and poorly dressed.

It was a typical working day. Andrei Petrovich was flicking his abacus, Olga Ivanovna was filling out file cards, and Simochka was happily chattering with Ofitzerov, a smart, well-dressed NKVD lieutenant whom Verochka intensely disliked. He seemed to her like Dantès.

Ofitzerov, bending toward Simochka's ear, was telling her something funny while looking out of the corner of his eye at Olga Ivanovna. At this moment Olga Ivanovna stood up and went to Andrei Petrovich for some sort of reference. Ofitzerov immediately sat down in her place and, sprawling out on the chair, continued to chatter with Simochka. Olga Ivnovna returned and asked Ofitzerov to free up her work place. Carelessly growling "wait," he continued to chatter with Simochka. Olga Ivanovna stood there confusedly with red spots on her face. She was outraged by his insolence but feared starting an argument with him and couldn't find the right words anyway. Finally she decisively took a step toward her table and started to say something, but at this moment Andrei Petrovich, observing the whole scene, called to her in a very polite tone:

"Be so kind, Olga Ivanovna, as to give me the summary for October 1942, number such and such . . ."

Olga Ivanovna searched for the summary, gave it to him, and then again wished to return to her desk, still firmly occupied by Ofitzerov, but Andrei Petrovich grabbed her arm strongly and began a long explanation, whispering from time to time, "Stop. Don't get involved!" Olga Ivanovna withdrew her arm, but Andrei Petrovich said in a sweet voice:

"My dear Olga Ivanovna, I wish that you would make file cards for all the issues of material value for 1941 through 1944. Yes, we'll need them to verify the balances . . ." Slowly and lengthily he explained. Verochka observed this scene, and Ofitzerov, who continued to whisper something funny to Simochka, looked at Olga Ivanovna from the corner of his eye.

Having kept this going for long enough in his opinion to teach the brazen Olga Ivanovna a lesson, Ofitzerov stood up, kissed Simochka's hand and, remarking to Olga Ivanovna, "Now sit down," he left the accounting office, with his uniform, eyes, and boots all shining and exuding the smell of perfume, wine, and the skin of a healthy wholesome male.

Everyone continued to work as if nothing had happened. About twenty minutes after Ofitzerov left the room, the workday ended.

For the whole twenty minutes Vera fidgeted in her chair and didn't know how she could go up to Olga Ivanovna, in what words she could express her outrage at Ofitzerov and Sima, as well as her sympathy for Olga. Not being able to think of anything, she waited for the right moment.

As always, Simochka was the first to flit away. Then Andrei Petrovich went out, waving a hand to Olga Ivanovna in good-bye and cheerfully saying:

"Learn the Kolyma ways. Things can be worse than this."

Olga Ivanovna also got herself ready to leave and pulled on some sort of old raincoat over her prison padded jacket. Verochka went up to her, embraced her, pressed her lips against her cheek and gasped:

"Oh, the skunk! Oh, what a skunk!" and quickly ran out into the street.

To her astonishment, her mother was not very outraged when Vera told her that evening about the incident in the office. Sophia Mikhailovna only shook her head sadly and said:

"Yes, Verochka, that is life here. When I go to treat a child, they are completely gracious, but deep in their hearts they consider us the lowest people. You must pretend that you don't observe their boorishness. Otherwise one can't live in Kolyma."

Vera had a friend at evening school—Ivan Kolosov. He was a *special settler.* Special settlers were people who had been sentenced to forced settlement in Kolyma without the right to leave. In 1945 and 1946 they were mostly Soviet POWs who had been liberated from German camps by the Soviet or Allied soldiers.

Ivan had fought from the beginning of the war until the end of 1943. He was at Stalingrad and even was decorated with the Order of the Red Banner. Then he was wounded. After recovering he again went back to fight, and at the beginning of 1944 he was badly wounded and taken prisoner. He lived through all the horrors of capture. The Americans freed him. Ivan told Vera how the prisoners recovered from Hitler's death camps in the American zone where you were well fed and free, but how strongly their homeland tugged at their hearts! How rumors circulated that everyone who returned to Russia from captivity would be sent to the camps. How he, an ardent member of the Komsomol, argued and demonstrated that this was enemy propaganda, that a person who had been badly wounded and taken prisoner wasn't responsible for that, and they should believe the Soviet officers who arrived to take the Russian prisoners home for repatriation. They said:

"Your country is awaiting you. Your families are awaiting you."

Ivan boldly stepped forward when the Soviet representative asked:

"Who wants to return to our country?"

The repatriates rode in a train decorated with the slogan "Your motherland awaits you!" In Negoreloye they were transferred to a freight car, locked up, and sent to Kolyma. In Vladivostok they sat for five months in an investigation prison. The majority ended up in the camps. Ivan was lucky. He had been captured after being badly wounded, and therefore they let him live free in Kolyma but without the right to leave.

And so Ivan, having fought with the army for almost four years, instead of living with his mother and brothers in a large Cossack village in the Kuban, instead of studying to become an engineer as he had dreamed, was working as a metalworker in an auto repair factory in Magadan and living in a dormitory where there was no entertainment but getting drunk. With horror he felt that the vodka pulled at him more and more. He felt moral injury, and his sense of justice that had been so rudely suppressed now boiled up in his soul. It just so happened that he broke loose in a terrible way. Somehow in answer to a rather typical observation that "you don't go to prison for nothing," he beat up an old person, a contractor. He was arrested for fifteen days and acquired the reputation of being a hooligan. In the winter of 1945 he decided to enter the tenth grade at evening school, and there he became friends with Vera.

The first thing she required of her friend was that he give up vodka once and for all. Ivan happily began to obey Vera. He stopped needing vodka because he had the joy of meeting this splendid girl every day.

When Verochka told him with outrage what had happened at the office, Ivan did not react the way Sophia Mikhailovna had. He ground his teeth, clenched his fists, and said:

"He'll pay for this, the skunk, just wait . . . And you, Vera, get out of there. Why should you be with those skunks? Come and work in our repair factory as a lathe operator."

And Verochka, without saying a word to her mother, went to the factory to work as a lathe operator. Now she and Ivan spent all day together—days at the factory and evenings at school. Sophia Mikhailovna of course found out about her daughter's infatuation. She spoke with her and tried convincing her that Ivan was an illiterate fellow who drank too much, was a hooligan, and had no perspective on life. For Vera nothing worked. And then when it was reported to Sophia Mikhailovna that Verochka and Ivan had been seen kissing on a small bench by the fence at the school, Sophia Mikhailovna went to the director of the Dalstroi administration and told him that her daughter was threatened with ruin because of some alcoholic boy, a special settler named Ivan Kolosov. The administrative director, whose children Sophia Mikhailovna had treated, gladly granted her this minor favor:

"Don't be upset, my dear. Tomorrow the wind will blow him away. Of course we must protect your charming daughter from this bandit."

And the next day Ivan was shipped off to the North to work in the mines. Verochka showed me a letter Ivan had left for her before he departed.

"Farewell, my Vera," Ivan wrote. "In vain I dreamed that my whole-hearted love would find a response in your heart, that I was and will be a real human being, regardless of my terrible, shameful situation. In vain I dreamed that I had found a friend, a wife for my whole life. I know that you love me, but your mother of course would never put up with the idea that her beautiful, intelligent daughter who has all the paths of education open to her, a life in the capitals, a daughter whom any doctor of science or colonel would gladly marry, would instead marry a man without rights, a man without education, a well-known drunk.

"Apparently I will live out my life with cursing and vodka, in hard labor, in filth. Farewell, my Vera. Farewell forever!"

"How did you answer this letter, Verochka?" I asked.

"I didn't answer it at all. I pulled myself together, jumped into a passing car, and went to him at the mine."

And here's how the rest of it went.

At the mine Verochka arrived on a Sunday morning. A truck took her to the canteen and there they told her that the brigade in which Kolosov worked was stationed in Barracks 2. She walked up to a low wooden building and went into the entryway. From the barracks one could hear yelling, snatches of song, and coarse laughter. No one heard her knock. She walked in. The living quarters were dark, narrow, and dirty. Along the walls were bunks with some kind of rags on the beds. About twelve men sat around a table. On the table was alcohol, pieces of herring on a newspaper, cigarette butts, and bread. Besides the men around the table there were two painted, drunken women each in the arms of two men.

Ivan sat with his back to the door, but Vera instantly recognized him and with horror watched as he drank alcohol from a glass, chasing it with water. One of the women took in Vera at a glance and hoarsely screeched:

"Vanka, I'll be fucked if that isn't your sweetie!"

Ivan turned around and seeing Vera, turned pale. Everyone made a racket:

"Vanka, right, she's yours! Whew, what a piece of ass!"

Ivan went up to Vera. The intoxication flew away from him. He took her by the hand and led her from the barracks.

"Why, why did you come? To make sure that your mother is right and that I am a drunk and a hooligan?"

"Don't be stupid. Go wash yourself and get dressed. I'll wait for you."

Ivan went away. A man of about thirty-five came up to Vera.

"Well, were you frightened to take a look at our life? And did you think there's anything to do here except drown ourselves in drink? But your Ivan is a golden boy, I say this to you honestly. He told me about you, I didn't believe him, but now I see he was right."

The man went away.

Ivan came out. He was pale, embarrassed, and shocked.

"Why did you come?"

Vera pitied him terribly.

"Let's go to the ZAGS so we can register our marriage."

Ivan lowered his head.

"Are you kidding me? There isn't a ZAGS here."

"It's all the same—I came here to marry you. Let's go to the director of the mine or to the head of the local NKVD. There must be some sort of person in charge here!"

"So it happened," Vera continued, "the way it has to without a ZAGS. We went to the head of the NKVD and the boss of the mine and told them everything.

"The boss gave Ivan three days for a wedding. The NKVD head wrote some sort of document saying that I was the wife of Kolosov. His comrades acted very delicately—everyone got out of the room. Where they huddled, I don't know. We lived together for three days. And when I returned home, what a blowup! Mama was nearly out of her mind. Of course I could understand her. She had suffered so much; she wanted a good life for me. Only she absolutely does not understand me. Here she is sending me to fetch my grandmother from the mainland, and she hopes I'll forget Ivan. Since our marriage isn't registered, it would be easy for us to separate. But I will never forget him. I do want to study and I will, but all the same, Ivan and I will get back together."

"And isn't he still a drunk?"

"No. You don't know him. He is strong and loyal. I told him to save his money so that I could come back to Kolyma." She smiled guilefully and happily. "Now he will begrudge spending even a kopeck on alcohol. And he's not at the mine for a century. The panning season will end. He'll work at the factory again and he'll study. No, my Ivan won't ever become a drunk. We'll get our way, we'll be together. Do I need a colonel or a doctor of science? No, I need Ivan, and he needs me! We'll get our way, we'll be together."

I looked into her bold, clear eyes and believed her. She would get her way.

Return

And so at the beginning of June 1946 I left Kolyma.

We traveled for a whole month: six days on the steamship, nineteen days on the train; we even waited for five more days at the port of Nakhodka while they organized a special train.

I eagerly looked at the people who had been on the other side during these years, surviving the war and not knowing about the camps. These people were coarse and worn out. I was surprised that in line for hot water, women were quarreling and crying out, "You—are you a human being or a militia man?" In our time (before 1936), *militia man* was not a swearword; in those days it was "My militia protects me."

Once a man came up to me on the platform, waved his hand toward the east, and said, "Are you from there?" He handed me a package of tea. "Take it, please, take it. Do you think we don't know how much you suffered for nothing?"

The man was wearing an old military jacket. He looked like a forty-year-old laborer.

I wired home from every stop where there was a telegraph, but they didn't come to meet me. On the last day somewhere around Riazhsk, our train was driven onto a siding and we had to wait eighteen hours. Then they took us by the circular railway line to the Rizhsky station, and on the morning of August 6 we arrived in Moscow.

No one met us. (That was the reason they had taken us in circles.)

I was so bewildered that I didn't know how to get home (and trolley car 25 went right to my house). A man told me he could take me home for two hundred rubles, and after a half-hour ride on the trolley, I was delivered home.

I went into my apartment. One elderly female relative was there. My mother, father, and children were at the dacha; my sister and brother had waited for me at the station for two days and nights and then went away to rest.

Within fifteen minutes my brother's wife came for me, and then within an hour all my relatives gathered and were amazed that I was not a gray-haired old lady and not in hysterics, that I didn't cry, didn't yell, but conversed like everyone else.

My sister-in-law told us that she and my brother had met many trains and had gone up to all the old ladies, thinking they would be me (and I was forty-four years old). I took off my camp dress. My brother's wife gave me her navy blue English-style suit and yellow knitted sweater. At that moment I was only glad I was dressed decently, but later it turned out that my chosen suit was unusually appropriate.

We went to the dacha. The children had been meeting every train for three days already. My sister told me that my daughter was wearing a light-blue dress and my son a yellow shirt. The train pulled into the Sokolovskaya station. My eyes searched frantically. There were many people on the platform, but I couldn't make out my own children. In the distance a boy and girl were running toward us, but I couldn't tell whether they were mine or not. When the train came to a stop, a tall girl, almost a young lady, rushed up to me (she was fifteen years old) and in an unnatural voice began to cry out:

"Mama! Mama? Mama!"

And then I heard my sister say: "Come on, Shurik."

And a young fellow came up to me. He was tall and awkward with a cracking voice. And he had eyes that were somewhat mine and somewhat my husband's. And he pursed his lips just the way his father had when he was excited . . .

We went through a little gate in the fence into our garden. On the terrace in an armchair sat Mama and behind her stood my older sister—a doctor with a hypodermic syringe ready. (She was afraid our mother's heart would not hold out.)

Mama had changed more than all the others. From a strong sixty-year-old woman who could wash a hundred pieces of linen and polish a floor better than a professional floor-polisher, she had become an ancient woman who couldn't get up out of her armchair.

"You, you," Mama said, and tears streamed from her eyes. "Lord, I've lived, I've lived to see you! You, you!"

I ran up, fell on my knees, and buried my head in her breast, in her arms, breathed in her scent.

"Mama!"

And she was afraid to disturb the joy of our meeting with a heart attack. She pressed her hands to her heart, cried without a sound, and said:

"I've lived, I've lived to see you."

My father was in a sanatorium in Bolshevo. He was blind in one eye, and in the other eye a cataract was developing. Before giving him an operation to remove the cataract, they had decided to build up his strength. The next day the children and I went to the sanatorium. My son and I sat on a bench in the garden, and we sent my daughter in to get her grandfather so that she could prepare him. Within several minutes my father's tall figure appeared. He was almost running, holding out his arms like a blind person, and crying out:

"Where, where?"

Ellochka was following after him and saying in bewilderment:

"Quiet, Grandpa, you promised me you wouldn't get excited!"

I ran up to him, took hold of him, and we both cried. People said:

"It must be his daughter who has arrived from the front."

In the evening at the dinner table I asked:

"Is it true that Stalin is very sick?"

No one knew but my son answered very meaningfully:

"I don't know if he is sick, but if he were sick and I had to give him my blood and die for him, I would do it."

I realized that this was a lesson and warning for me, and I fell silent. I remember my son's words from another time. I was recounting how a fellow in our freight train stood by the open door of the cattle car with his jacket flung over his shoulders. Somehow the jacket flew away, the fellow jumped after it, and so he was left behind by the train. My son observed:

"Probably his Komsomol ticket was in his pocket. I would have jumped too."

Another time I asked him:

"Shurik, did you remember Papa and me and our old life? Did you remember us?"

He answered brusquely:

"No, I don't remember anything, I never remembered anything."

And then within two weeks:

"Mama, did you choose to wear a blue skirt and yellow sweater on purpose?"

"Why do you think that?"

"Because you left in a blue skirt and yellow sweater, and I was sure when the door opened you'd come in wearing a blue skirt and yellow sweater. And that's how it turned out."

Only then I remembered how I had been dressed when I was arrested. And he remembered. That meant he did remember.

My relationship with my daughter was very simple. We shared a bed and at night she would snuggle up to me with her tender young body, half child and half young woman. I would breathe in the aroma of her hair, her lips, and it would feel as if I had never been separated from her for even one day. She was convinced that she had to tell Mama everything, and I quickly found out all her fifteen-year-old secrets, sorrows, and joys. She was a clear, charming creature and poured out to me a flood of unending sweetness.

With my son it was more complicated. I was afraid to tell him what had been revealed to me on the other side. Probably I could have convinced him that many things in the country were not quite right and that his idol, Stalin, was very far from perfect, but after all he was only seventeen years old. If I had explained everything to him and he had agreed with me, would he be able to applaud at the mention of Stalin, would he be able to write letters to Stalin, calling him a wise genius and saying that in our country there was justice?

And if he could not, he would be ruined!

And if he could, what a breakdown, what double-dealing, what a double life! No. I could not doom him to that. So I was afraid to be open with him. But somehow I gradually won over his soul. He observed me attentively. Within three months he said to me:

"Mama, I like you."

"What do you like about me, my son?"

"I am glad that you are not like Aunt Sonia."

Sonia was our distant relative whose husband, once a very important person, had been arrested. They evicted Sonia from her apartment in the House on the Embankment, but for some reason they didn't send her away from Moscow.

She went around to her friends and relatives, begging, crying, and reminiscing about their former grandeur. Shurik couldn't endure her ingratiating tone, the way she curried favor, her sensational gossip, her pathetic efforts to restore her fading beauty with lip gloss and some sort of lilac powder. In her time she had been abroad and now said in a whisper how good things were there and how bad everything was with us.

My son's feelings were correct. Even then it didn't seem to me that everything was so bad with us. Oh, how I loved Moscow where I was living as if on the edge of a volcano, how I loved our life even though I was excluded from it, even though I detested, how sharply I detested, those who had disfigured our beautiful life, who had gagged our mouths and tied our hands.

Having stayed with my family for two weeks I knew very well that I had to go somewhere two hundred to two hundred fifty kilometers outside Moscow where I could be registered. But everything around us was so peaceful. We lived at the dacha, where there wasn't a single unfamiliar face, and it seemed as if no one was paying any attention to me.

Several times I tried to leave. Once I even set out for the city of Gus-Khrustalny, took a room there, and was registered. I began to look for work, which wasn't easy. And then my landlord said to me:

"Go along to Moscow, Olga Lvovna; if they ask for you, you'll get a telegram from me on that very day. Many do that here."

I paid him for three months in advance, went back to Moscow, and continued to live with my family.

My mother was like a child. She cried when I went away and said:

"Why do you leave? No one will find out you're living with us. And if they do find out, we'll say you came here to take care of your sick mother. Who will judge that?"

I thought painfully about the fact that at the dacha I was relatively safe, whereas at home in the city where so many people knew me, conversation would begin. Someone would figure out that I was living without a permit. They'd come and seize me. Under the best of circumstances, I'd be doomed to isolation, exile, homelessness, not knowing what to do with myself. Sometimes they said that people who didn't have permits were seized and sent away within twenty-four hours, and under a repeat violation, could even be sent back to the camps. It would be better to leave. But where to go? How?

How many times I froze at the slightest knock or unexpected phone call and naively hid myself behind the cabinet! At night I would swear to myself that I would leave, but in the morning I sat by my dying mother's bed again and reassured her:

"Don't be afraid, Mamochka, I won't leave, I'll be with you!"

The bitterest moments for me were with my dearly beloved father who in his eightieth year didn't understand contemporary life very well. More than once I found him on a small bench near the fence of our garden with some old man or old woman in an absorbing conversation, and these old people would gaze at me with tears in their eyes and say, "You poor innocent sufferer, finally you're rewarded by fate! You have such splendid children, such parents!"

"Papa, you've been talking about me again! I already begged you to be quiet!" I reproached him.

"You're such a strange one! Ivan Matveevich"—or Maria Petrovna—"is a person of splendid character; he is so sympathetic to you, and you suspect that he might denounce you!"

After the dacha, we moved to the city, into the apartment on Petrovka Street, where I had lived for sixteen years before my marriage. Naturally many knew me and my grievous history. I tried not to go out into the street during the day. But my father had many splendid friends there too, and old people came up to me in the courtyard more than once and secretly whispered to me, "Don't be afraid, no one will report you, you can live peacefully, you poor innocent sufferer!"

You can imagine how peacefully I lived, but all the same I didn't have the strength to leave my mother who was confined to her bed nor my blind father nor (probably this was the most difficult) my children, whom I had never loved so deeply as in this period of mutual reacquaintance, closeness, and discovering of each other.

The most amazing thing was that I lived in Moscow on Petrovka Street for three years and no one denounced me, although dozens of people knew of my existence. For three whole years I lived in uninterrupted terror.

I must say that I began to think about Nikolai more and more often. At the beginning the reunion with my children and relatives completely excluded all thoughts of him. He wrote me rather dry short letters. (He didn't really know how to write expressive letters.) I even had the suspicion that another woman had come into his life. He was still rather young (forty-four years old), handsome, and charming. Besides that, some bitter feelings about the way we parted still dwelt in my heart. We had said good-bye in a somewhat strange way. We were waiting for the driver who was supposed to take me away. Nikolai was playing chess with a friend. When the car arrived, he called to his friend, "Don't go away, we'll finish the game." He took me to the car, kissed me, and returned to the game. This farewell hurt me a great deal. I still could not forget the chess game and his indifference to my departure. I was hurt. Although he had said, "Wait for me, I will come to you," I didn't give these words much significance. They sounded simply like, "Good-bye." Besides I knew that leaving Kolyma was practically impossible, especially for a man. Much later I realized that Nikolai's behavior when we said good-bye was a screen. He was too proud to let me feel sorry for him.

So while I considered our relationship finished, he began from that very first day to explore all possible paths for leaving Kolyma. Having received refusals at all official levels, he wrote his friends (several of them had rather high positions), but no one could help him. So two years went by. Finally he got lucky. He became ill with flu and a young woman doctor took care of him. She was not a prisoner but had been sent on assignment to Kolyma not long before, along with her husband who was also a doctor. She didn't suspect what kinds of people in what numbers and under what conditions were kept in the camps. Nikolai enlightened her. At first she was horrified and had doubts, but it was impossible not to believe Nikolai. He had a special gift for telling things in a way that made all doubts fade away. She fell under his influence, came often to see him, and they became friends.

When all efforts to get permission to leave Kolyma ended unsuccessfully, Nikolai discovered that his doctor friend was putting together a group of tuberculosis patients to dispatch to the mainland. He tried to persuade her to include him in this group. She was against it for a long time, realizing that along with everything else, he might become infected. But Nikolai said that then he would simply die. He had decided to go on a hunger strike and not go to work, in order to receive an article 58, point 14, indictment (for sabotage of production). Knowing Nikolai, she realized that he would certainly do this, and so she gave in. She sent someone else's mucus for analysis, and Nikolai was included in the group.

They traveled under terribly unsanitary conditions. On the steamboat they were put in a small cabin where they slept right up against each other. The dishes weren't washed but simply splashed about in cold water. Naturally Nikolai got infected, although his strong physique didn't allow the illness to appear for a long time.

And so one beautiful day Nikolai appeared at our home on Petrovka Street.

Our meeting with each other was very warm.

My parents and children liked him very much. My daughter listened to his tales openmouthed, since he was a great storyteller.

It was illegal for him to live in Moscow, just as it was for me. One of his friends worked as the director of a little factory in a small town two hundred kilometers from Moscow. Nikolai went there, got a job, and rented a room. He often visited us in Moscow and asked me to come with him, but I couldn't make myself part from my children and parents, and I continued my illegal existence.

Even Mama insisted that he take me away with him, as she saw how afraid I was to live in Moscow without a registration permit and how I hid at every ring or knock. They had begun to arrest people during this period in Moscow. People said that for Stalin's Seventieth Jubilee, they were cleaning up Moscow. I knew some other people who lived without documents like me. We all went into a spin. Several immediately left town. (All the same, it made no difference; they were arrested just the same in the villages.) In my small circle there were two suicides—Olga Radovich and Lipa Kaplan ended their lives. I realized that I had to leave.

The possibility of living legally without fear of being checked or denounced and living with Nikolai, whom not long ago I had considered lost forever—what happiness this was!

We decided to leave. Nikolai bought train tickets for August 30, and he was supposed to come for me.

On August 29, as I sat at the dacha beside my mother's bed peacefully reading a book to her, two young people came in wearing well-tailored suits and asked me to follow them . . .

I saw how horror contorted my mother's face. She began:

"She doesn't live here, she is visiting her sick mother. I am sick, I will probably die soon . . . She is visiting . . . She . . ."

Mama began to have a heart attack. She gasped for breath and in the intervals when she could breathe, she clung to my hand and continued her useless white lie, continued to protect her child.

"She is visiting . . . I am dying . . . Let her go . . . She doesn't live with us . . . She was visiting . . ."

I carefully tore my hand away from Mama and stood up.

"I will come with you."

My father came in. He looked around with his half-blind eyes. Just recently he had had a cataract operation, and he could barely see. There were tears in his poor eyes.

"Comrades, I'll explain to you, she has come to visit her mother."

They didn't listen to him.

"Her mother is sick, her mother, and I can't see. She has come to visit her mother."

I never saw either my mother or father again. Shortly after my second arrest they both died.

"Get your things together, certainly you know what's necessary; you don't need to be told."

I went to the closet.

Why should I take my things? Maybe my children can use them. It's completely clear that I will not survive. To live through it a second time? No. I didn't take anything except a towel, a toothbrush, and a pack of cigarettes. I was absolutely certain that I must die.

But how?

Second Arrest

And so on August 29, 1949, I was arrested a second time and taken to the prison at Malaya Lubyanka. They didn't file a guilty sentence against me, and for a month they didn't call me for an interrogation.

Finally they called me in and the investigator told me that in the city apartment where my children lived a search had been made and a sheet of paper had been taken on which something was written in German. He handed the paper to me. What was written there I couldn't make out, but I recognized my son's handwriting. With horror I remembered that my son had read *Mein Kampf* by Hitler. Maybe he had written out some citation from this book.

"Who wrote this?" the investigator asked.

Without thinking I answered:

"I did!"

"Translate it."

A simple task! I know practically no German, and my son's handwriting was illegible. What to do? I painfully peered at the sheet of paper and suddenly made out several words. It was a poem by Heine called "Lorelei," which I had learned in school. A load was taken off my mind.

"I made a mistake," I said. "I didn't write this. It was written by Heine."

The interrogator's eyes caught fire like those of a dog finding the trail.

"First name, patronymic!" he yelled.

I was so happy that I even wanted to joke.

"We used to simply call him Heinrich," I said. "I don't remember his patronymic."

Either there was something written on my face or the combination of the words *Heinrich Heine* reminded the interrogator of something, but he was silent and rang. An armed guard came in.

"Take the prisoner away."

He led me out.

And so my second investigation ended. They didn't call me again. They didn't indict me. But my neighbors in the cell told me that to all appearances I was a *repeater*. Many were arrested and they only threatened them with exile. In other words, our fate wasn't as terrible as going to the camps. In exile people lived freely and could be employed; they just had to stay in one place, and every week had to report to the commandant. It was terrible to think that you could be sent to a remote village, so far away that you wouldn't see your family, but all the same you could put together some sort of life, and it wasn't the torture of the camps.

I already dreamed that I would work, read, possibly find some friends and a place of my own. I had suffered so much from my illegal life in Moscow over the past three years when I had expected to be arrested at any moment.

However, I still didn't have a sentence, although I had already been in prison for two months, and I was very afraid. What if something suddenly changed and I ended up in the camps? This fear could have been the end of me, if I had not firmly decided that I would not go to the camps but would end my life. I didn't fear death. I was too exhausted already with life; the thought of ending it was calming to me.

At the end of October they called me to get my things together and took me to Butyrka prison. It was three o'clock in the morning. In prison there were new procedures: before entering the cell one had to wash. The prison supervisor took me to the shower.

"Wash yourself," said the supervisor. "I will turn on the water." And she went out of the shower room, locking the door behind her.

I trustingly stood under the shower, and suddenly totally cold water began to flow. I wanted to run out, but the door into the dressing room was locked. I knocked and cried out, but no one answered, and icy water continued to pour onto me. Finally the door opened and the shower was turned off.

This little episode somehow took away my last bit of patience. I shivered from the cold and could not calm myself. Tears poured from my eyes.

We went into the cell. All the bunks were occupied, and no one lifted her head.

"Sit down on the bench," said the supervisor. "We'll be getting up in two hours."

I sat down. I was shivering all over.

Suddenly a woman got up from one of the beds.

"Come to my bed, we'll lie together."

I lay in her warm bed, but I continued to shake. I answered her questions about my life story with difficulty.

"We won't languish in prison much longer. In 1950, there'll be a war, the Bolsheviks will be overthrown, and we'll be free."

"Why do you think that?"

"Do you remember that the First World War started in 1914? The sum of these numbers is fifteen. The Second World War? 1941. The sum of these numbers is the same. The third world war will be in 1950, with the same sum. A soothsayer in Warsaw told us this, and her predictions always come true."

What a character! Whom had I fallen in with?

In order to change the subject, I asked her what her name was.

"Wanda."

"Are you Polish? You speak Russian very well."

"Before the war started I had a chance to study in a Russian high school. Later I became a special student of Russian."

"And when were you arrested?"

"After the war, and they gave me a twenty-year sentence."

The thought flashed across my mind. Might she have studied in a school for spies before the war?

"What kind of work did you do in the camps?"

"I was the person on duty in the barracks. I have a bad heart!"

It was clear to me who she was. For a comparatively young woman to get the job of duty person, she had to have been a stool pigeon. And as for her heart? Who on earth would pay any attention to that in the camps anyway! In order to shorten my conversation with her, I pretended I had fallen asleep. In the morning, thanking her for the nighttime refuge, I left her and went to the most distant corner of the cell where they gave me a bunk and I tried to have the least possible contact with her. She noticed my disaffection and was offended.

By a strange coincidence I had ended up in cell 105, the same cell in Butyrka in which I had been imprisoned in 1936. In the past thirteen years the place had changed a lot. In 1936 the cell had been dirty and stinking, with rags drying on strings, and people crying, screaming, talking, walking around all night, and sleeping side by side on plank bunks. In 1949 everything had been transformed into a prison of perfect orderliness. The walls and floors were sparkling clean, people slept on separate beds with mattresses, and even for some minor shift in the schedule, one could be put in an isolation cell; every morning a doctor came in and checked with a white handkerchief to see if there was dust anywhere. For doing a poor job of cleaning, the day guard was also threatened with the isolation cell. In a word, prison culture had achieved perfection. One could imagine a blackboard on the wall showing a Socialist competition with other similar institutions. It was terrible. Now this was not a catastrophe or an earthquake as it had been in 1937 but an orderly existence, established to last for years to come.

After breakfast in the cell, a brawl broke out with hysterics, crude profanity, and bowls thrown on the ground. The performance was put on by Maria Ivanovna Sinitsyna, a gray-haired, fat, messy, screeching old woman who let forth streams of terrible profanity.

"What's going on?" I asked. "Why don't you stop her?"

"Oh, she is so nervous. She already spent ten years in the camps, and this is her second arrest."

(I realized that she, like me, was a repeater, arrested for dispatch into exile.)

At this moment the woman screamed:

"Don't try to stop me. You haven't suffered anything yet. Look, when you get to the camps, you'll see if you pay attention to the niceties there."

Everyone squeezed into a corner in a panic and watched reproachfully as a young woman timidly tried to challenge Maria Ivanovna:

"All the same, even though you're nervous, you don't need to act so crudely and swear. Everyone here is exhausted and anxious."

The old woman threw herself on a bed sobbing and yelling, and everyone gazed at her, depressed and upset, seeing in her their future.

I sat on a bed and began looking around at my comrades in misery.

The whole group of prisoners was drastically different from those I remembered from 1936.

If members of the Party or wives of members of the Party had made up the majority in 1936, now they were only about 10 percent. Many were women arrested for love affairs with Germans (the so-called Under-the-Fritzes). There were members of some religious organization, most of them almost illiterate peasants, who even had their own pretender to the throne, a certain Mikhail, who was clearly not the same age as Mikhail Romanov and couldn't possibly have been he. A lot of prisoners were Latvians and Estonians who hated Russians and held them in contempt. They kept apart from the other prisoners. There was a group of Communists who, all things considered, should have been arrested in 1937 but had somehow been spared, and they all agreed that the arrests of 1937 were just. The proof of this they saw in the fact that they hadn't been arrested in 1937 and so had not been affected.

It was only this small group that, in a very weakened state, was going through a crisis similar to what we had gone through in 1937. That is, their worldview had collapsed. They were in a weakened state because they had been inoculated more than once. Without admitting it to themselves, they had lost their absolute belief in the justice of Soviet power that we all had shared. Hundreds of times already they had substituted the word *expediency* for the word *justice*. They had accepted the ridiculous argument that even though a given person is innocent, he must be eliminated from life for the sake of higher goals. They had thoroughly accepted the idea that *if you cut down a forest, wood chips fly*. And though it was terrible and painful to become a wood chip, there was nothing unnatural about it.

The most horrible was the group of children.

They had been about six or eight years old in 1937 when their parents were arrested. Now they were eighteen to twenty years old. They were arrested because they were children of those arrested in the 1930s, and they were sent into exile for five or ten years. They were members of the Komsomol, had been studying, and didn't know what their parents had done, but they terribly wanted to show that they were just like all Soviet girls or even that they were among the best, although their parents had been stigmatized. Almost all of them were excellent students. They were active in the Komsomol. They dreamed of achieving great exploits so that everyone would recognize them as loyal Soviet people.

At first I couldn't understand where these girls had come from, but then I learned what a real horror it was. I imagined my daughter in these bunks, frightened and not understanding anything. Even worse, I imagined my son, understanding everything, disillusioned with everything, with deathly melancholy and fear in his eyes.

That was when I turned gray!

I asked everyone if they had seen a tall slim girl named Ella, and some answered that there was such a girl. Much later I realized that not all the children of purged parents had been arrested but only those who had happened to become visible; for example, those who, being forbidden to enter the university, had somehow managed to enter anyway or those who had been denounced for their free statements. They arrested the children of very important criminals on no grounds at all. I came across the children of Kosior, Kosarev, Artem Vesioly, Bukharin's brother (who was crazy enough to take his father into his home—also Bukharin's father, of course), the daughter of Rakovsky, and even a group of children of powerful MGB workers. Happily my husband didn't belong to the enemies of the people at this rank, so my children were not arrested.

I looked at my companions in misery and pitied them with an aching pity because I knew these people were condemned to that fearful road to Calvary, which I had already walked. They tried to bring forward evidence of their innocence and hoped that they would sort things out, but I knew the verdict was already written and that all of them were doomed.

Here sits a forty-year-old, well-preserved literary woman. Even here she is rather elegant, wears silk pajamas, arranges her hair, and pencils her eyebrows with a match. Finding out that I have already served time in the camps, she eagerly asks me if it will be possible to continue her profession in the camps.

"Well, is there a wall newspaper or some sort of cultural work?"

Poor woman! I clearly see her future. There she is, having lost all her elegance, awkwardly digging in the earth or raking straw. There she is in quilted pants walking in close formation, and criminals beside her swear at her because she walks with mincing steps and slows down the pace . . .

An older woman engineer comes up to me. Authoritatively, but seeking support, she says:

"They do use technicians according to their specialties, don't they? It would be stupid not to utilize one's cultural capabilities, wouldn't it?"

I imagine her weaving baskets or cleaning toilets, and sidestepping I say:

"Sometimes yes and sometimes no."

Olga Pavlovna Kantor takes me aside. She is a journalist, an old member of the Party. In 1937 she spent a year in her dying mother's village, and the arrests swept over her workplace without her. Upon returning she found her editorial board emptied out but, since she hadn't been harmed, she was surprised at how blind she had been not to have seen the undermining activities of enemies at her workplace.

From that time on she lived in blissful certainty that everything was as it should be. She fought, received the Order of the Red Banner, and nearly perished in the Nazi encirclement. If she hadn't accidentally escaped, she would have died with a peaceful soul.

But having survived, she was arrested in 1949 and went down the terrible, well-trodden path of 1937.

She took me aside.

"You inspire trust in me. You went through all this. In what way do you think one should write so that the message would get to Stalin? He of course knows nothing about this, but through what means could one write to him?"

Oh, how many have written to Stalin! How many have called out to him, as if to their last hope, as if to a holy man who could not deceive anyone!

If one were to make an exhibit of letters to Stalin, it would make a stronger impression than an exhibit of gifts, and what had really happened would sink into someone's brain!

How could I tell this to a person I didn't know very well? She could report me to the investigator, and I would be sent back to the camps for article 58, point 10, agitation against Stalin, instead of into exile!

But I very much wanted to explain this to her—a person such as she deserved to be better informed and to see the truth for what it was.

"I respect Comrade Stalin even more than you do," I answered. "As the leader of the government he cannot be unaware of what everyone else knows. Probably he has access to the prisons. If something isn't clear to him, he can go and talk with the people who have been arrested, and he can watch how the interrogations go. The disasters are too massive and the prisons can't hold all the criminals. No, I respect him too much to consider him a fool whom everyone can trick. It is his will, it is his responsibility. It is his strategy."

"It is terrible! One cannot live then! In his name we died in battle. To lose belief in him is to lose belief in the Revolution."

"But could it be that he and the Revolution are not one and the same?" I put forth this Mephistophelian question and leave her to think of these things on her own. To explain is dangerous. One can only hint in private so that, if this conversation is reported to the investigator, I can deny that I said it and only assert that everything is done according to the will of Stalin, and that is completely legal.

I go up to a charming twenty-year-old girl, an Estonian called Aino. The story of her young life shocks me. During the war, when Estonia was under the Fascists, Aino and her friends warmly sympathized with the Red Army, were happy with every defeat of Hitler, and welcomed the Red Army as liberators. Even before the victory Aino and four boys, her friends, went to Moscow to study. Aino had a very good voice, and she was accepted at the conservatory. The boys entered technological institutes. They lived in various dormitories, and every evening they got together at the Pushkin monument. In July they went to Estonia for vacation. What they saw there horrified them.

Whole villages had been sent into exile, people had been arrested who had fought the Fascists, and there were endless denunciations and purges.

Observing this they decided to fight for Estonia. But how? Should they write a letter to the United Nations, describing all the injustices?

Because she knew English, Aino wrote the letter. But how to send it abroad? They searched for a way but could not find any. One day when Aino was sitting at their usual meeting place by the Pushkin monument, a man came up to her.

"I have seen you several times with your friends," he said. "How pleasant to see such friendship! You were speaking in Estonian. I lived there. Of course I don't know the language, but I realized that you're Estonian. I love Estonia very much."

He began to praise Estonia and Estonians, and this immediately won over Aino.

She told him what was happening in Estonia at that time. He sympathized with her so warmly, was so outraged, that she decided to share with him their intention to write a letter to the UN. He approved of her plan and said that he could possibly give the letter to the American embassy. She promised to bring the letter the next day.

He went away. The boys came. They were happy with her success.

On the following day Aino brought the letter, and that night they were all arrested. The investigator had the letter in his hands. He had to establish who had written it, that is, who was the most guilty. They called in all of them one after the other, and every boy said, "I wrote the letter!" They called in Aino and she exposed them all:

"Call them all in and make them write two lines in English. You will see right away that they don't know English and could not have written the letter. But I can write the whole letter for you right here."

The question was cleared up.

The investigation, however, had only just started.

They were trying to find out who had reported the facts they were investigating about unjust arrests, eviction of whole towns, and so forth, in Estonia. They arrested relatives and friends of Aino and the boys. They brought charges of treason to the country, of terror and espionage. The investigation ensued according to all the rules: weekly deprivation of sleep, many days of questioning on a conveyor belt (in which the investigators changed but the questioned person had to stand on swollen legs and couldn't even lean against a wall), isolation, beatings, simultaneous confrontation with witnesses, with unhappy people who gave up and signed false denunciations.

Aino had gone through all that. In the cell she was very restrained and feared to involve anyone else in her terrible case that was growing like a snowball. However we were experienced people, and at the least hint we understood the situation. All the women imprisoned in our cell warmly pitied and loved Aino.

There was one more quality about her that captivated everyone.

Once I asked her to softly sing. She began to sing romances by Tchaikovsky, Schubert, Grieg, and Bulakhov in a soft sweet voice. But what a voice it was! Pure as crystal, expressive, tender. The cell froze. We were afraid to breathe for fear of muffling her singing.

A guard came up to the glass and listened, not interrupting her. When she finished, he opened the little peephole and barked for order:

"Be quiet! Do you want to be sent to isolation?"

Every time the guard who loved music was on duty, Aino sang to us, and only if the authorities came would he open the little window and shout: "Be quiet! Singing is forbidden!"

I cannot communicate what Aino's singing meant to us! A little piece of life, a reminder that there still was beauty in the world in spite of the cursed prison.

But alas! Within several days they told Aino to get her things together to leave. She hardly had any things. But all the inhabitants of the cell wanted to give her something, although we ourselves had hardly anything. Someone gave her a pair of stockings, someone a handkerchief, someone a scarf, someone a towel. Saying good-bye to Aino, many cried. I was gathering her gifts into a little sack when Aino came up to me.

"How good you all are!" she said with a flood of true love. Then she was quiet and softly said, "But what slaves you are!"

The door opened and they led Aino away. She disappeared forever from my life.

A girl comes into the cell. An emaciated girl with pigtails and legs as thin as sticks. She seems to be about sixteen or seventeen. The girl looks around and moves in my direction. I immediately turn and walk away from her. No, my nerves just can't stand it. I don't have the strength to look into her childish eyes from which tears are pouring. The whole day I try to avoid her, but in the evening I discover that she has arranged herself on the bunk next to mine. She lies on the bunk bed, clumsily smoking and crying. Her skinny chicken-wing shoulders wince. It's impossible not to talk with her. Her name is Valia. Today is her birthday, and she is twenty years old. Hers is a simple story:

"I was seven years old when they arrested Papa. Mama was so desperate that my aunt and I had to guard her so she wouldn't throw herself out the window. She shared everything with me, although I was only seven years old. She talked endlessly about how good Papa was, how they were torturing him, how terrible it was to live. Then they arrested Mama herself. My aunt took me in. I had to say that my Papa and Mama had died probably because my aunt had intimidated me, I don't remember. I always just knew that if they found out my Papa and Mama were in prison, something horrible would happen. Maybe they'll hit me or swear at me, nobody will play with me. I always tried to do better in school than the others, to be best of all, so I can *show* them. But what? I don't know, but I have to prove something so I won't be afraid of everyone and won't feel depressed.

"I felt depressed and inferior until I was in the upper classes when I stood out as the best in our schoolwork. They praised me too much. And then I fell in love. He too had parents who had been purged, he too hid this from everyone, but with each other we were open. He loved me, admired me, and said he realized right away that I was the victim of terrible injustice. And everything that had seemed to me to be a disgrace became valuable in his eyes. I loved him. And now everything, everything is finished?"

God, how sorry I felt for Valia! How I pitied all these girls who didn't believe in justice, who didn't see the smallest glimmer of light in the black abyss into which a mysterious dark evil force was hurling them.

Gradually, a young girls' club gets organized on my bunk. I am very much afraid of getting sent to a camp instead of into exile, but I don't have the strength to restrain myself from comforting my girls. I swear to myself, give my word to hold myself back, and then say a word to one or the other that pours balsam on the wounds of their poor little hearts. If the investigator finds out about it he'll send me to the camps for ten years.

"Silly girls," I say. "You think your life has ended, but you're only twenty years old. Within five years *he* won't exist, and you'll be twenty-five, and your whole life will be before you."

The girls' choir answers me:

"You're a cockeyed optimist. Can't you see that the problem is with the whole system rather than about just one person? He will go, but his comrades will remain. You don't think you'll elect a new government, do you?"

"It goes against nature and it can't last long!" I say.

"You probably thought that in 1937, but twelve years have passed, and still it goes on!"

The argument looks convincing, but with all my heart I know that it will not be so. I know because when I was free I didn't run into a single person whose belief in justice was uncracked. I know because I can see a difference between the inhabitants of this cell in 1936 and those in 1949. I remember how in 1936 everyone, myself included, had faith in the infallibility of Soviet power, the Soviet court, and especially Stalin—faith that made us think of our own insubstantial sins and those of our comrades because it was easier to blame ourselves than our Soviet power and especially *him*, whose name was synonymous with Revolution, Socialism, truth, and justice.

I know that of what once seemed to be an indestructibly strong tree, there remains only bark, and inside everything is rotten—one push would be enough to make this colossus collapse.

I know this absolutely, and this knowledge, this certainty must be passed on.

I love these girls with their clear eyes that may quickly turn into dull, hopeless prison stares. I love them and pity them, pity them with a sharp stab in my heart. I gaze at them and imagine my own daughter who also may be lying on a prison bunk in insane fear and seeking support and consolation in the eyes of older people. And with all the strength of maternal love I give these girls my whole soul. I want to infuse them with good spirit and faith in life, in humanity.

I beseech fate that around my daughter there may be a person with the kind of love, the kind of faith I have, a faith that her life isn't over, a faith that many young boys and girls, now sitting in luxurious apartments with fathers involved in this dark business, will someday be envious of our poor children with their terrible stories, children lost in prisons, driven from their studies, from the Komsomol, from the society of those who are similar to them, like lepers.

Young skeptics from my girls' club mock me and I receive the title "Unique Optimist," but then at night first one and then another comes to me under the blanket. They nestle close to me with their thin girlish bodies, they cry and demand that I swear to them that I won't just comfort them, but that I firmly believe they will live. They so much want to live!

They demand that I reassure them, that it is possible to preserve a purity in their lives even under terrible conditions and that they will find real love, and I swear to them that they will live, and I caress them as I would my own daughter and snuggle up to them and talk with them about what is most important—getting beyond this abyss, holding onto oneself, and not losing one's self-respect.

They tell me about a certain boy, Vasia Petrov, the son of a Bolshevik who had been executed. Vasia was then recruited by the MGB. He mingled with children whose parents like his had been purged. He reported every word of dissatisfaction, every puzzled question that came out of the young people's circle. Through his reports many of his comrades were arrested.

I knew Vasia's mother from Kolyma. She was a splendid, honest woman. She talked a lot about her son, about his exceptional kindness, sparkling talents, and integrity. I loved him without ever meeting him. And here he was playing a terrible role, written for him by people whom he had trusted.

He probably did it because he was trying to show that he could rise above his personal tragedy, that he, like Pavlik Morozov, was ready to destroy his own father and mother in the name of Communism. Poor fellow! He believed that he was doing this for the sake of Communism. They deceived him. And here he is tossing now on a prison bunk, and he would prefer to be decapitated rather than to report that Shura said his father had been wrongly shot or that Petia said people live badly on the collective farm or that Mania said the university doesn't take Jews.

I eagerly ask my girls what he is like, this boy? And strangely enough they are lenient with him. The general opinion is that he's a nice person, but a rose-colored idiot.

In the mouths of my young friends, who consider themselves very wise, this expression is used to describe naive kids who believe anything written in the newspapers and act straightforwardly according to their beliefs.

He's a rose-colored idiot . . . But my son is also a rose-colored idiot. I was afraid to open his eyes. I was afraid his youthful integrity and passion had perhaps prepared him for a similar fate. It scares me. I beseech God, in whom I don't believe, that my son should be just like silly little Valia, sitting next to me, whom everyone swears at because she boldly speaks the truth to the investigator's face and says that she won't talk with scoundrels.

She feels like a heroine, although she is horribly afraid of the dark isolation cell with rats where she has already been thrown three times for her heroic deeds, although she cries bitter tears at the thought that all the girls are going into exile, but for her the investigator has promised the camps because of her bad behavior.

I also swear at her and demand that she act diplomatically and respectfully. But I admire her and want my son to be just like her and not like poor Vasia Petrov, because Vasia is ruined.

It is hard to believe, but these four months in Butyrka in 1949 remain in my memory as a bright time. I lived with such inspiration, with such an exertion of soul. I felt myself to be so needed. The girls stuck to me like chicks to a hen. With the women for whom the camps lay ahead, I tried to convince them that even in the camps not everyone was like Maria Ivanovna with her hysterics and cursing, but there were also normal people there. I tried to comport myself so they would see that one could survive even the most terrible camp in Kolyma and remain human. Into this darkness I brought them a bit of light, and this was the best thing I did in my whole life.

I am so happy that this was part of my life!

Then I changed.

Prisoners' Transport to Karaganda

In the middle of December 1949 I was exiled to Kazakhstan. We were sent in a Stolypin train as far as Kuibyshev, and in Kuibyshev conditions in the transit prison became extremely difficult. A cell designed for two hundred people had been hastily converted from a horse stable. It still had the ineradicable smell of horses and manure that, in combination with the stench of the slop bucket and a huge number of overcrowded, unwashed, sick bodies, created an unbearable atmosphere. When they led us into this cell and we found a place on the bunks, there were two hundred of us. But then they brought in more and more; women lay in the passageway, under the bunks, on top of tables, and under tables. We gasped for breath in the stench. They gave us neither books nor any kind of medicine. In this enormous cell, fights and hysterics blazed up.

"When will they get us out of here," we asked the guard, but he only threw up his hands and answered very naively:

"What can I do, all the prisons and camps are overcrowded. No one will take you. Whose fault is it that you are such a mob?"

Yes, exactly, whose fault is it?

It is understandable that when they finally called us to continue the journey after a month of waiting, we were glad. "It's worse, but it's different," said our Ukrainians, and we all agreed with them.

But when they took us far down the track in the early twilight of a January day to the train standing on a siding and then stuffed us into the freight car, it was really horrible. The temperature was at least thirty degrees below zero. It was five o'clock in the evening, already getting dark.

When, on the heels of the other women, I scrambled into the freight car by an attached ladder, it seemed pitch-dark to me. The freight car was frozen. Getting used to the darkness, we noticed innumerable cracks through which the winter evening grew gray. There was a small portable stove in the freight car, but neither firewood nor matches. The bunks were covered with a layer of ice. I was warmly dressed, and my relatives had given me a quilted blanket. Everyone who had warm things began to untie their knotted parcels and bundle themselves up. Next to me I noticed a young girl who had already attracted my attention when we were in the truck that had brought us from the prison to the train.

She had a sweet, brave face. She seemed to be about twenty-three or twenty-four years old. She was dressed in a summer cotton chintz dress and a padded camp jacket. On her legs were darned and redarned stockings and prison boots. I called her to me under the quilted blanket, and we got to know each other. Her name was Olia Kosenko. She snuggled up close to me but simply could not get warm.

"Olia, why are you dressed like this, why do you have no warm things?"

"The bitch of an investigator didn't let me have parcels from home because of my insolence. Here I'm left as I was in the summer when they arrested me. They gave me the jacket and boots for the road, that's all."

We sat in the dark and freezing freight car for several hours. Finally one could hear some movement; they were walking on the roof, and in the neighboring freight car they slammed the door bolts. Our door opened too; the guards and an electrician came in and hooked up an electric light. Then they threw us an armful of wood and matches, went out, and bolted the door. There wasn't much wood, and we didn't know when they might give us more, but all the same we lit the small portable stove and warmed up a bit. It turned out that in the darkness the best places near the stove had already been taken. A group of Latvian women who didn't speak to us sat there giving us to understand that they didn't know Russian. (Later it turned out that they did speak Russian but were so angry with Russians that they didn't want to speak even with us.) A mother and a daughter from western Ukraine were in the freight car. They had ended up in prison because their son and brother, a Banderite, had gone into the woods but had come back to his mother for bread. His mother kept repeating:

"Well, how could I not give it to him? If your son came to you starving, wouldn't you give him something to eat?"

She was very sick, had apparently become worse in the cold of this freezing freight car, and coughed badly. With us there was yet another prisoner, an experienced old nurse. She thought that the woman had a touch of pneumonia and asked the guard to call a doctor, but that didn't happen. This nurse, Vera Samoilovna Lokkerman, had an interesting past. Before the Revolution her brothers were well-known Mensheviks. One, it seemed, was even a member of the Menshevik Central Committee. In her youth Vera Samoilovna also participated in her brothers' work and in 1905 she was arrested on the Krasnopresnensky barricade with weapons in her hands.

Because of her young age (she was fifteen in 1905) she got off with just being sent into exile in Siberia. Now she was a stout, unhealthy, sixty-year-old woman no longer involved in politics. But unfortunately she had a beautiful room in a three-room apartment. The two other rooms were occupied by a man who worked for the MGB and very much wanted to live in a separate apartment. Nothing was simpler than to put his neighbor in prison and occupy her room, and so it happened.

In Vera Samoilovna's indictment it was written, "Involved in anti-Soviet activities since 1905."

It took us sixteen days to get to Karaganda. At the beginning we were frightfully cold and then, when we were on some sort of siding, our train stood next to a car loaded with coal. Suddenly our guard, a Ukrainian who sometimes exchanged a couple of words in Ukrainian with Olga Kosenko, opened the door, gave Olia a bucket—she had been appointed freight car leader—and commanded her:

"Go collect as much coal as you can."

Olia jumped up and was able to gather about twenty buckets of coal. Then the door closed, but we came back to life. We noticed that people from several other freight cars had also gathered coal.

I remembered Lev Tolstoy wrote that one can tolerate Russian rules only because everyone breaks them; if they didn't break them, life would be simply unbearable.

If we hadn't gathered coal with the blessing of the guard, we would hardly have gotten to our destination alive, since the norm for fuel was one armful of firewood a day.

Olia and I made a bed, cuddled up together, and talked with each other for whole days.

Olia's sentence was terrible: twenty years. According to her the investigator who "dumped it on her" was infuriated by her fearlessness, her unwillingness to submit, her fighting, and her shrill, sometimes coarse words.

She was very unlucky in the investigation. She had been arrested in 1947 with a group of philology students from the University of Kiev.

The investigator didn't want to rest on the laurels of the MGB from 1937, and so he thought up a grandiose terrorist scheme to separate Ukraine from the USSR. Olia seemed to him a suitable figure for giving the necessary evidence. He fabricated and tried to force her to sign monstrous protocols making dozens of her comrades guilty.

He also thought of a link with the Gestapo, which allegedly enlisted a group of Ukrainian young people during the war. (Incidentally, during the war fifteen-year-old Olia acted like a heroine. In order not to get sent to Germany, she infected herself with trachoma, knowing the Germans would not take such sick people.)

The investigator thought that being threatened, beaten, and put in solitary confinement with inquisitions on the conveyor belt day and night, as well as promises of freedom and not exile, would break down this fine, now twenty-three-year-old girl, but he was wrong. He got nothing out of her and rabidly promised:

"I am going to throw twenty years of hard labor at you."

This promise he kept, adding one more thing—one day after her interrogation was already over, he called her in and asked:

"So, have you been shedding tears over your obstinacy?" And in answer to Olia's words, "I haven't cried and I don't intend to," he started laughing and added, "Well, let's bet on whether you'll cry! Your fiancé has been arrested, and I requested that I be his investigator."

Here he triumphed. Olia fainted. Her fiancé was from her village. He didn't even know any of the accused and had come to Kiev in order to take parcels to the prison and inquire about Olia—in other words, he thus very unfortunately let the authorities know of his existence.

While this terrible investigation was going on, eight months went by, and the only good luck brightening Olia's existence was a neighbor in the cell, an old woman named Maria Gertsevna who comforted Olia, supporting her and relating to her like a mother. Olia often reminisced about Maria Gertsevna and told me:

"All the same I've been lucky that I could brighten my spirits around her, and now I have met you."

Poor girl, she could still find the word *luck* in the language!

And now I should tell you about one side of our friendship that gave me some bitter moments. This intelligent, brave, bighearted girl was infected with a miserable illness: she was an antisemite. Olia told me endless stories about the way Jews knew how to manage things. In her village the Jews ran the stores and arranged soft jobs for all their relatives. Her friend's investigator in the Kiev prison was a Jew, and what a scoundrel he was, and so forth.

When I pointed out that her investigator here had been Ukrainian, and where could one find a worse butcher, she answered:

"Oh, Olga Lvovna, you don't know them. In Moscow there are very few of them, but in Kiev you can't avoid them!"

I could have shortened these painful conversations by saying that I myself was a Jew. But then this foolish girl couldn't have stayed with me. She would freeze and starve without the food and blanket sent to me by my Jewish relatives. So I put up with her talk until Karaganda.

On the sixteenth day of the transport the guard entered, called out several last names, and said:

"Get your things together, within two hours we'll be arriving."

There were only five of us lucky ones going into exile. The rest, with huge sentences from ten to twenty years, were going to Novorudnia to the diamond mines, a camp with the most terrible regime. We began to get our things together. Olia gazed at me with eyes full of tears.

"Again I am alone!"

We sat in a corner on a bunk.

"Olechka," I said, "I need to talk with you. You've tormented me terribly these sixteen days, since I am a Jew." Olia cried out, covered her face with her hands and through her fingers I saw how her cheeks, ears, and neck flamed.

Our train came into the station. I stood up. Olia threw herself on my neck, all in tears.

"You've taught me such a lesson! Forgive me! I swear I will always remember it."

I never met Olia again. They said that she died in Novorudnia. If this is not true and if these lines fall under your eyes someday, please respond, Olia! I often remember you with pain and sadness. Ahead of you lay years of terrible torment. I hope to God you were still alive in 1954 or 1956.

Please respond, Olia!

In Exile

In exile I was lucky. I ended up in Karaganda where I could find work and where there were many members of the exiled intelligentsia. Valia Gerlin, whom I had liked so much in Butyrka, was also sent to Karaganda. In Karaganda Valia soon married Yura Aikhenvald, also exiled, so friends turned up right away for me.

There was the question of arranging work. I certainly didn't want to look for work in my specialty (economics)—what a thought that I would have to fill out forms and try to pull strings so they would take me with my previous conviction . . .

I decided to go to work in a dressmaker's shop where they made padded jackets on an assembly line. For this work my qualifications were sufficient, since I was actually the daughter of tailors. They were freely hiring exiles, and I worked there for three months before the events described below.

We worked in two brigades of forty-four people each. There were two brigade leaders, two mechanics who adjusted the machines, two watchmen, and two women who cleaned up. But for some unknown reason there was only one storehouse, and the two brigade leaders eternally argued. There was never a regular system. Every month they checked what materials remained, and each time one of the brigade leaders would have to pay for a shortage and insist that the other had taken several jackets for her team account.

We worked in two shifts. The night shift began at five o'clock in the evening and ended at one o'clock in the morning. Walking around Karaganda at that hour was dangerous—your clothing could be stolen and even worse. Therefore we stayed for the night in the shop and had to sleep on the tables. All night long the girls whispered together and flirted with the guys.

It was completely bewildering how the work went. Each brigade was required to make 125 quilted jackets per day. This was very little for forty-four people, but we almost never fulfilled our plan, since the assembly line worked extraordinarily irregularly. Almost every hour there was down-time for one or another operation. I sat sewing sleeves onto the jackets, but often there weren't enough sleeves for the jackets or jackets for the sleeves. Often it turned out that there weren't any needles or buttons. The salary was miserable—two hundred to three hundred rubles in old Soviet money and the same pay for complex operations (sewing on the sleeves and the pockets) as for sewing on buttons, cleaning the jackets with a brush made of twigs, and so forth. But the girls weren't discouraged. During their downtimes they slept on the piles of material (after a sleepless night) or sewed and knitted.

I busied myself with calculating the downtimes and thinking about how to avoid them. I talked with the best workers, asked them how much they could do if there weren't any downtimes, if their machines weren't breaking down so often and a mechanic nowhere to be found. More and more I wanted to organize the work more effectively.

And then it happened that after another fine for a shortage our two brigade leaders (young girls who had finished sewing school in Alma Ata and had been sent to work in Karaganda) talked with each other and, not having been paid, hopped on a train and ran off. We arrived at work in the morning and found the storehouse locked. The director of our shop, Anisia Vasilievna Korneva, began to talk with various workers, asking them to take on the leadership, but no one agreed to, fearing to be respon-sible for this business and having to pay fines for shortages.

We didn't work for three days. Then I made a decision. I went to Anisia Vasilievna, who did not know me at all, and I told her that I had a pro-posal. I would become the brigade leader but on one condition. Instead of two brigades there should be one. I myself would choose who in the brigade would stay and who would be fired. I myself would oversee the norms and tariff pricing. In tight spots I might need five additional people. I was sure the plan to produce two hundred fifty quilted jackets a day could be fulfilled by one brigade.

Anisia Vasilievna was astounded by my impudence—I had proposed that I would be the brigade leader and also had set conditions. In addition I was an exile and it wasn't quite right for an exile to have such an *important* position. I must say that Anisia Vasilievna was an uneducated person but with natural intelligence, inquisitiveness, and a belief in human beings, even exiles. She, of course, was taking a risk in agreeing to my reforms without asking for the approval of the authorities. But her position was untenable—the shop had stopped functioning. She agreed.

I can't say I wasn't scared—what if nothing comes of it, what if the girls refuse to work so hard, when I have fired forty people and broken all the rules of a work system that has somehow squeaked by for decades? Taking into account my situation, everything, of course, would fall on me, and they would create a new charge of sabotage against me . . . But I also very much wanted to work like a human being in a normal way.

I started by gathering the workers together (those who were left after a staff reduction). I explained to them that they would be working now with no downtimes, and they would earn much more. And I was introducing different payments for different levels of work. I finished this way:

"Girls, it's tiresome for you as well as for me working in such disorder and having to sleep on the tables during the second shift. I can save you from this, but I can't stop the thievery. Of course I've fired the major thieves but maybe not all of them. I put you in charge of controlling the thievery but, if I have a shortage after the first accounting, I will quit because I have no money to cover it."

The girls accepted my proposition. Amazing as it may seem, in the very first month we fulfilled double the plan, and not only did I have no shortages but there were additional economies in thread, our eternal sore point.

By the way, there was an incident that completely reassured me with regard to the thievery. I was sitting in the office of the local deputy director, Satenov, and we were conversing together peacefully. Suddenly two of my girls burst into the office dragging a third (Satenov's aunt, incidentally) and screaming:

"She was hiding thread in her bag!"

The woman compulsively clutched her bag and would not give it up. Suddenly one of the girls lunged at the bag, and out of it rolled four big factory bobbins (each one with twenty-five spools). I said:

"You are fired."

Satenov wanted to work out a deal in this affair. But I said firmly: it is either she or I. He had to agree with me.

I worked with enthusiasm. After the physical work of the camps, this was organizational and creative. Within two months we were making three hundred quilted jackets a day. Then a comical thing happened. Knowing of my results, Anisia Vasilievna said to me:

"Olga Lvovna, for every quilted jacket I lose ten kopecks. Now you have figured out how to make so many of them that I am going completely broke."

She finally understood and was happy after I explained to her how much the overhead had decreased since, instead of two brigade leaders only one remained, instead of two mechanics, two cleaning women, two watchmen, there was only one of each. And the payments for housing, lighting, accountants, and so forth were now divided not by one hundred twenty-five but by three hundred quilted jackets.

Such was the educational level of the boss at our production site.

As soon as I had settled into my place of exile, Nikolai gave up his work, his friends, his more or less orderly life, and came to join me in Karaganda. That was of course the major event in my life of exile. We rented a room with a kitchen and Nikolai started work. Again I had a family, I could live peacefully, without fear of my passport being checked, and I could recover from the strain of my illegal existence in Moscow.

In the summer my children came to us for vacation. My daughter became friends with Nikolai, was enchanted with his manliness, his fearlessness. In my opinion she was drawn to him as to a father. In Karaganda our social group began to develop—Valia and Yura Aikhenvald, Alik Volpin (Yesenin), and several friends from work, also exiles. We often went out to visit them and they would come to us. In short, if you didn't count the humiliating procedures for checking in with the MGB, it was a normal human life.

But alas! Very quickly I realized that I was on the edge of an abyss. In the three years that we had been separated, a determination to confront power had been ripening in Nikolai. Coming from the peasant class, he understood well what price had been paid for dekulakization. As a military professional he could not forgive Stalin for destroying the commanders of the army right before the war. And much more! He could not forgive the torture during investigations and the persecution of Russian soldiers who had been taken captive by the Germans but had freely returned to their country, and so on and so forth.

He talked about all this not only with his closest friends but also with the young people at work who were drawn to him. This went on for a whole year. Nikolai felt inspired and, in response to all my supplications to be careful, he answered that he wanted to die in a fight and not like a despicable slave.

On April 29, 1951, he was arrested.

In the investigation he tried to co-opt his investigator, who was extremely intimidated by him. He threatened the investigator that he too might wind up as an enemy of the people.

And again a terrible time began for me. Lining up with parcels at the prison. Fearing that I myself would land in prison again, this time because of my second husband. I didn't have the strength to survive this a second time.

For the two months of his investigation I didn't enter my home—it was beyond my strength. I lived with Valia Gerlin and Yura Aikhenvald. When I found out what his sentence was, I came to them utterly sick and lay on the bed. Half delirious, I saw Valia enter the room with an unknown man. I didn't hear what they were talking about. The sounds of separate phrases reached me: "They robbed . . ." and children's laughter with giggling and snorting. "Well, something will work out, it's all nonsense. I'd better read you some poetry." And he began to recite.

He recited "Jacobin," "Ode," "Bride of the Decembrist," "The Banners," and much more.

Never had any poetry made such an impression on me. I was so beaten down, so humiliated with my situation—carrying packages to the prison for two months as well as receiving impudent condolences at work, such as, "Your guy has landed in prison again." And most important were the speeches about the trials and the articles in newspapers throughout the country and the world, saying that the Revolution, the holy Revolution had saved *them,* but those who opposed it (I and those like me) had been crushed, had fallen—we belonged in a manure pit. And suddenly I heard from my comrade, that pariah, an outcast like me, words full of dignity:

> He was crushed by that heavy force
> Against which he had launched the battle
> As an equal,

This seemed to me to be about Nikolai.
And this one was about Stalin.

> He stole the Revolution
> And arrayed himself in its banner.

And the ode where he sings of his Revolution with a strength and passion that an official hack writer could never dream of:

. . . And maybe I should launch an uprising?
But against whom?
And the enemy keeps watching, he is wearing glasses and is well fed,
With a pencil behind his ear . . .
Look!
> There
> I see him clearly!
Fire!
> Point blank!
But careful, my friends . . .
He has hidden himself behind the red banners
And we are not allowed to touch those banners!
And all the same I rush about,
> Breathing is difficult.
What is the point of useless moaning,
The disgusting one is making its way toward your throat like a slug,
But we may not touch him:
> The banners!

I stood up, went to the table, and saw Mandel. At this time he was twenty-five years old. He was dressed remarkably: yellow-checked trousers, the right size for a giant and shortened at the pants hem but with the crotch down to his knees. His jacket was blue and had once been nice, but it was now so old and dirty that when I later washed it, it came completely apart at the seams in my hands—it was held together only with dirt. His fat homely face with strange eyes (his pupils were an irregular shape, as if jagged), his childlike laughter, the unbelievable appetite with which he ate the simple food Valia offered him, his way of forgetting to eat and beginning again and again to recite poetry, and then again throwing himself on the potatoes and cabbage, and then again forgetting about the food and talking, talking—all that pleased me tremendously. For the first time in two terrible months I was distracted from my pain, and I gazed at him. He was already on a *ty* basis with Valia and Yura. I asked if they had been acquainted in Moscow. It turned out that Valia, a student in the literature department of the Pedagogical Institute, knew him in Moscow from hearing his poetry readings, but he didn't know her. Valia was walking in the street [in Karaganda] and saw a bewildered Mandel, whose suitcase had just been stolen with all his clothes and money in it. She walked up to him and asked:

"Are you Mandel?"

He was tremendously happy:

"And do you know me, girl?" After that he explained to her his circumstances and invited himself to her place. He explained to me at once that he was absolutely not guilty, that he had been robbed. And again he recited poetry. I understood right away that this was a genuine talent before me. But how careless he was. He had known Valia, Yura, and me for only a few hours, and he was reciting such poetry! Each of them could cost him ten years in the camps! And a painful fear for him, strange to say, a kind of maternal love for him at first glance, a desire to protect him, to help him in some way, took hold of me.

We suddenly realized that it was already midnight.

"Where will you spend the night?" Valia asked.

"Somewhere here at your place," Emka answered simply. But this was completely impossible. Valia and Yura had a room of about nine square meters with their bed and a little folding cot where I had been sleeping, but the biggest difficulty was with the landlady who constantly swore that she had rented the room to a couple but that a third person (I) was now living there. Then I said:

"I have a room and a kitchen. If you wish, I'll give you the key. But bear in mind that I haven't been in the room for two months since my husband's arrest. You can settle yourself in the kitchen. I will also come over there right away."

"Something always turns up for Mandel," said Mandel. He hesitated for a second, and then said, "Give me the key."

So we lived together for more than a year, like mother and son.

Very quickly Emka told me about himself. He came to Moscow in the spring of 1951, after three years of exile in the village of Chumaki near Novosibirsk. He arrived ragged, neglected, filthy, starved for culture, and starved for Moscow. In searching for a way to settle in Moscow, he arrived at the apartment of the writer P., the editor or member of the editorial board at that time of some journal. P. happened to be in Kislovodsk. The writer's daughter, Vera, opened the door to Mandel. Vera was a graceful well-groomed woman of about thirty, living with her father and daughter after a divorce. Vera invited Mandel in, fed him, and offered him wine. They conversed (Mandel was a great master of conversation), and in short, a wild romance very quickly blazed up.

The romance lasted about two weeks, at the end of which Vera said her father was returning, and it was time for Mandel to disappear. Leaving the safe and lavish apartment of P., Mandel again felt that the earth under him was shaky. Registration was not possible, finding work was not possible, and there was nowhere to live or simply spend the night. And suddenly the crazy thought came into his head that he had to go to a city where he could live legally and even with some advantages in relation to the majority of the established population—the exiles. In short, he appeared in Karaganda.

In order to understand how great Mandel's naïveté was, one had to listen to his tales about "my girl Vera." He planned to invite her to Karaganda as soon as he had gotten work and rented a room.

"But she has a daughter," I said.

"I'll adopt her."

"Do you really think that Vera will come here to be with you from her Moscow apartment, from her affluent comfortable life, in order to be the wife of Mandel who has no rights? Will she be willing to live on the pittance you'll be able to earn?"

"She loves me."

He wrote to her in poetry and prose and waited for her. There was no answer to his letters. But suddenly my Mandel clouded over and stopped speaking of her. Within a couple of days he admitted to me that he had received a letter and gave it to me to read. Vera wrote that she was surprised by his proposal and grateful to him for the minutes of passion and rapture that had thrown them together. But it had been just an episode in their lives that she enjoyed looking back on and that should not be repeated. And she had a request of Mandel: She had been offered work at *Ogonyok*, but she couldn't somehow think of a theme for an essay or a short story. Could Mandel think of a theme and send it to her?

This episode was later expressed in his poetry where there are these lines:

> Have you forgotten that a Russia exists
> In which I live somewhere . . .

He did not send her a theme for a short story.

During this period Mandel wrote all day long. His productivity was extraordinary. But alas! He couldn't even get a position as a newspaper correspondent, not to speak of the fact that no one wanted to print his poetry even on the most innocent themes.

The appearance of Mandel in my life in a certain sense saved me. He brought me back to life. Now there was someone I needed to take care of. I delighted in him as a poet but worried about the casualness with which he chose listeners and his openness with almost unknown people. To my reproaches he answered, "Don't be afraid, I have an eye for it! I don't read my poems to everyone. I see right away who is a good person and who is a scoundrel." He was probably right that he had an "eye for it" because he was never denounced, but my agitation was considerable.

I thought about Nikolai continuously—during the day and especially at night. For I knew all too well what prison was like. Occasionally I condemned Nikolai, for how many times had I warned him not to get involved in politics! And both he and I well knew how it would end. But he didn't want to abandon the struggle, and he ruined both himself and me.

I sent him money and he wrote me his short, dry letters, all the drier because we both knew that they went through the camp censor. But one day, a year after Nikolai's arrest, a girl (a nonpolitical prisoner) who had been liberated from the camp came to me. She brought me a letter from Nikolai written on a large handkerchief that she had carried in her bosom, where it was hidden from searches.

This letter I carry with me to this day, and more than once it has been wet with tears. In it for the first time he revealed his tender soul:

> Greetings, dear Olia . . . I so very much want, my dear, to say something tender, sweet, and loving to you. But really I can't, I am not a poet, the words of love don't come from my burning lips. No, I am not a crude person. But I firmly believe, my dear one, you can understand me because you know that it isn't a question of words and that my qualities are somehow different, they are in my integrity, in my honor . . . And this is dearer than the usual lisping about happiness and love.

> Leaving you, somewhere, probably for a long time, I don't feel unhappy and I don't retract a single one of my actions, thoughts, or words. I know how to love the people who are worthy, who are strong, brave, and honorable, people who don't ask for mercy, who don't lower themselves to a request.

> Darling Olia . . . I am well and I firmly believe in our good fortune, in our beautiful human future. I wish, my dear, that you too won't be pulled down into pessimism or panic. Wait for me . . . Our paths are laid out, and we cannot and will not change them, no matter how hard it is for us. Death and the tears of my people are greater than our own sorrows. No matter how hard it is, remember that it isn't easier for others, and for us it isn't more difficult than for others.

This girl will tell you all about how our time goes by, about the details of life. And now I wish you all the best, my beloved, my dear one. I kiss you deeply, deeply. Your Kolia. June 16, 1952.

I remembered everything he had done for me. How, because of loving me, he had twice helped me go to my children. How, risking his health and life, he tore himself from Kolyma and came to me in Moscow. How he threw away an orderly predictable life outside Moscow and came to me in exile in Karaganda.

All I was able to do for him was send him as much money as was permitted, write short letters that would pass the censors, and wait.

I lived as I could, became friends with Mandel and the Aikhenvalds, and prayed to God that Stalin would die and that the country would change.

On August 1, 1951, I turned forty-nine. Emka Mandel, Alik Volpin, Valia Gerlin, and Yura Aikhenvald visited me. For a present they brought me a bottle of port wine. I completely forgot that Alik was not allowed to drink. I poured half the bottle and we drank to the birthday girl. Alik wanted to propose the second toast.

It was summer, one window was broken, and always whenever four or five exiles gathered together, agents (MGB workers) prowled around under the windows.

And so Alik proposed a toast.

"I drink," he said in his loud, creaky voice, "I drink to Stalin's dying like a dog!"

My guests blew away like the wind. I remained alone with Alik.

"Quiet! You will ruin both me and yourself! Be quiet!"

"I am a free person," Alik replied importantly, "and I will say what I wish. I drink to Stalin's dying like a dog!"

I wanted to cover his lips, and somehow I hit him on the mouth, with the result that he very amenably fell to the ground, but even so he quietly, clearly, and definitively repeated:

"I drink to Stalin's dying like a dog. I am a free person. You can't close my mouth."

I again hit him on the lips, and he continued to repeat his toast, but more and more quietly.

In panicky terror I simply began to beat him on the mouth, on the cheeks, wherever I could, and he continued to mutter one thing or another. Finally he stood up and said to me:

"I despise you, as I despise the MGB," and he went out.

Very quickly, Mandel, Valia, and Yura returned. It turned out that they had run out under the window to see if the agents had appeared, but they hadn't. Then Alik went out. They followed him to see where he went and, when they were sure he had gone home, they ran back to my place.

The next day Valia came to my house and said that Alik wasn't at work, and when she went to his house, she saw that he had been beaten with such bruises under his eyes and on his lips that he couldn't go to work.

"Vavka," I said. "Go to him, take him yesterday's pirog that he didn't eat, and beg his forgiveness of me."

Valia fulfilled her assignment and returned with a volume of Lermontov that Alik sent me as a gift, inscribed, "To a dear Tiger Daughter-of-a-Lion who does not beat a man's eyebrow, but hits him in the eye." But unfortunately the incident wasn't over yet.

Within about five days he had recovered and went back to work. His school was situated close to the sewing factory where I worked as the boss of the shop. He often would pick me up after work, and we would walk home together. Seeing that he was whole and unharmed, I called out to him from afar:

"Ah! You came! So you're not angry with me?" To this question a loud answer echoed throughout the whole sewing shop:

"Do you really think that scoundrel Stalin can make us quarrel with each other?"

You can imagine my reaction.

Long, long nights I didn't sleep as I waited for the MGB's reaction to Alik's words. There wasn't any reaction.

Once I even shared my fear with one of the workers. She said to me, "We all heard his words, but we decided to keep quiet and act as if we had heard nothing."

How good my girls were!

Kerta Nourten

I got to know Kerta Nourten in the fall of 1953 when she appeared in Karaganda after having served ten years in prisons and in the camps. At that time she was already about fifty years old, but to me she looked like a really young woman, as if she were perhaps thirty-five. She enchanted me right away with her unusual charm. It turned out that we had a lot in common. Like me she had an enormous interest in life, in the fate of the nation, and in people. And like me she could not withdraw into her own pain. We talked for hours about how life would change after the death of Stalin. We discussed what the changes would be and what our place would be in that new life. We became friends and she told me her story. Her parents were from Finland. Her father, a member of the Bolshevik underground, ran away from exile in Siberia and emigrated to America. Kerta was born there. And incidentally when we met she said to me:

"Well, you won't forget my name—it's from 'The Snow Queen.'"

"But there it is Gerda!"

"But it's the same name, only in Russian for some reason it is pronounced differently."

Her mother was an actress. Kerta's mother tongues were English and Finnish. Her father made her study Russian—Russia was his spiritual homeland.

In 1917 the family of course left for Russia. On Lenin's recommendation, Kerta's father participated in creating the Karelo-Finnish Republic and apparently became its president. The family lived in Petrozavodsk. Kerta studied in Leningrad in a special school for theater.

Brought up by her father to be a professional political worker, Kerta could not think of herself as existing outside of the Party, outside of public activities. She joined the Party and became an active, I would even say an orthodox, Communist for whom the sense of Party loyalty was highest of all. Such character, such extraordinary fluency in three languages, and such exceptional charm and lightness in social relationships made her of the highest interest to the NKVD. They proposed that she enter a school for intelligence agents, and she completed the program.

Kerta married but quickly divorced and settled with her son at her parents' home in Petrozavodsk. She worked as an actress in the theater.

Kerta's father died and was buried with great honors in Petrozavodsk.

Meanwhile the Finnish War was approaching. The appropriate organs of the Party proposed to Kerta that they send her to Finland. It was not a simple decision for her to make. To give up her son and her mother. To give up the work she loved. At this time Kerta was already a well-known and very successful actress; she was even known abroad. She passionately loved her creative work and felt that a great stage career lay before her.

To give up everything. To take enormous risks. But her sense of Party loyalty won out. The Party is sending me—I cannot refuse. Kerta agreed to go.

There for the first time she encountered the badly organized work of the NKVD, of which she had previously had such a high opinion. They of course presented her as a foreigner—one of the major conditions of her work was to have absolutely no connection with the USSR. According to the story, she was to be an American. At the last moment before her departure she remembered that she had a Russian watch on her wrist. Some guy from the NKVD was sending her off. He also forgot about the watch and it was his lapse. Kerta suggested that they quickly exchange watches—he had a gold Swiss watch. She was surprised that he did this with much dissatisfaction—she was risking her life, and he felt bad about a watch!

However this was not the NKVD's last act of carelessness. When Kerta jumped from a parachute into Finland, she discovered with horror that they had forgotten to include a shovel, and she had to bury her parachute by digging with her bare hands in the snow. The next strange thing was that apparently they had thrown her out of the plane thirty kilometers from the place she needed to be. She should have landed next to an estate, the owner of which was an agent of the USSR whose task was to help her get settled and connected. Kerta had to walk several kilometers to reach a railroad line, which alerted the village inhabitants to her arrival. When she finally got to the Soviet agent's place, the agent waved her hands at her:

"Quickly go away! War has begun, the authorities are so strict, there is so much to fear!" She had to leave.

Kerta went to Helsinki and began to study cosmetics in order to have a profession. She was able to get involved in political work and recruit an old Finn who was the father of five children and a member of the Communist Party. With his help she was able to establish a connection and began to make radio transmissions. But it didn't last long.

Clearly they had begun to follow her after that flashy arrival in Finland. She hadn't noticed it. But one sad day her door suddenly opened and several people appeared. They made a search, found her portable two-way radio, and arrested her.

Kerta went to prison. Her description of this prison is rather curious. A three-story building stood in the center of the city. On the first floor was a café, on the second floor some sort of family lived, and on the third floor was a prison in which there were fourteen people. The food wasn't bad, and those who had money could order from the café—every evening they were given coffee and pastries. The prisoners were treated politely.

An investigation began. First of all they wanted to find out what country she was from. She presented herself as an American and fooled them. Kerta charmed the investigator who was obviously not indifferent to her. Someone said to him that the woman he was investigating reminded him very much of the Russian actress Kerta Nourten. Kerta at that time was about forty years old, but according to the story she was supposed to be twenty-six, and she didn't look any older. When she was asked the direct question, whether she was The Nourten, she smiled and playfully answered:

"I heard the name of that actress many years ago. Today she would have to be no less than forty. Do I look like such an old woman?"

The investigator immediately rejected this suggestion.

At this time, in spite of the good conditions of the prison, Kerta began to experience some psychological problems, probably from overexertion. She was tormented by auditory and visual hallucinations, as well as by memory lapses. In her investigation she told the invented story about herself and suddenly forgot the date of her fictitious birth, the place she was born, and so forth. I am writing about this because of what came later. I have never heard anything like this ever again, but I vouch for the exact way Kerta told the story.

One day Kerta woke up with a sharp pain and realized that they were giving her some sort of injection. Then she lost consciousness for a while, and upon awakening she heard her own voice. She was speaking Russian and telling the truth about herself, about how she had recruited the Finnish man, and about the agent who was the owner of an estate.

After such evidence, she really couldn't resist the investigation anymore. There was a trial. Kerta and the Finn she had recruited were sentenced to death and the female agent to ten years of imprisonment.

Kerta reconciled herself to her fate; she only wished that everything would soon be over. She was tormented with guilt because of the Finn and his five children who had trusted her.

During this time, 1940 went by and the end of the Finnish War drew near.

The sentence for some reason wasn't carried out right away. They took Kerta from the prison in Helsinki to a monastery where she was alone. She received no books or newspapers. The only diversion was visits from the monks. Perhaps before her death they wanted her to reconcile with God.

Finally, however, they told her to get her things together and took her to the director of the prison. She was fully convinced that she awaited death by execution.

In the room behind the table sat an elderly man, apparently the director of the prison. On the table was a clock, the hands of which showed quarter to twelve.

"Sit down," said the man.

Fifteen minutes went by. The clock struck twelve. He stood up and told her to stand. He said:

"The war is over. You and the others who were condemned have been pardoned. The only thing you must do is leave Finland today. Forever. Go into the next room; your possessions are there."

Kerta went out. There her things were hanging in perfect order. She dressed. They told her that her cousin Nourten wanted to see her. Kerta agreed.

Outside the monastery a young man who looked like her father awaited her. This was the son of her father's brother, a professor at the university. Together they went to the railroad station. Nourten went up to the window and bought a ticket for Sweden. Kerta categorically refused. She was going to Leningrad. Her son and mother were in Russia, and in addition she had to tell them about how outrageous her departure from Finland had been and had to affirm that she wasn't guilty.

"You do not know your country," Nourten said to her. "You will be put in prison, and you won't be able to prove anything!"

They argued for the whole day. When the train for Leningrad arrived he would not let her get on, and she would not get on the train for Sweden.

Finally he realized that he could not convince her, and he put her on the Leningrad train.

In Leningrad at the station they were waiting for her and took her straight to prison. They made her take a cold shower, and they pushed her into a completely empty cold room. Her hair was still wet and she was freezing.

"They'll come for you," they told her. "Wait."

She sat until morning, writhing in pain, freezing, and outraged by the way she had been welcomed.

In the morning the door opened and a woman in a uniform came in. She was carrying a bowl of steaming hot cabbage soup.

"Aren't you freezing?" the woman asked cheerfully. "Now you'll warm up."

Kerta walked up to her.

"Thank you," she said. "Now I'll warm up!"

She took the bowl and unexpectedly poured it on the supervisor's head.

Hot cabbage soup clogged her nose and eyes. She screamed and the guards rushed in. They beat Kerta and dragged her to the basement where an insane asylum was apparently housed. There Kerta found out what a Soviet prison was like!

They were starving. There were so many prisoners that they could not lie down, and it wasn't always possible to find a place to sit. The crazy people would steal bread from each other. There were no doctors. There were fights and cursing. Finally someone told Kerta that a medical commission came there once every half year. The healthy ones were transferred to prison, and the sick were prescribed treatment. The commission was supposed to come in about two months.

Kerta firmly resolved to get herself out of this basement. She pretended to be healthy, although she was certainly sick. She suffered from hallucinations and lapses of memory. For the medical commission she got her clothing in order, combed her hair, and appeared before the commission as a charming, tranquil young woman.

She succeeded in deceiving the commission. They released her from the insane asylum, tried her in absentia, and sentenced her to the camps for ten years.

In the camps Kerta found out the fate of her son. (Her mother had died during the war.) He was serving a sentence for participating in a gang. Kerta succeeded in connecting with him, and through exchanging letters she realized that he had received absolutely no education and couldn't write grammatically. She dreamed that when she got her freedom, they would live together, and she would educate him and win his love.

In 1956 we were all rehabilitated except for Kerta. She stayed on alone in Karaganda. Later, dreaming of seeing her old home and her father's grave, Kerta went to Petrozavodsk where she found that her father's grave had been removed and everything had been destroyed.

Returning from Petrozavodsk, Kerta stopped off with me in Moscow. I well remember her story and her condition.

Trying to have her father's grave restored, she had gained an audience with Otto Kuusinen. In his time Kuusinen had emigrated to America, had become friends with her father, and frequently came to their home. Little Kerta had often sat on his knee.

The visit to Kuusinen made a terrible impression on Kerta. In front of her was a dried-up old man, his skin tightly covering his skeleton. He was almost completely deaf, and an assistant repeated her questions loudly in his ear. He did not recognize Kerta, did not remember her father, and could not understand what she wanted at all. Finally in order to end the meeting, he said they would do everything. Of course nothing was done. Kerta was shocked that a person in such condition continued to be a Politburo member and govern our country!

Soon after finishing his sentence, Kerta's son came to join his mother in Karaganda. But alas! He came with a wife who was a common criminal and who immediately observed, "You want to educate him so he can get rid of me? That will never happen!" She grabbed the textbooks prepared for him and threw them in a hot stove. Kerta's son was silent. It was clear that the criminal was the head of the family.

They took up residence separately, of course. Her son once in a while secretly dropped in without his wife knowing. Kerta lived in a communal apartment. Her relationships with her neighbors were good and they loved her. She worked as a kind of bookkeeper for an institute. Since she was a talented person she easily mastered this profession and even found satisfaction in her work. She did everything well.

Occasionally Kerta felt pain in her heart. Her neighbors helped her. But one evening she came home late and everyone was already asleep. They heard the way she paced around the room, coughed, and sometimes moaned. They did not dare to go into her room. And in the morning they found her lying on the floor dead. She had had a heart attack. She died without help and alone. I don't remember the date of her death.

That's all that I know about Kerta. If I have forgotten something, it might only be the dates. I vouch for the essence of Kerta's story.

The Doctors' Plot

Rumors of the arrest of a group of doctors began to reach Karaganda in 1952. Loathsome rumors about Joint, an international organization of Zionists, were also spread about.

The secretary to the director of our sewing shop, Natasha Vakula, told us that she had seen with her own eyes how they had opened a package from America at the post office that was addressed to someone named Rabinovich. In the package there was cotton padding, and thousands of typhus-bearing lice were crawling in the cotton.

At a general meeting a dressmaker stood up and told us that she remembered from childhood how the Jews had killed a young Christian baby and used his blood to make matzo. Her presentation was met with an embarrassed silence, and someone said:

"Well, that hasn't been proven. Don't speak of it."

With this our discussion of the matzo incident ended.

In general the mood seemed to be leading up to a pogrom.

At this time I was the manager of a sewing workshop that produced clothing. I also kept track of workers' salaries, a task for which I sometimes had to sit in the office. In the office I was the only Jew and the only exile. When I came in the lively conversation would stop and all glances would turn toward me, as if I were a murderous doctor, a member of Joint, and a consumer of bloody matzo.

One night I had the pleasure of hearing a masterpiece by a famous Soviet journalist on the radio: *Murderers in White Lab Coats.*

The next day I went to work as if to an execution. When I came in, the lively conversation again stopped and all eyes, as usual, turned toward me.

I sat at my table and began to turn the adding machine, to make calculations.

Our bookkeeper, Maria Nikitichna Puzikova, came in a little bit late. She was the most socially elite woman of all the workers in the office. Her husband was a member of the regional Party Committee, and all the Karaganda elite gathered in her home, a fact that she reported to us every morning:

"Yesterday the secretary of the Party Committee, M. M., an important official from Moscow, came to our house," and so forth.

Today Maria Nikitichna shone like a new penny.

"Goodness me," she said. "What a terrible thing! What lack of vigilance! How could they have let those Jews into the Kremlin and trusted them with the health of our leaders! Sergei and I didn't sleep all night after we heard the report from *Pravda, Murderers in White Lab Coats,* on the radio."

Maria Nikitichna flew out of the office and within a minute returned with a newspaper in her hands.

"Olga Lvovna, read this article aloud to us, you read so well!"

"As I recall, you completed junior high school, Maria Nikitichna, and should be able to read it yourself since I don't have time," I answered. (My university diploma was a cause of suffering for Maria Nikitichna, since she could only compare it with her certificate for completing seventh grade.)

The head bookkeeper took the newspaper and began to read the celebrated article aloud.

Our director, Anisia Vasilievna, was a good person. A semiliterate girl from the village, and then a maidservant who was politically active, she later became a Party member. She was promoted in the Party hierarchy and became one of the leading women of Karaganda. She possessed a naturally inquisitive mind and, in spite of her adoration of Stalin, to whom in her opinion she owed her happy career and life, she evidently wanted to understand what kind of people we exiles were. She loved to converse with me, but she checked up on every one of my words. Once I said that Marx was a Jew. Soon there was some sort of anniversary and, in a big article on Marx in *Pravda,* it was written that Marx was a German. Anisia Vasilievna reproached me:

"Look, Olga Lvovna, I believe your words since you are an educated person, but apparently you told me something that wasn't true."

"And whom do you believe more, Anisia Vasilievna, *Pravda* or Lenin?"

"Well, of course I believe Lenin unconditionally."

I went to the Red Corner and took out a volume of Lenin with the article "Karl Marx," where Lenin said that Marx was a German Jew. *Pravda* was put to shame, and Anisia Vasilievna did some thinking.

Once she asked me:

"Well, explain to me what it was that these Jewish doctors wanted? Do they find their life in the USSR so unbearable that they have to kill our leaders?"

To this I couldn't find an answer, so I said:

"In my opinion they were just crazy. I can't explain it otherwise."

Certainly I couldn't tell her that this whole affair had been fabricated, that none of these crimes had been committed.

I would end up with another sentence for agitation against the Soviet state if I said that.

So I lived in an atmosphere of hostile curiosity, hate, and persecution.

In spite of our misfortunes, four other exiled women and I decided to celebrate the New Year of 1953. One of these women, Ida Markovna Reznikova, worked at our dressmaking shop, and the other three were nurses.

We prepared a tasty supper, baked a tart, and got hold of a nice bottle of wine. It was time to sit down at the table, but one of the women, Gita Abramovna, for some reason hadn't arrived.

I decided to go get her. She lived nearby. When I came into her room, the light was off. At first I couldn't tell if she was home or not. I turned on the light and saw Gita sitting silently on the cot. Her single most valuable possession, a down feather quilt, had been taken off the cot. Next to the cot lay a wrapped and addressed package.

"What happened, Gita? Why have you taken the feather quilt off the cot, what is the package about?"

"Be quiet!" said Gita. "Leave quickly. Probably today or tomorrow they are going to arrest me. They already called me for questioning and asked about my brother who ran away from Poland to Palestine in 1939. When my husband and I were arrested, he sent my daughter money. They say this money is from Joint. Everything that I have I am going to ship to my daughter, if I have time."

"Well, all the more reason for you to come and greet the New Year with us. Who knows if we'll ever see each other again, and they don't serve tasty food in prison. Come on, let's go!"

"No, you'll just end up in prison again because of me. I am already a marked woman!"

I just barely managed to bring her to my place. Then we enjoyed ourselves a bit, drank wine, ate well, and decided that maybe nothing bad would happen.

"And now I drink a silent toast to my greatest desire, and I ask all of you to join me," I said. We drank silently. Later it turned out that for four of us our greatest wish was that Stalin would die in 1953, and only Gita, an old and faithful member of the Party, had wished that in 1953 there would be a revolution in Italy and France.

Until March 5 when our wish was fulfilled, and even during the first few months after the death of Stalin, nothing changed. That same fear of arrest (Gita was not arrested) and the same stupid articles in newspapers. But on a truly beautiful day, April 4, 1953, during my lunch break I went out to warm myself in the sun, and suddenly Ida Markovna, in tears, ran out of the workshop, threw herself on my neck, and gasped to me that just now on the radio they had transmitted the news that the whole trial of the doctor-poisoners was a fabrication of Riumin and his accomplices. Our happiness was limitless. We cried and dreamed that we would also get rid of our terrible sentences so that we could return to our children.

In a happy mood I went to the office and heard the last few words from a little speech Maria Nikitichna was making: "Americans have a lot of money. They can buy whomever they need!"

The words flashed like lightning through my brain: "Now I'll show you, you bitch!" I went up to the door of the director's office and said loudly:

"Anisia Vasilievna, come out here! This was a rude act of insubordination, very uncommon in our relationships."

"What are you saying, Olga Lvovna?"

"Just what you heard. You and Anna Petrovna (our Party organizer) must come out here together."

They came out.

"Just a minute ago Maria Nikitichna said that the Supreme Court had been bribed by the Americans. I spent eight years in prison because I hadn't denounced my husband, and I don't want to sit in prison any longer because of Maria Nikitichna. She used words discrediting the Soviet Court that fully fit under article 58, number 10. Usually this is punished with ten years' deprivation of freedom. Here everyone has just heard these words and can confirm them. I will not go to the MGB, but here before witnesses I inform you. It's up to you to go to the MGB."

Everyone turned to stone.

"Maria Nikitichna, how could you say such a thing?" exclaimed Anisia Vasilievna.

"Oh, I don't know, I don't know, I wasn't thinking!" Maria Nikitichna cried and ran home.

Of course Maria Nikitichna received no judicial consequences or unfortunate sentence. She was beaten so badly by her husband, a member of the regional Party Committee, that she didn't come to work for four days and then appeared with bruises covered over with powder.

Still I could not stop myself from going to Anisia Vasilievna with satisfaction and saying:

"Anisia Vasilievna, I ask you as a member of the Party why Riumin and his accomplices slandered innocent people and put our country to shame with this idiotic trial? Was Riumin living so badly under the Soviet system that he had to commit this crime?"

To this poor Anisia Vasilievna mumbled something about American spies. And then I received even more satisfaction from a popular street song that quickly responded to the events of the day:

Dear Comrade Vovsi,
I am sincerely happy
That it turns out now
That you are not guilty!
For no reason you languished
In a damp prison cell,
And you hadn't even tried
To bring down our Soviet system.
Dear Comrade Kogan,
Famous doctor,
You are anxious and deeply moved,
But now don't cry!
For no reason they upset you,
You, a doctor of science,
Because of this scoundrel Lidka Timashuk
You labored, you toiled,
Never closing your eyes
While this plague of an informer
Denounced you.
A rumor now spreads among the people—
It was all nonsense.
Live now in freedom,
You, our doctors.

The workers in our shop went around for a long time with upset expressions, as if they had lost a football match for the championship of the USSR.

The Death of Stalin

There was a conference in the director's office.

Except for me there was not a single exile there.

During the meeting a woman worker burst in without knocking: "Anisia Vasilievna . . ."

"Why did you come in without permission? Leave the room."

"But Anisia Vasilievna . . ."

"I told you we are busy. Leave the room."

"Stalin is dying."

It was as if a bomb had exploded. Anisia Vasilievna screamed, began to slump to one side, and fainted.

Everyone in the room turned around and looked at me. I was terribly afraid that my face might express something it wasn't supposed to, and I covered it with my hands. I began to shake. I said to myself, "Now or never."

And what if all my splendid well-founded calculations prove to be wrong, bursting like a soap bubble?

And what if some Malenkov, Beria, some devil or evil type suddenly takes over this colossus and tries to prop it up with still more millions of corpses? And if so, it will endure for another twenty years or so, enough for my lifetime, and then that's it.

Now or never!

I felt that my shoulders were shaking.

Then I heard them talking about me: "What a hypocrite—pretending to cry, and when she uncovers her face, her eyes will be dry."

210

Everyone went around as if crazy. Suddenly everyone became hyper-vigilant. For instance, from a hundred kilometers away a woman arrived who had made an appointment months before for a fitting on March 5.

"Today we are not doing any fittings," I said. (I was responsible for the shop that day.) The woman began to argue that it was a working day. I persuaded her to go away. Later the MGB called me, and they wrote down everything she had said, as well as her name and address. She never showed up at our shop again.

One brave general got drunk in a restaurant and said it would have been better if this had happened fifteen years ago; it would have been easier to fight. For that he was sent to the camps with a sentence of twenty-five years.

It seemed to me that now when perhaps the end was in sight, they would seize me and finish me off.

Everyone was wearing mourning rosettes.

I thought with anguish, "Wear one or not wear one?"

Anna Petrovna, our Party organizer, called me in and stuck a rosette on my dress.

"You should wear it," she said.

I was then afraid to take it off and wore it longer than anyone else, until Anna Petrovna came up to me and took it off herself. We listened to the government funeral on the radio. Beria spoke:

"We know how to do business."

Yes, he knows how.

Malenkov said:

"Let our enemies inside and outside the country remember that our vigilance will not weaken."

I remembered . . . I think things had never been so hard as during the year of Stalin's death, when little by little somewhere, somehow things began to become clearer and show signs of life.

Nikolai Adamov—The End of the Road

Ever so slowly the sky grew clearer after the death of Stalin. Only a year later in 1954, they began to terminate eternal exile sentences and give passports, of course with an indication of previous convictions and denial of the right to live in thirty-nine cities. For some reason I was the very last to have my exile terminated, and I lived completely alone in Karaganda for some time. All my friends had left, and time stretched out unbelievably slowly. Arriving home from work I would lie down to sleep at eight o'clock (from disgust with life, as Mandel used to say) and at three o'clock in the morning I would wake up, read, suffer, and wait for morning.

Finally for me too exile ended, and I went directly to Jezkazgan and Nikolai's camp.

There were rumors about this camp. There had been disturbances, and the prisoners had refused to work, demanding that there should be a review of their cases, that Malenkov should come to inspect them, and that the camp regime should be changed. People even said that tanks had been called in.

Arriving in Jezkazgan, I found out that all that was already over. They had liquidated the insurgents, the disturbances had quieted down, and there had been great changes in the camp rules. Relatives were now permitted to visit for a week, and for this purpose they arranged accommodations with two exits: one for prisoners into the zone, the other for visitors to exit into the street. Nothing like this had ever happened in the camps before.

I entered a narrow room where there was a bed with a table and two stools. With a beating heart I sat down . . .

The door opened and Nikolai came in.

I recognized him only with difficulty. In four years he had turned into an old man, eaten alive by tuberculosis.

I stayed with him for a week. In all of my terrible life this week was one of the most painful.

At the end of the week one of the bosses arrived and said that Adamov could be released for health reasons, if I gave a signed statement that I would care for him and file no grievances against the camp.

Of course I signed this strange statement, and together we returned to Karaganda.

A new stage of life began in Karaganda for Nikolai and me. His health improved noticeably; he got better, stronger, and again got into political arguments. I have to say that we often saw events very differently. Our temperaments were very different. He was a fighter, a fearless person, and I was frightened to death. We often had arguments.

In this period in Karaganda I again began to write the memoirs that had been interrupted by my second arrest. I remember I finished the chapter "Liza" and read it to Nikolai. He very much disliked it.

"Your Liza is a traitor. Her daughter asks her how she can live, asks her if she took money from *them*, but Liza is afraid they won't take her daughter into the Komsomol (may it go to the dogs!), and she answers, 'Yes, I am guilty.' She betrayed not only herself but all of us! She said all of us were guilty—the spies and the terrorists. Is this the way to write about that time? You must write so that the walls tremble, so that the roof falls on their despicable heads! And you feel sorry for Liza! Poor Liza!"

I could not agree with him and could not write it otherwise. I was never at all political. I just deeply pitied my comrades in their unhappiness, and I hated our executioners.

At this time rumors flew about that many people were being rehabilitated, and we decided to leave Karaganda in order to apply for rehabilitation. I went to Moscow and Nikolai to Voronezh, where he had been convicted and where his case was filed. Arriving in Voronezh, Nikolai not only was rehabilitated rather quickly but rejoined the Party. When the secretary presented him with his Party card at a Party gathering and congratulated Nikolai, he answered:

"It's not me who should be congratulated. I should congratulate you that people like me are returning to the Party."

The Party group was shocked.

Nikolai was given an apartment in Voronezh. He also registered his niece, a Voronezh university student, so that she could share it with him.

Right away many friends turned up from the Komsomol and the Civil War who also had been purged at the same time as him but hadn't yet been rehabilitated. Nikolai tried to help them. His home was full of people whom he cared for, who respected him and who recognized him as their leader. He was in his element. He arranged to go to work. His niece worshiped him and he worshiped her. She kept house and he lived in a family where he was the chief and idol, which he needed.

During this time he came to see me in Moscow several times, but he couldn't find a place for himself in our family. He was different from my circle, and he felt this sharply. And I couldn't leave my family. I was consumed with caring for my sick elderly sisters, grandchildren were born, and it seemed to me that through them it was as though my children were returning to me; they filled up my life. So we lived each in our own family; we wrote to each other and sometimes got together.

Nikolai's tuberculosis grew worse and worse. He was often sick. One day I received tragic news from his niece: he had fallen ill with pneumonia, was taken to the hospital, and died there.

He was sixty-two years old.

Rehabilitation

In 1955 I came to Moscow to seek rehabilitation. Everything stretched out terribly slowly. For the rehabilitation application they required proof from all the places I had been registered after liberation from the camps. And I myself didn't remember where and how many times I had been registered. I had lived in Moscow illegally, and I had obtained a residence permit through paying money here and there. They required a reference from each workplace, but at work they didn't give references very often; probably they had certain instructions in this connection.

Finally I submitted my application for rehabilitation. My case fell to the prosecutor Ivanov, a man with dull eyes who spoke in a wooden voice. Every time I came into his office after having waited in line for five or six hours he said:

"Your case will be examined in its time. The waiting list has not gotten to you yet."

Once he opened a cupboard and showed me a whole library of cases in identical folders.

"Here is the professor's case for which you and your husband came in. You see there are more than a hundred participants, and all the cases must be examined."

"And are many of the participants still alive?" I asked.

He hedged.

"Some are alive."

"So maybe you should start with those who are living. Otherwise I'm afraid no one will live long enough to have her own turn."

So it dragged on until the Twentieth Party Congress. After the Congress, at the beginning of March, I went to the Supreme Court and found out that my case had been transferred to another prosecutor. Unfortunately I don't remember his name. They told me to write a brief description of my case. I wrote: "For twenty years I have been waiting for justice. Will I be waiting for this until I die or not?"

They let me and my brother's wife, who went everywhere with me, in to see the prosecutor. A cheerful young man met us. He was about thirty-five years old and apparently a military man. I gave him my application.

My sister-in-law, who previously had not seen what I had written, was horrified and began to make excuses.

"She is so nervous. Please excuse her."

He smiled broadly.

"No wonder you are nervous. It's not hard to understand why. Now your case will go quickly. I think it won't be more than a month."

"But they're going to send me out of Moscow. Yesterday the militia came and told me to leave Moscow within twenty-four hours."

"Hide yourself, hide from the militia. It will end soon. Can you live in a different place for a short while?"

"I can stay with my sister."

"Give me the telephone number there. I'll call you."

On March 8 the telephone rang, and the cheerful voice of my prosecutor said:

"You are going to receive a gift on the eighth of March. Your case has been reviewed, and you will receive a rehabilitation certificate at the office of the Supreme Court. You'll be informed of the day. I congratulate you."

When I went for my certificate on the day indicated, there were about twenty people in the waiting room, almost all women fifty years old or older. One was a very old Ukrainian woman with a half-crazed look on her face. She kept whispering something to herself. A man of about forty sat by the window and smoked.

They called us in turn. People came out of the office and again waited for something. When they called my last name and that of my husband, the man sitting by the window gave a start. I went in and received my certificate of rehabilitation. They told me that I had to wait in the waiting room, where they would give out certificates for passports and money.

My certificate stated the following:

June 6, 1956 No. 44-03393/56
Certificate

The Plenum of the Supreme Court of the USSR has reviewed the case of the guilt of Olga Lvovna Adamova-Sliozberg on May 24, 1956.

The sentence of the Military Board from November 12, 1936, Resolution of the Supreme Court of the USSR from November 21, 1940, and Resolution of the Special Conference of the MGB from November 19, 1949, in relation to Adamova-Sliozberg is canceled, and the case is terminated for lack of evidence.

Presiding officer of the judicial staff of the Military Board
Colonel of Justice   P. Likhachev

I had been arrested on April 27, 1936. That means I had paid for this mistake with twenty years and forty-one days of my life.

When I returned to the waiting room, the man sitting by the window came up to me.

"Tell me please, did your husband teach the history of science at the university?"

"Yes, until 1936."

"I was his student. What a teacher he was! I have never encountered such broad erudition, such brilliant presentation style, and such great love for his subject in any other man."

We were quiet. A soldier came out and began to distribute the certificates for receiving passports and compensation.

They gave me two months' salary for me and for my husband and an additional eleven rubles fifty kopeks equal to the one hundred fifteen rubles that my husband had had on him at the moment of his death.

The old Ukrainian woman receiving her certificates screamed wildly:

"I don't need money for the blood of my son. Keep it yourselves, you murderers." She tore up the certificates and threw them on the floor.

A soldier handing out certificates came up to her.

"Calm down, citizen . . ." he began.

But the old woman again began to shriek:

"Murderers!" She spat in his face and fell into a fit. A doctor and two aides ran in and carried her away.

Everyone was quiet and depressed. Here and there loud weeping could be heard.

I could not hold onto myself. Sobbing suffocated me. The man came up to me.

"I also received a certificate of rehabilitation for my father. For a lack of corpus delicti . . . He too, like your husband, was an exceptional human being."

We went out together. My companion took me home. He asked:

"Do you have a son?"

"Yes," I answered.

"Does he resemble his father?"

"Very much."

"Well, at least that is good."

His kissed my hand and went away. I went into my apartment from which the militia could no longer snatch me. There was no one at home and I could cry without holding back.

I cried for my husband, murdered in the basement of Lubyanka at the age of thirty-seven in the full flower of his strength and talent; for my children, who grew up as orphans labeled children of enemies of the people; for my parents who died of sorrow; for twenty years of suffering; for friends who did not live to be rehabilitated and are buried in the frozen earth of Kolyma.

STORIES ABOUT MY FAMILY

My Relatives' Struggle for My Children

I wrote a book of memories called *My Journey,* in which I tried to communicate the tragic fates of my cellmates, almost all of whom were completely innocent but fell into the terrible clutches of the MGB. I wanted to bring out the way people whose mouths had been closed had been slandered. The reader will judge if I have been successful in doing this.

Reading through what I had written, I suddenly realized that I had said almost nothing about one particular fate. This was the fate of my family, their many-year struggle for my freedom, and the way they overcame their own fear of also falling behind bars. And how many families there were like that! How many mothers spent days in endless lines waiting for information and trying to deliver packages! Waiting in lines to meet with important officials, begging them to review the cases of their children! How many grandmothers and grandfathers, knowing of the horrible conditions in orphanages for the children of enemies of the people, suffered from not being able to help their grandchildren! How many of them were willing to share their last piece of bread in order to send packages to the camps!

I want to describe this struggle using the example of my own family.

When my husband and I were arrested in 1936, we had two large, nice rooms in a communal apartment. Our children were six and four years old. Mama heard that the children of people who had been arrested were sent to children's orphanages and that their apartments were given to members of the NKVD. So my parents' first task was to save our children. Mama very quickly succeeded in exchanging our two rooms for an eleven-square-meter room in a large communal apartment on Petrovka Street, where my parents and my sister Elena lived with her son.

They registered the children; the room belonging to them was unenviable, and Mama, having calmed herself a bit, turned all her energy to interceding on my behalf. But alas! One terrible day three men arrived and the oldest asked:

"Are the children of the enemies of the people Zakgeim and Sliozberg living here?"

"Yes," answered Mama, frozen in horror.

"We have come for them. There is an order to take them to a children's home."

Mama shoved the children into their room, locked the door with a key, and put the key in her bosom.

"Do you have an order to arrest me?" she asked.

"No," one man answered. "We don't plan to arrest you; we came for the children."

"Well then," Mama said, "You can arrest me, you can kill me, but as long as I live, I will not give the children up to you!"

My father stood with his back against the door of the children's room. On his face was written, "As long as I live, I too will not give up the children!"

Apparently the NKVD did not expect such a rebuff. They were used to encountering fear and submissiveness. The senior one exchanged with his comrades looks that said, "Let's not fight with the old people!"

"Well, come on, we can just as well come back with an order."

Evidently he was not a bad person and had not completely lost his conscience. He could have pushed back and broken the door. But he only threatened to do that. However one should bear in mind that this was still only 1936, when the punitive machine had just begun to grind. And my parents' rebuffs worked.

Horror hung over my family. They began to search feverishly for a way out. They decided that the only person who could help was Vladimir Arkadevich Tronin, my sister Polina's husband. He was a hero of the Civil War, a medal holder, a friend of Frunze and Kuibyshev, and at this time a member of the Collegium Ministry of Water Management and Irrigation (and probably he was even a vice minister of a People's Committee). I once saw his Kremlin permit, upon which it was written that he was a "Member of the Government."

Everyone waited anxiously until Vladimir came home from work. Would he agree to speak for these children of enemies of the people? Vladimir Arkadevich, without hesitating even for a minute, promised to do all he could. And in fact in a short time he succeeded in obtaining permission for the children to be placed with their grandmother and grandfather under his supervision. Tronin was appointed to be personally responsible for raising them. In this way my children were saved and never knew what it would have been like to have been orphans. They grew up among loving people who took the place of parents for them.

I must say that Vladimir Arkadevich really did pay a lot of attention to my children. They often stayed at my sister's home and at the Tronins' dacha. When the war began, the Academy of Sciences of the USSR (where Tronin was working) evacuated the children to a camp in Borovoe, a health resort in Kazakhstan. Tronin, regardless of a number of complications, included three children on his list—his son and my two children. He considered himself to be their guardian. In the Party Committee he had some rather unpleasant conversations with regard to his protection of the children of enemies of the people. My sister Polina told me the comical ending to one of these conversations. Searching for another argument, the chair of the Party Committee said, "Can you imagine if a Fascist protected the children of an arrested Communist?" To this Vladimir answered, "But I am not a Fascist—I am a Communist."

Elena Lvovna Sliozberg

My older sister became a mother to my children. When I returned to Moscow ten years later, I didn't notice even a grain of preference for her own son. She loved them all equally. Her relationships with mine were colored by pity and fear—what if something completely unexpected happens to them, how will I be able to endure it?

Elena's son, Dima, was ten years older than my children. A kind boy by nature, he had absorbed the family's love for my children and related to them as if they were his natural brother and sister. Elena told me that Dima received two little pieces of candy for breakfast at school every day. He always brought them to my children. Elena once said to him, "Dimochka, why don't you eat these little candies once in a while yourself? Certainly with everyone around you eating them, you might really want them a lot."

"No, Mama. They are little children, so they want them even more!"

I love my nephew very much, but a feeling of deep gratitude is mixed with my ordinary love because of his love and care for my children. I will never forget these little candies.

My sister Polina also related to my children beautifully. Over a period of ten years twice a year (on the children's birthdays) she sent them packages by mail on which it was written, "From Mama." Once my daughter wrote me in the camps: "Mama, how did you guess that I was dreaming of a little bed for my doll? You sent me exactly what I wanted! Thank you!"

I was endlessly grateful to all my relatives for their relationships with my children. But I knew that absolutely no one could relate to them better than Elena. She was simply a mother to them. Thanks to her they didn't know what it could have been like to be orphaned.

And what a doctor she was!

When I returned, her life was very hard. She would get up at six in the morning in order to be able to give Mama her injection, put a mustard plaster on her, help our half-blind father, and get to work by nine o'clock. She worked in a little hospital for riverboat workers in the village of Nagatino. To get there from Petrovka Street she had to ride three trams for an hour and a half each way. Returning home at eight o'clock in the evening, she immediately went to Mama and then took care of the housekeeping (for a family of six people). She lay down to sleep on a fold-out cot next to Mama's bed because almost every night Mama had heart troubles. Elena had to get up and give her injections and oxygen. So she was chronically deprived of sleep.

When I arrived in 1946 of course I took on all the domestic work, even learning to give Mama injections. Now things became easier for Elena. But all the same she never was fully rested. She always dreamed of Sundays when I didn't allow others to wake her before eleven o'clock.

Suddenly one Saturday she said to me:

"Tomorrow wake me up at six o'clock. I have to go to Nagatino."

"Why?" I wondered.

"They brought in a one-year-old baby who was suffering from worms. I wrote a prescription for him with a dose of 0.01. But the nurse, Katia, said to me, 'We have some of that medicine left here. Why should the mother go to the pharmacy? I'll give it to her.' I agreed. And then when I was already at home I realized I never had treated a one-year-old for worms and that in the office I had only a dose of 0.1, which I'd prescribed for older children. This dose could kill a one-year-old baby, and I had recommended that the mother give him the medicine morning and evening. Tomorrow morning I am going to them to see if I can correct this."

"I'm coming with you," I said to Elena.

We arrived at Nagatino at eight o'clock in the morning. Everyone who saw us was amazed that Elena had come on a Sunday. Everyone urged us to drink a cup of tea. It was extraordinarily pleasant for me to see how the residents of Nagatino loved and respected Elena.

The house where we had to go stood at a distance. With sinking hearts we knocked. A young woman opened the door; she was washing the floor. She joyfully invited us into the house and was amazed that Elena had come on a Sunday and so early. Elena had thought of something.

"And I am guilty, Elena Lvovna," said the woman. "You told me I should give him the medicine night and morning, but I brought it to him and he was fast asleep. I hated to wake him. And now he is still sleeping!"

I felt relieved from the bottom of my heart. We heard the baby's little voice. The mother ran and got the charming baby, who could already stand on his fat little legs.

"He has already begun to talk," the mother said. "Petenka, tell me, who is that?" she asked the child.

Petia pointed his finger at Elena and said:

"Baba."

"Well, isn't he a smart one? And he didn't say 'auntie.' He sees that this is an older woman, and he said, 'Baba.'" And she kissed his little legs. "Maybe this isn't right, but it seems to me that there is no better child than my Petia."

Elena and I listened to the mother and imagined what could have happened if we had been too late. Elena asked the baby's mother to show her the medicine the nurse had given her the previous evening. Elena put it in her bag, and wrote out another prescription, underlining the dosage of 0.01.

"I think," she said, "that this would be better for him."

When we left our legs nearly gave way with the agitation we had just gone through. We went to the nurse, Katia. I had never seen Elena so furious!

"You are fired!" she screamed. "You could have killed the child! Don't think for a moment that you'll ever be able to find work as a nurse anywhere else! I will tell everyone why I fired you. You'll be kept as far away from medicine as possible!"

Katia cried, swore she would now verify the prescription three times, asked for forgiveness, and swore on the memory of her mother never to forget this terrible event.

Elena and I went home. Within a half hour Katia arrived. She implored Elena to forgive her. Elena saw her remorse and of course forgave her. No one ever found out about this event.

I should say that although Elena was a clinician (during this period she led the outpatient clinical department of the hospital), she never refused to treat children, and all the women of the village preferred to bring their little children to her. Children loved her very much. And I also want to say that Elena had a real gift for diagnosis. She had an unusual empathy for the sick. I know of several occasions when the picture was very unclear, but she diagnosed appendicitis and saved people's lives.

I remember one particular occasion. In the village of Nagatino lived a woman named Anisia and her ten-year-old son, Vasia. Anisia was different from the others in that she always stood for *truth,* and she was loudly indignant about any injustice. (This detail is important in light of what happened later.) One day Anisia came to Elena with Vasia, who was crying, and said that the child had been crying all night; his stomach hurt. Elena examined him and it looked to her like appendicitis. She called the surgeon. The surgeon was young, inexperienced, but very self-confident. He took a look, felt Vasia's stomach, and categorically said, "There is no appendicitis; he ate something bad for him. Give him castor oil and everything will be fine."

But Elena did not allow him to be given castor oil; she was very anxious about Vasia's condition. She decided to go with them herself to a children's hospital. All along the road Vasia cried. At the hospital they accepted him immediately. The doctor took Vasia in and told Elena and Anisia to wait in the waiting room. They waited rather a long time and began to get nervous. Finally the doctor came out and said to Anisia:

"Thank God you have such a doctor. The child could have died. We did an operation at the last minute; the appendix was about to rupture. But your surgeon wasn't really to blame—the appendix was lying under the liver; he couldn't feel it; great experience is necessary for this. Come back and visit your son in two days, and within a week he'll be running around again."

Then he came up to Elena, kissed her hand, and said, "Thank you."

Anisia of course told everyone about this event, praised Elena, and cursed the young surgeon.

This was in 1952. Then the vile campaign against the so-called murderers in white lab coats began. In the hospital where Elena worked there was a meeting about this. A representative of the Ministry of Health let it be understood that a Jew could not be the director of a department. Everyone was so frightened that no one dared speak out. Only Katia tried to say what a good doctor Elena was, but no one supported her.

Then Katia left for the village, where she gathered about twenty women together, and they went to the regional health center. The women protested against the removal of Elena from her leadership position. Anisia screamed, "She saved my son!" Another said, "My mother had a heart attack, and she spent the whole night with her giving her injections and massaging her heart. She had left her own mother to rescue mine from death. Can people like that be murderers?" Someone shouted, "In other hospitals in order to get a good doctor, you have to give ten rubles or a box of candy as a bribe. But if you go to Elena Lvovna with candies, she'll swear at you and chase you away!"

In short, the order to fire Elena was delayed. And then she herself decided to retire. A grandson was born in her son's family, and her health began to deteriorate.

But still, in Moscow and at the dacha, if someone was sick day or night they would run for help to Elena. So she remained a doctor to the end of her life.

She died in 1967 in her seventy-second year.

The Children

I am eighty-eight years old. More than half a century has gone by since my life was shattered in 1936. I survived the whole cycle of prison, camps, and exile.

I am very glad that I wrote about what I had experienced while the impressions were still fresh, beginning to write back in 1946 after being released from my first arrest, having been in prisons and camps for eight years, and then spending two years without the right to leave Kolyma. I wrote at night, trembling with fear because when we were liberated we had to sign an agreement of nondisclosure. Now I wouldn't be able to write that way because even the most vivid experiences fade with the years. Of course I do remember Kolyma, the fifty-degree-below-zero temperature, starvation, and hard labor (for four years I chopped down trees in Kolyma!), but not other details.

But one thing lives and to this day is still burning painfully in my memory. The children!

When they arrested me, my son was six years old and my daughter four.

In prison I slept badly. Exhausted during the day, I would fall asleep around midnight and almost always saw the children in my dreams. I played with them. I kissed their feet, their little necks and heads . . . At four o'clock I would wake up as if from a stabbing pain in my heart—yes, they had taken my children from me and maybe I would never see them again!

The first year after my arrest I received no news at all from home, and the investigator threatened that, if I did not help the investigation (in other

229

words, sign false evidence against my husband), they would put my children in a children's home and possibly change their last name in order to save them from my degenerate family. They were very small, especially my daughter. They would of course forget their last name, and I would never find them . . .

Within a year I received a letter from Mama. Learning that my children were living with her, I calmed down somewhat.

In the cell almost everyone was a mother, and conversations about our children tormented the soul. I've already written earlier in my memoirs of the massive hysterics elicited by the weeping of a woman who was new to the cell and whose child had been left behind.

We agreed not to speak of our children.

During the day I somehow distracted myself—I read and busied myself with learning mathematics or English with my cellmates or teaching others.

Only during the sleepless hours of the night, from four (in our cell you could hear the striking of the clock) until six (wake-up time), I allowed myself to remember the children.

I always remembered Shurik as weak and unprotected. I was overwhelmed by an aching pity for him. But I was astonished by the workings of his mind.

When he was four years old my husband brought home a poster with images of evolution: from a frog coming out of the sea, to some sort of creatures, to monkeys, and finally to humans. My son kept asking me:

"And who is that? And how could a frog come out of the sea if he still didn't have legs?"

Deeply convinced that Darwin's theory was irrefutable, I somehow tried to explain it all to him, and when I couldn't explain something, I said:

"Look, Papa's coming, he'll tell us everything."

One day my son asked me:

"And who gave birth to the frog?"

"It was some kind of small fish who gave birth to him."

"And who gave birth to the fish?"

I again thought of something, and in the end got back to the worm.

"And who gave birth to the worm?"

"A very, very tiny microbe," I answered.

My answer seemed to satisfy the little boy. This conversation was in the early spring. But later in the fall on a walk he suddenly asked:

"Hmm . . . And who gave birth to the tiny microbe?"

"We'll ask Papa," I said, not knowing what to answer, but amazed that at the age of four and a half he had been thinking for five months about a puzzle that science has not yet solved.

Ellochka was a completely different child. She always came to my memory in a kind of glow of joy and tranquility. Once in Kolyma in a moment of sharp melancholy and despair I wrote a poem that I dedicated to her:

You grew, my golden buttercup,
Like a flower on a slim stalk.
People spoke of you
And said that you would tread lightly on the earth.

I gave birth to you lightly
And nursed you with ease.
That is why I loved you
With a tranquil love in those days.

But half a world lies between us now
And you come only in dreams,
With large blue eyes
You smile at me brightly.

And you come quickly and lightly.
I see this in a dream every night,
And nodding your dark blond head,
You walk away carefree.

I have no voice, no strength
To turn you back, to hold you.
And now your mother has come to love you
With true love.

Once I was taking a walk with Ellochka. Shurik was sick and had stayed at home. A man came up to us.

"Oh, what a girl!" he said. "What's your name?"

"Ellochka."

"And how old are you?

"Three."

"What a smart little girl!"

"No, it's my brother Shura who is smart. I am stupid but very pretty!"
The man was amazed.

"Well, how about that! Well, you certainly don't need to worry about her. She'll never be without boyfriends."

Another memory.

One time we all went as a family to visit my husband's mother. Ellochka was three at the time. For some reason she didn't have a real doll but only small gray rubber ones.

On my sister-in-law's table stood an amazing tea cozy shaped like a doll in a green silk dress with light brown braids. Ellochka took hold of this doll and for the rest of that day we didn't hear anymore from her. She went into a corner with the doll and played with her uninterruptedly, putting her to bed, feeding her, and rocking her. When it was time to go home, she categorically refused to give up the doll, clung to her, screamed, cried, and said that she was going to live with her grandmother and would play with the doll. Grandmother wasn't quite willing to give the doll away since it belonged to her daughter and meant a lot to her.

We could not reason with Ellochka. Finally my mother-in-law said, "Well, I will give you the doll; only we must wrap it up." She took the doll and quickly returned with it wrapped in newspaper and tied with string. The whole return trip Ellochka held her treasure to her heart. Arriving at home I opened the package, and—oh alas!—the doll was not inside. There was some kind of rag wrapped in the newspaper, and what happened to the child! She screamed and cried so much that I could do nothing with her. Until twelve o'clock at night I talked with her and told her we probably had lost the doll on the streetcar. Tomorrow I would go and find it. Nothing helped. Finally she was exhausted and fell asleep, but she continued to gasp and sob in her sleep.

The next day I got up at seven o'clock, and before eight I went to the department store. There I bought a wondrous doll in a green dress with two fair braids. Arriving at home, I found my husband sitting on Ellochka's bed and trying to quiet her, but she pushed him away and cried bitterly.

"Here is your daughter," I said, giving her the doll. Ellochka threw herself on me, took the doll in her arms and, as if wishing to be alone with her, ran into the farthest corner, turned away from us, and in a sort of throaty, low-pitched voice said, "My dear one! My life! My joy!"

My husband and I were stunned. I glanced at him. He was an exceptionally reserved person, but there were tears in his eyes.

"Just think," he said. "Such a little one, but how strong the maternal feeling is in her!"

My sister's friend, who had once been a children's writer, posed the question to then six-year-old Ellochka: "What will you be when you grow up?" Without thinking, she answered, "I will simply be a Mama." Her answer enchanted everyone and the nickname "Simply Mama" stuck solidly to Ellochka.

Every night I called forth the most minute episodes from my previous life with the children, talked with them, dreamed of their future, and trembled with fear for them.

Now my son is a professor and my daughter is a docent. They teach at institutes for higher learning, love their work, have children and grandchildren. So fate turned out happily for them, but this is a very rare case. For the majority of those who shared my misery, their children's lives were destroyed.

Yudel Ruvimovich Zakgeim

I have written about almost everything that I saw and lived through. Almost. But I have not written about one person—my husband. As soon as I would begin to write about him, my heart would break. I thought, "I'll write about him later, but now I'll write about something not so painful . . ."

Not long ago on television I saw a dumping ground for human remains. (You couldn't call it a cemetery.) The television showed the bodies of prisoners who had been killed, bodies of enemies of the people. And suddenly the narrator picked up a skull. A bare skull with a round hole in the brow above one eye. It seemed to me that this was my husband's skull. All night I could not sleep. Before my very eyes my husband stood with a bullet wound in his forehead.

Now almost no one is left among the living who knew him! Except for me. I had put off writing about the memories, protecting myself from them. But now I cannot put them off any longer. I am already eighty-eight years old and, if I don't write about him, no one will.

But my heart is breaking! Let it break. I shall begin to write.

Yudel was born in 1898 into a very religious family in the town of Vitebsk. At home they spoke only Yiddish. The boy went to a Jewish school since school children were required to write on Saturdays at the gymnasium, and that was a great sin. One of the teachers, however, saw the boy's great ability and convinced his father to send his son to the gymnasium after he had finished the Jewish elementary school.

Later on I found his report card from the school. In all subjects he had received a five, but in Russian a two or a three. However, after a year or two he mastered Russian. At that time the First World War began. The Zakgeim family became refugees. They went to Samara where Yudel finished the gymnasium. After the Revolution he moved to Moscow and entered the biology department of the Krupskaya Pedagogical Institute.

Very quickly Yudel's unusual talent revealed itself. By nature he was a brilliant orator, and at the institute they used him for propaganda. Coming out of a religious environment, he knew the Bible and religious history thoroughly, although he had become a convinced atheist. His public profession became the propaganda of atheism. Zakgeim, like many others in this period, honestly thought that the morality of Communism was based on an incomparably higher morality than that of religion.

In 1925 a letter came to the institute from the Party's Central Committee with a request that someone be sent to Moscow University as an instructor in Marxist ideology. They sent Yudel, not even letting him finish his studies at the institute. So he became a teacher at the university without receiving the diploma of higher education, but that bothered him very little.

In 1931 he was already a professor in the Department of the Dialectics of Nature, at the same time fulfilling the duties of professor in the Department of History and Philosophy and running the offices of the Natural Sciences Department (as was written in his employment record book). In 1935 someone was verifying the scientific educational credentials of teachers, and suddenly it was revealed that Zakgeim did not have a diploma of higher education! The rector of the university, who knew Yudel very well, called him in and ordered him to write and defend a dissertation within three months. The task was almost undoable. The thing was that Yudel had one special attribute: he spoke brilliantly. But he wrote with great difficulty. The moment he sat down at a desk with a pen in his hand, his ideas would scatter; in no way could he put them together in an organized way. So I decided to help.

We had a habit of going for a walk after the children had gone to sleep, and he would tell me about his work, his lectures, and the problems of science. Nothing was more interesting to me than these stories of his. I even began to understand a bit myself about the natural sciences. And so we decided to work together. He created an outline for his dissertation and chapter by chapter told it to me. I would write down the abstract, write it out by hand, and give it to a typist. Yudel had only to edit the printed version. The rector's requirement was fulfilled, the dissertation was written, and within three months he defended it. Its title was "Development of the Physiology of the Higher Nervous Functions in the Eighteenth Century." The decision of the commission was "to award Zakgeim the degree of candidate in the biological sciences and to propose that he continue this work toward the degree of doctor of science." Alas, he had less than a year to live.

Many years later my son wanted to find this dissertation in the university archives, but he was not successful.

Yudel was a very affectionate father. With his daughter he was completely helpless. Often when he was preparing for lectures and sat surrounded by books, she would come up to her father and announce, "I want to play horsey." He unhesitatingly put aside his book, seated her on his neck, and jumped around the room.

"You are spoiling the child," I said.

"It is so interesting for her to ride a horse and so pleasant for me to feel her chubby little legs on my neck!"

He paid very careful attention to his son. In Shurik's little head, in his endless "why" questions, Yudel often perceived serious thoughts that seemed to him to be signs of giftedness in the boy.

I remember one time when Shurik had fallen sick and lay in his little bed with a temperature of thirty-eight degrees. I sat near him. On the little marble table beside his bed lay the thermometer.

"Mama?" Shurik asked. "Tell me how a thermometer works."

I was glad. I couldn't answer every one of his questions, but this time it was something simple. I told him that mercury expands when it is heated and goes up the little glass pipe, and the degrees of temperature are marked on a scale.

At this moment his father came into the room

"So how are things?" he asked, taking the thermometer from the table and saying, "Thirty-eight again? It just won't go down!"

Shurik quickly responded:

"Then Mama didn't tell me the right thing about the thermometer!"

"Why?" I asked.

"If it was the way you said, the thermometer wouldn't say thirty-eight anymore! Look, it's been lying on the cold table for a long time, and the mercury should have gone down!"

Yudel explained how a thermometer worked and then privately teased me, "You let a five-year-old boy show you up! This is what happens when one is dazzled with novels and poetry? Not being able to explain how a thermometer works! But Shurka is a fine fellow!"

I never knew anyone who loved pedagogical work the way Yudel did. He taught the history of biology. Looking at a certain period, whether the sixteenth or the eighteenth century, he tried to teach it so that the students would feel they had lived in this epoch, felt its art, religion, and daily life. In 1935 the two hundred fiftieth birthday of Bach took place. A choir came from Leningrad and gave two concerts: the Saint Matthew Passion and the B Minor Mass. Yudel decided to take his students to the Passion. He gathered them in an auditorium (I was there too) and talked about the creativity of Bach, about the content of the Passion. He had a good though small voice and absolute pitch. He even sang several themes from the Passion. The next day we all (about fifteen people) went to the conservatory.

I think that without this preparation none of us could have experienced this magnificent concert so ardently. Until this day I remember the profound feeling. I couldn't hold back my tears during the performance. It was the same with the others.

In that same winter he took his whole class to an exhibit of paintings from the seventeenth century. (The students were studying the history of the natural sciences in the seventeenth century.) The paintings were based on biblical subjects, but who in the 1930s knew the Bible? Yudel explained the paintings and the artists so interestingly that a large crowd gathered around us. Everyone wanted to hear this tour guide.

Yudel loved it when one of his former students would come to our place, sometimes even coming to Moscow for just a couple of days. He was always trying to give him the best place to sit and was extremely hospitable. They would talk for hours about life and would work together. After the student left, Yudel would boast like a child:

"You see how they remember and love me!" He himself very much loved and respected his students. He was interested in their lives and creative destinies.

In addition to his pedagogical work at the university, Yudel had another preoccupation. In 1925 he organized a scientific discussion group on the history of medicine. In 1935 this group was still meeting regularly. By that time its members were already doctors and even professors. Usually they gathered once a month and gave reports about their work and about foreign medical achievements. I remember the words of one professor of surgery: "I have no time now because I am so busy doing surgery. But when my hands grow weak, I will write about our circle. And for ten years no one has left it! It's a cultural phenomenon and really a rather rare one!"

This discussion group had its enfant terrible. Unfortunately I don't remember either his first or last name. This man was of small stature and very thin. His nickname was "the forty-five-kilogram professor." I'll tentatively call him Valery, although I think he had another name. Valery was an anti-Darwinist. He thought that, under strict testing from the point of view of philosophy and natural science, Darwin's theory would not hold up. Everyone fought with him, called him an idealist, a bourgeois philosopher. They said he would end up in religiosity. The only person who didn't preach to Valery was Yudel. I once asked him:

"Why don't you explain to Valery that he is not right? You certainly know Darwin so well!"

"He knows Darwin better than I do. But besides he knows philosophy and natural science even more brilliantly. How could I teach him? Do you know how intelligent and talented he is? There is a broad road ahead of him. His name will go down in the history of Russian science next to the names of Mendeleev, Pavlov, and Timiriazev!"

Yudel was wrong. This conversation took place in 1935, and on March 10, 1936, Yudel, Valery, and six weeks later even I and the majority of the members of their discussion group were arrested.

I remember the investigator asked me if Valery had come to our house and what opinion my husband had of him. Naively thinking I was saying something useful for Valery, I answered:

"My husband considered him an extraordinarily knowledgeable, talented person. He said Valery would be an extraordinary scientist . . ."

And to that the investigator cynically answered:

"They are all smart people. We certainly need that type. Fools aren't worth much."

Much later I found out that Valery died during the investigation, and Yudel received the sentence of ten years without the right to correspondence—this meant the death sentence. And from that time on I have dreamed that they are beating Valery's splendid head with sticks but that Yudel's sadistic executioner is shooting him not in the back of the head but in the brow, in order to enjoy the horror on his face just before death . . .

I lived with Yudel for only eight years of my long life. Not everything was smooth in those eight years. He was absolutely unable to cope with the problems of daily living. The difficult decision-making tasks (both then and now), such as changing a broken windowpane, repairing the roof, renting a dacha, and so forth, always fell to me. But these small things are not memorable. I remember only eight years of life with him, years that were filled with deep happiness.

Almost a half century has gone by without Yudel among the living, and the grief for him, the dreams about him do not leave me.

They will be with me forever.

The Origin of a Family Name

My father-in-law, Ruvim Yevseevich Zakgeim, was a taciturn Jew, immersed in holy books. Sometimes he would noisily argue in ancient Hebrew with other old people. The argument had to do with differing interpretations of the Talmud, and it had already heatedly engaged Talmudists, living in their own special world, very far from the questions of everyday life, for several thousand years.

Once I asked:

"Why did you give your son (my husband) the name Juda?"

"And you don't like it?"

"It is associated with betrayal."

"What betrayal? What are you talking about?"

"Juda betrayed Christ, and his name is a symbol of betrayal."

"What nonsense! Juda is the name of our Jewish people. How could you not like that name? I don't understand!"

He rejected Christianity wholeheartedly. Nothing was written about it in his holy books; it was too contemporary for him.

In 1930 my father-in-law solemnly entered my room where I sat by my newborn son's little crib.

"I need to talk with you. Will you circumcise the child?"

I knew my baby's grandfather had prayed to God that I would have a daughter because he realized that a boy would not be circumcised, and for him that would be a tragedy. It was difficult for me to refuse the old man, and I decided to hide behind my husband's back.

"No, Ruvim Yevseevich; even if I agreed to it, your son would never permit me to do it."

"If you agree, we will do it without his permission."

Grandfather was inciting me to crime. Poor thing! How much he would have suffered if he had decided to go against his adored son!

"No, I can't do that," I said categorically.

"But your son will not be Jewish! Do you understand what that means?"

I did not understand. It seemed to me completely unimportant whether my son was Jewish or Chinese, as long as he lived under Communism! I never thought that when my son was forty there would be such a thing as the "fifth point" and that his grandfather needn't have worried. His grandson wouldn't be able to call himself anything but Jewish even if he wanted to.

"Do you know the origin of our family name?"

Grandfather pulled out of his pocket an old leather case decorated with the Star of David and an inscription in Hebrew. In the case lay a scroll of parchment. He solemnly read me a text in Hebrew that I could not understand, and then he translated it.

The contents of the writing were as follows:

In the seventeenth century in the shtetl of Ruzhany before Easter, the dead body of a Christian baby was found. The whole Ruzhany Jewish community was accused of a ritual murder.

The powerful prince to whom this shtetl belonged announced that he would erase the whole community from the face of the earth if they did not give up the murderers within three days.

Three whole days and nights the community prayed in the synagogue for salvation, and on the morning of the fourth day two old men went to the prince and confessed to being the murderers.

They hung the old men on the gates of the castle.

The community drew up two documents and gave them to the families of the men who were killed. One of these was in my father-in-law's hands. It attested that the old man (so-and-so) was not the murderer but that he had given his life in order to save the community, that the synagogue of Ruzhany would pray for his soul eternally, and that his family would receive the last name of Zakgeim, which is an abbreviation of *zerezh keidesh reim*—Hebrew for "his seed is sacred." His offspring would continue from century to century, and if the next in line was not a boy, then the daughter when she married would transfer this family name to her husband.

Grandfather read the document to me and looked at me questioningly.

"If he is not circumcised, I cannot give him this document, although he is the heir of the family."

I very much wanted to receive this scroll and felt very sorry for the old man who hoped so much that now I would not hold out.

But I did hold out. Offended, he left the room and took his treasure with him.

Grandfather died long ago. During the war the scroll disappeared. The latest Zakgeim, the son of my son, will soon be one year old. He is learning to walk. He can't yet keep his balance and is still very unsteady on his chubby little legs. I look at him and think how many storms have passed over humanity since the seventeenth century when "unto the ages of ages" this document was given to the Zakgeim family . . .

One Zakgeim, chairman of the Administrative Committee of Yaroslavl, was savagely murdered in 1918 at the time of the White Guards' mutiny. Four Zakgeims were killed in the war. Several were killed in the ovens of Auschwitz.

My husband was shot in the basement of Lubyanka in 1936.

And all the same the baton is handed on. In this tiny little being flows the blood of his great-great-great-grandfather who gave his life for the community.

What awaits him at the end of this terrible twentieth century and the even more terrible twenty-first century?

And is it possible that fate will carry this family on unto the ages of ages?

About National Feeling

I am a Jewish woman.

I belong to Russian culture. More than anything in the world I love Russian literature. I don't know Yiddish. Religion is alien to me. Mama was born in Moscow and my father in Smolensk, from whence he was brought to Moscow at the age of thirteen. Both my grandfathers were soldiers for Czar Nikolai and served in the army for twenty-five years, receiving for that service the right to reside in all the cities of Russia, and so the world of the Jewish Pale, the world of the Jewish shtetl, was not known to me or my parents. I always considered Russia to be my homeland.

In my youth I didn't look like a Jewish girl, and frequently I overheard antisemitic comments. For example, when I was fifteen I lived with Mama in Kislovodsk where Mama worked as a dressmaker. A woman came up to me in the park and offered me twenty tickets for the spa. There was a shortage of tickets, and I gladly bought those she didn't need.

"Today I'm leaving," she told me, "and it's too bad that I didn't use the tickets. For two hours I've been running around the park looking for a Russian face. There seem to be only Yids around here. They have taken over all of Kislovodsk!"

I gave her the money, and as I said good-bye I told her:

"I know this will upset you. You sold the tickets to me, but I'm a Jew."

She snorted and ran away.

In order to avoid similar situations, I always tried at first acquaintance to make some reference to my nationality.

I am very sensitive to the slightest appearance of antisemitism. The sufferings of the Jewish people bother me deeply.

Do you know what *cantonists* are? Probably only very vaguely. I will cite evidence from Herzen, who encountered this terrible phenomenon and wrote about it as I, of course, am not able to write.

Here is an account of a conversation between Herzen and an officer in a village near Vyatka:

> Herzen: "Whom are you taking and where to?"
>
> Officer: "Oh don't ask; it makes my heart break. Well, it's my superiors who know all about it; our duty is just to carry out orders and we are not responsible, but, as a human being I say it is an ugly business."
>
> Herzen: "Why, what is it?"
>
> Officer: "You see, they have collected a crowd of cursed little Jew boys of eight or nine years old. Whether they are taking them for the navy or what, I can't say. At first the orders were to drive them to Perm; then there was a change and we are driving them to Kazan. I took them over a hundred versts farther back. The officer who handed them over said, 'It's dreadful, and that's all there is to it; a third were left on the way.'" (And the officer pointed to the earth.)
>
> "Have there been epidemics or what?" Herzen asked, deeply shocked.
>
> "No, not epidemics, but they just die off like flies. A Jew boy, you know, is such a frail, weakly creature, like a wet cat; he is not used to tramping in the mud for ten hours a day and eating dried bread—and also they are among strangers, no father nor mother nor petting; well, they cough and cough and then they die. And I ask you, what use are they? What can they do with little boys?"
>
> They brought the children and formed them into regular ranks: it was one of the most awful sights Herzen had ever seen, those poor, poor children! Boys of twelve or thirteen might somehow have held up, but little creatures of eight and ten . . .
>
> Pale, exhausted, with frightened faces, they stood in clumsy soldiers' overcoats, fixing helpless, pitiful eyes on the garrison soldiers who were roughly getting them into ranks. And these sick children, without care or tenderness, exposed to the icy wind that blows unobstructed from the Arctic Ocean, were going to their graves.

Herzen took the officer by the arm and saying, "take care of them," threw himself into a carriage. He wanted to sob; he felt that he could not hold up.

And both my grandfathers were cantonists. My mother's father, Schneider, died long before I was born, but my grandfather Aaron Sliozberg lived with us until I was ten, and I loved him dearly. My grandfather often told my nanny and my grandmother (my mother's mother) about his childhood. I was three or four years old then; he didn't realize that I listened to his stories and understood a lot of them. At night I couldn't sleep, and I thought about how they had taken grandfather from his father and mother, how he had suffered, how afraid he had been of the evil commanders!

My older sister added one more thing to my fear. She read me a chapter from *Uncle Tom's Cabin* where they sold a young Negro boy, and the mother ran away with him across a river into Canada, jumping across the ice to escape the pursuers. In my head everything got mixed up: the calamity of my Jewish grandfathers and the disaster of the Negro woman, Eliza. I somehow decided that I too might be taken from Mama. I too was not like my Russian girlfriends. I was someone without rights! This fear tormented me for a long time. I somehow never talked with anyone about this, but at night I thought about it, worried, and suffered.

Increasing my torment even more was the fear of a Jewish pogrom. In 1906 a pogrom was expected. Some women ran up to us and said that on the outskirts of Samara the *pogromshchiki* had gathered carrying portraits of the czar and crosses, and shouting, "Beat the Yids! Save Russia!" They had already smashed up and looted a little shop and killed an old man. Niania dressed my sisters and me and wanted to take us to the house of an acquaintance who had agreed to hide us. My cousin, a student named Misha, threw off his jacket and sat on a stool at the door in his white undershirt. In his hands he held an ax. Mama told him to hide himself or "let them take everything," but he answered stubbornly, "The first to force his way in here, I'll put an ax through his head."

Frequently people kept running up, telling the details: they are coming by Zavodskaya, by Nikolaevskaya, they are coming, coming . . . Mama sent Niania for a carriage driver and went to see the governor's wife. She was a dressmaker for her and more than once had gone to her house for fittings. The governor's wife didn't know about the pogrom, was horrified by Mama's story, called her husband, and told him about it. He called the chief of police. They spoke in French, but Mama understood that they were arguing about something. Then the governor said, "Don't be afraid. The police will disperse them." They really did disperse them, and the pogrom did not take place. But in my soul the fear lived on for many long years.

In 1909 for the third time my cousin Lev wasn't admitted to the gymnasium. For a Jew to be accepted he had to get fives in all the entrance exams. Normally 2.5 percent of all students accepted into the gymnasium could be Jewish. (For this reason S. Y. Marshak was not admitted to the gymnasium the first time, although he astonished everyone with his capabilities). Everyone scolded Lev, but he, poor thing, definitely had received a four or a three in some subject and was not accepted by the gymnasium. He was three years older than I, but I was already eight years old and had to begin thinking about a gymnasium.

Right next to our apartment was Khardina's private gymnasium. There was a preparatory class where they took eight-year-old girls. But Mama, in order to avoid paying eighty rubles for that year, didn't want to let me enter the preparatory class. I read fluently and my handwriting was weak, but my sisters could prepare me. Mama wanted me to start studying right away in the first grade.

One morning I went out to play with my neighborhood girlfriends, but they told me they wouldn't be playing today since they were going to take exams for the preparatory class of the gymnasium. "Well, I'm going with you," I said and not asking Mama I set out for the gymnasium.

The exam began.

"Who knows how to read?"

Everyone knew how, but I had already read several novels by Jules Verne and Mayne Reed, and of course I received a five for my reading.

"Who knows how to count?"

I even knew the multiplication table—my memory was good. Again a five.

"Who knows how to write?"

This was worse. My handwriting was very bad. I tried my hardest, but somehow an inkblot appeared and then a second one! The teacher came up.

"Show me, did you make an inkblot?"

Alas! I received a three for handwriting. I was defeated, since they hadn't taken Lev into the gymnasium because of a four! (I didn't know that in Khardina's private gymnasium there were no quotas for Jews.)

"For the last exam," the teacher asked, "who knows how to recite poetry?"

Everyone raised her hand. The teacher at first asked other girls to recite, and then she called on me.

"With expression?" I asked.

"Yes, of course."

I recited a fable *with expression*. I twisted my behind; I stood on tiptoes; I rolled my eyes; with a thin voice I praised a crow. The teacher smiled.

"Wait a moment," she said and called the teachers who had come into the large teachers' room for the break: "Come in here a minute. I have an artist here with me. She is reciting poetry."

I was put on a table. Here I completely outdid myself. The teachers laughed. I remember one old teacher who took off his glasses, wiped his eyes with a handkerchief, and groaned, "Oy, I can't, oy, I can't . . ."

I finished "The Crow and the Fox" and then asked:

"Should I recite more?" I recited "The Dragonfly and the Ant" and was ready to continue because everyone was laughing and praising me, but my examiner cut short the presentation, lifted me off the table, and said:

"Tell your Mama you are accepted into the gymnasium." Very satisfied I was walking home, when suddenly a thought pierced me: "They don't even know I'm Jewish! And I got a three in handwriting!"

I returned to the school and went to the teachers' room. They were drinking tea, sitting around tables. I sweetly curtsied to one side and then to the other.

"Excuse me," I said, "I am Jewish. Will I have a competitive exam?"

They all laughed.

"You won't have anything; you are already accepted."

Very content, I again curtsied twice and went home.

One of the most terrible impressions influencing my childish soul was the Beiliss Affair. At that time I was already eleven years old. Papa read the liberal newspaper *Russian Word* aloud every day. There they printed the speeches of the public prosecutor (Wipper), the lawyers (I've forgotten their names), and the interrogations of the witnesses for the prosecution and the defense.

Beiliss was accused of murdering a ten-year-old boy, Andrusha Yushchinsky, with the aim of draining all his blood and using it for preparing matzo.

Basically they accused the entire Jewish people of murdering Christian babies for ritual purposes. The czarist government and the newspapers that followed the ideology of the Black Hundreds hotly supported this wild accusation. The Russian intelligentsia stood for the defense of Beiliss.

The court had appointed jurors who were specially chosen from illiterate peasants in the hope that it would be easy to persuade them to decide against the Jews, who were foreign to them and had crucified Christ.

But the defense was so brilliant that it was able to demonstrate that Andrusha's mother (Vera Cheberiak) herself was involved in the murder of her son. (She was a member of a criminal gang that Andrusha threatened to turn over to the police.) The jurors realized that Beiliss's guilt had been cooked up, and they delivered a verdict of not guilty.

I still remember a feeling of infinite gratitude to the Russian intelligentsia and love for Korolenko, who wrote articles in Beiliss's defense . . .

I remember how my father and I took a walk in the street after the news of the verdict and how people we hardly knew, Jews and Russians, hugged us and greeted us. It was a happy moment.

The Revolution had seemed to have swept national feelings from the soul like a broom. What difference did it make who we were: Jews, Russians, Tatars, or Chinese?

Alas! In the future we still had to live with the discriminatory slogan "Rootless Cosmopolitans" and the trial instigated by *Murderers in White Lab Coats,* and even now in the present day Pamyat has bloomed.

My Great-Granddaughter's Gift

On the first of August 1990, my eighty-eighth birthday, I received many gifts: books, flowers, and candies. They lay on the table in the garden. I was looking at the books. Suddenly I saw my five-year-old great-granddaughter, Tania. She was running to me, waving a piece of paper.

"What is it, Tanechka?" I asked.

"I drew a picture for you. It's a present."

"Let's see it."

I glanced at the paper. It was a drawing of a log cabin, drawn the way children draw, but long. Under the roof was a row of windows, each one with a grille. On the door was a large lock.

"What is it, Tania?" I asked, shocked.

"What is it? It is a prison! Have you forgotten that you were in prison for a long time and were very sad there?"

"Well, it may not be wise," I thought, "but we do say so much in front of children, and they really do understand everything!"

And maybe it is wise. I certainly learned what a pogrom was when I was four years old. Perhaps my hatred of pogromists was pressed into my soul forever, wherever they may be active—in Azerbaijan or Armenia, Tbilisi or Vilnius.

A Dream

On the first of August 1991, I will turn eighty-nine years old. This will be in two weeks.

My old age is happy. In the family everyone gets along well with me; I don't have any serious illnesses; I can still read, but with each day weakness increases and strength flows away, like water from a cracked vase. Perhaps for that reason the certainty came to me that my eighty-ninth birthday would be the last one in which my family and friends would gather with me.

I am not afraid of death; apparently I am very tired of living. But I am afraid of the torments of death that I have witnessed in my long life. One of my friends, dying of cancer, prayed to be given poison; she wasn't able to bear the pain. Another became blind and lived for many long years in complete darkness. I am afraid of these torments and dream of an easy death.

I was thinking about it and suddenly saw myself in Samara where I was born and lived until I was eighteen.

I sat on the big terrace by the Volga River. Next to me was a friend of my father, a doctor.

"Perhaps I should call the guests to the table," I said. "Dinner is already prepared."

"No, your son himself will organize everything," responded the man with whom I was talking.

On the radio my son's voice announced, "At this very moment eighty-nine years ago our Mama was born. She has survived a difficult and long

249

life and has remained a person of great value. She spent twenty years in prisons, camps, and exile. In her whole life she never received a single award, medal, or star. However, I am wrong . . . In her sentence, which has been preserved and which Vyshinsky signed, they call her a hidden conspirator who never in any way helped the investigation or the court. This phrase Mama considers of the highest value. We drink to her life!"

"And she can still dance!" exclaimed the doctor, and firmly took me by the hand. The music sounded. The doctor and I took several rhythmic steps. And suddenly I saw my first husband, Yudel, at the end of the terrace! I tore away my hand and ran to him, and he met me halfway.

He embraced me, kissing my hands and cheeks. I smelled his eau de cologne, the reagent he worked with in the laboratory, and felt his skin. I was happy . . . In this moment the doctor said, "She has died!"

And the voice announced, "What an easy death! What happiness is written on her face!"

I thought, yes, what a good death. I died in the arms of the person whom I loved! I recognized his smell, which I had not smelled for fifty-five years!

In this moment I awoke in my room in Moscow, my beloved Volga was not there, and my beloved husband was not there. It had been a dream. How sad!

Translator's Notes

~

Instead of an Introduction

4   *enemies of the people*   The term used for people who were arrested during the Stalin purges of the 1930s.

A Wood Chip

5   *kulaks*   The kulaks were relatively successful farmers who lost their land and livestock during the period of agricultural collectivization, from 1929 to 1933. Many were sent to Siberia with their families, and millions died from famine. Their land and possessions were nationalized and became part of the Soviet collective farm system.

6   *digging a canal*   Probably a reference to the White Sea Canal, which was built by prison labor in the 1930s to connect the White Sea with the Baltic through various northern rivers and lakes.

The Beginning of the Road to Cavalry

8   *God did not save!*   Line 16 from *In Memory of A. I. Oldoevsky* (written in 1839) by Mikhail Yurievich Lermontov (1814–41), Sliozberg's favorite poet. She quotes him frequently throughout the memoir.

9   *Don't you understand? They took him.*   The secret police.

10   *a conference of the Stakhanovites*   Stakhanovites (named after a Soviet miner, A. G. Stakhanov) were Soviet laborers who received recognition for their extraordinarily high levels of production.

10   *in Nevele*   A city in the northwest near Pskov.

10   *once more I would be carrying packages*   Family members usually took food and warm clothing to prisoners.

Lubyanka Prison

13   *Trotskyite*   Many innocent people were arrested and accused of being supporters of Trotsky, a revolutionary who competed with Stalin for leadership of the Party after Lenin's death in 1924.

13   *Kirov*   Leader of the Party in Leningrad. His assassination in 1934 led to many false accusations and arrests.

15 *Komsomol* Communist Youth Union. Membership in the Komsomol was an entrée into educational and professional opportunities for young people during the Soviet period.

15 *Maria Ilinichna Ulianova* Lenin's youngest sister.

16 *Gorki Leninskie* A little suburb of Moscow where Lenin lived when he was sick and where he also died. It is in a group of low hills and is not to be confused with the city of Gorky to the east.

17 *after several days someone knocked on the wall* A coded communication system that Russian prisoners have used for centuries.

17 *in Gorky* An ancient city on the Volga, originally called Nizhni Novgorod but renamed after Maxim Gorky during the Soviet period.

17 *dialectical materialism* A required course for all Soviet university students.

17 *Life has become better, life has become more joyful now, thank God, as we work by the light of a splinter!* This was a takeoff on Stalin's slogan "Life has become better, life has become more joyful under Communism!"

The Investigation

19 *Porfiry from "Crime and Punishment"* The investigator in Dostoevsky's classic novel.

20 *Allilueva* Stalin's second wife, Nadezhda Allilueva, who committed suicide in 1932.

20 *Bukharin* Nikolai Ivanovich Bukharin (1888–1938), an early revolutionary and comrade of Lenin, who took a stand against Stalin's collectivization of agriculture in the late 1920s, was expelled from the Party and put to death after a "show trial."

Methods of Investigation

23 *GPU* Precursor of the NKVD, the secret police.

A Mother's Gift

24 *Decembrist* In 1825, a group of noblemen, the Decembrists, plotted an uprising against Czar Nikolai I. They were apprehended; some were executed and others were exiled to Siberia where they, their families, and their descendants lived out their lives.

24 *the eighth point* This refers to article 58, point 8, of the Criminal Code of the Soviet Constitution, which forbade terrorist acts against the state.

Butyrka Prison in 1936

26   *Black Maria*   In Russia this police transport vehicle is called a *Black Crow.*

27   *Trekhgorka*   A factory that is famous for its woven fabrics.

28   *a gap of about forty centimeters*   Just under sixteen inches.

29   *Nelli*   Many Soviet girls during this period were named Ninel (with Nelli as a nickname). *Ninel* is *Lenin* spelled backward.

29   *matrioshka*   A *matrioshka* is a stout peasant girl nesting doll with three or four identical dolls stacked inside her.

30   *Tarusa*   A small town near Moscow.

30   *she was refused a passport*   All adult Soviet citizens were required to have an internal passport in order to travel within the country.

31   *two thousand kilometers*   Approximately 1,243 miles.

31   *Socialist Revolutionary*   The Socialist Revolutionary Party was established in 1901 and grew out of the Russian populist movement.

31   *Georgian Mensheviks*   The Mensheviks were a faction of the Russian Revolutionary movement that emerged in 1903. They tended to be more moderate politically than the Bolsheviks.

32   *Papulya*   Daddy.

33   *Kaganovich*   Lazar Moiseevich Kaganovich (1893–1991) was an early Bolshevik leader, a rigid Stalinist, and secretary of the Central Committee of the Communist Party at the time of Sliozberg's arrest.

36   *Yagoda*   G. G. Yagoda (1891–1938) was head of the secret police and Stalin's chief prosecutor for the early show trials of the Great Terror during the mid-1930s. He himself was arrested and shot in 1938.

36   *Yezhov*   Nikolai Ivanovich Yezhov (1895–1939) was Yagoda's successor and prosecutor after Yagoda's arrest in September 1936. Yezhov was arrested and shot in 1939.

38   *November 7, 1936, had arrived.*   November 7 was the anniversary of the Revolution and a major holiday in the Soviet Union.

39   *Pugachev's Tower*   Yemilian Ivanovich Pugachev (1742–75) was the leader of a Cossack rebellion against Catherine the Great in 1773.

39   *November 12*   The Russian edition gives "November 15" here, though Sliozberg wrote elsewhere that the trial began on November 12, and her certificate of rehabilitation issued on June 6, 1956, gives November 12, 1936, as the date of her sentencing.

The Trial

40   *Heinrich Heine*   Heinrich Heine (1797–1856), nineteenth-century German romantic poet.

40   *Vyshinsky*   Andrei Y. Vyshinsky (1883–1954), prosecutor general of the USSR from 1935 to 1940. He presided over the major show trials of the Great Purge.

41   *troika*   Any threesome or, in this case, a triumvirate of judges or political leaders.

41   *Ulrikh*   Vasiliy Vasilievich Ulrikh (1889–1951) was the presiding judge in many of the major show trials during Stalin's Purge.

Solovki

44   *Solovki*   An ancient monastery on an island in the White Sea that was used as a prison during the Soviet period.

44   *SLON (Solovki Camp of Special Designation)*   The word *slon* means "elephant" in Russian.

45   *Monakhov*   The prison commandant.

47   *The white night*   In the North during the summer solstice the sun sets very late at night, and these bright evenings are called the white nights.

48   *Of the five*   The text says "ten women." Translator's change.

48   *Chinese Eastern Railroad (CER)*   The Chinese Eastern Railroad was built as a joint Russian-Chinese business venture between 1897 and 1907, and the two countries ran it together from 1924 to 1935. In 1935, the Soviets sold their interest in the project, and the railroad workers had to choose whether they would settle in the Soviet Union or in China.

49   *four hundred grams*   About fourteen ounces.

49   *two-square-meter cell*   About twenty-two square feet.

51   *coarse bands of cloth*   These were the same ragged cloth bands that prisoners used to wrap their feet inside their boots.

51   *Yelisarova*   Anna Ulianova Yelisarova was Lenin's younger sister.

51   *Barbusse*   Henri Barbusse (1873–1935), French Communist writer.

54   *mainland*   Prisoners referred to the world outside the camps as the mainland, although Solovki actually was on an island.

Kazan Prison

55   *Kazan*   Kazan is the capital city of the Republic of Tatarstan, located about five hundred miles east of Moscow on the Volga River.

55   *size forty-four*   Russian shoe size forty-four is the same as U.S. men's sizes eleven to eleven and a half.

56   *Instead of food, for which he pleaded.*   From "The Beggar" by Lermontov.

58   *Ivanovo*   A city northeast of Moscow.

58   *Furmanov*   A commissar in the Red Army and a famous Soviet writer.

60   *Baku*   The capital city and largest port in Azerbaijan on the Caspian Sea.

Liza

63   *intelligentsia*   The intellectual, educated, often dissident class in czarist Russia.

63   *Nezhdanova*   A famous Russian opera singer of the 1920s and 1930s.

64   *Ilych*   Lenin's middle name or patronymic. He was often referred to as Ilych.

64   *Young Pioneer*   The Young Pioneers was a Communist organization for children.

Suzdal

66   *Kolyma*   Kolyma is the region in far northeastern Siberia where many Gulag camps were located.

67   *Vladimir*   Vladimir and Suzdal are ancient cities northeast of Moscow.

69   *Perhaps it even would be funny.*   The last two lines are from a poem by Lermontov called "To A. O. Smirnova" (1840).

70   *Chaliapin*   F. I. Chaliapin (1873–1938), Soviet opera star of the 1920s.

70   *Rachmaninov*   S. V. Rachmaninoff (1873–1943), Russian composer of the romantic period.

Transport

72   *Glinka and Tchaikovsky*   Mikhail Ivanovich Glinka (1804–57) and Petr Ilyich Tchaikovsky (1840–93) were Russian romantic composers of the late nineteenth century.

73   *Eugene Onegin*   A novel in verse written between 1825 and 1832 by Pushkin.

73   *Woe from Wit*   A popular comedy by A. S. Griboedov (1795–1829), a writer and diplomat of the nineteenth century. Educated Russians can still recite much of his poetry by heart, and many lines have become popular aphorisms.

73   *Pasternak*   "Lieutenant Schmidt" was a popular poem by Boris L. Pasternak (1890–1960), published in the mid-1920s.

73   *My uncle—high ideals inspire him . . .*   The beginning line of *Eugene Onegin.*

74   *old woman who looked about fifty*   Sliozberg was born in 1902 and was thirty-seven years old at this time.

Magadan, My First Camp

76   *Magadan*   The city of Magadan was founded in the 1930s, and it became the port of entry for all the far east Siberian Gulag camps. People arrived there by steamship from Vladivostok, and then were sent north to the Kolyma region.

77   *construction area of the town*   Starting with this paragraph, Sliozberg begins to write in the present tense, giving the narrative more immediacy.

78   *kisel*   A fruit and potato-starch drink.

79   *Cossack*   The Cossacks were a group of martial people who lived in the southern steppes of Russia.

79   *blat*   The system of protection or bribery that operated in the camps.

Altunin

81   *Voronezh*   A large city in southwestern Russia, not far from Ukraine.

82   *Soltz*   Member of the Party's Central Control Commission.

82   *Big Whiskers*   Nickname for Stalin.

Igor Adrianovich Khorin

83   *fifty degrees below zero*   Fifty degrees below zero centigrade is about fifty-eight degrees below zero Fahrenheit.

83   *politicals*   The prisoners arrested for trumped-up political crimes, as Sliozberg had been.

84   *zek*   A *Zaklyuchonniy* was a prisoner. Inmates of the Gulag camps were referred to as *zeks*.

84   *numbers on government bonds*   A required government lottery. Winning numbers were published in the newspapers and could be redeemed for cash.

85   *Blok*   A. A. Blok (1880–1921), symbolist poet of the early twentieth century.

85   *Tiutchev*   F. I. Tiutchev (1803–73), Russian poet of the nineteenth century.

85   *Akhmatova*   Anna Akhmatova (1889–1966), a Russian poet and widow of Gumilev, a symbolist poet who was shot in 1921. Their son, historian Lev Gumilev, was arrested and imprisoned during the late 1930s. Akhmatova's most famous poem, "Requiem," was dedicated to the victims of the Great Terror.

85   *Turgenev*   Ivan Sergeevich Turgenev (1818–83) was a major Russian novelist and playwright.

86   *Smolny Institute*   The Smolny Institute was an excellent school in St. Petersburg for the daughters of the nobility. Its building became the headquarters for the Bolshevik Revolution in 1917.

86   *White Sea Canal*   Many political prisoners with forced labor sentences were sent to the far north to dig a canal that connected the White Sea with the Baltic through various rivers and lakes. They were forced to work under terrible conditions.

86   *fortunate status*   In other words, he was arrested as a true criminal and had no political charges against him. Therefore his sentence was shorter.

86   *Aristocrats*   A propaganda play about the White Sea Canal and the way criminals were taught to become responsible members of society by working there. Soviet playwright Nikolai Feodorovich Pogodin (1900–1962) was the author.

86   *Mayakovsky*   Vladimir Vladimirovich Mayakovsky (1893–1930), Russian poet and stylistic innovator. After the Revolution in 1917, he supported the international Socialist movement. He committed suicide in 1930.

88   *Balmont*   Konstantin Dmitrievich Balmont (1867–1942), Russian symbolist poet.

88   *Nekrasov*   N. A. Nekrasov (1821–78), nineteenth-century Russian poet born into the Russian nobility. In his poetry he describes the tragic peasant life in Russia.

88   *taiga*   The word *taiga* refers to the more barren northern regions of Russia, south of the Arctic tree line and just south of the tundra. For much of the year the sun does not rise far above the horizon in the taiga, winters last six to seven months, and temperatures vary between fifty degrees below zero centigrade and thirty degrees above zero centigrade year round. Summers are short but may be warm and humid.

Mama

90   *K. Simonov*   Konstantin Simonov (1915–79), a Soviet writer whose poetry was especially popular during the Second World War, when many recited it from memory.

90   *minus thirty-five*   Minus thirty-five degrees centigrade is about minus thirty-one degrees Fahrenheit.

91   *40.5 degrees*   A temperature of 40.5 degrees centigrade is about one hundred five degrees Fahrenheit.

Galia

92   *six hundred grams*   About twenty-one ounces of bread.

92   *eight cubic meters get stacked*   Throughout this chapter, Sliozberg shifts in and out of the present tense.

92   *five kilometers*   A little more than three miles.

Bread

95   *one kilogram*   A little more than two pounds.

Basia

97   *a hundred and fifty centimeters tall*   Just under five feet tall.

99   *Yagodny*   Yagodny is a village in the Kamchatka region.

Polina Lvovna Gertzenberg

101   *Sejm*   The lower house of the Polish parliament.

101   *the Russian-Polish negotiations according to which all Poles arrested on Polish territory after 1939 were to be released*   This was the Sikorsky-Maisky Pact of 1941, which gave amnesty to Poles being held in Soviet prisons and camps.

101   *couldn't return from Kolyma until the ocean was navigable*   The port was frozen for most of the year.

101   *the zone*   The prison compound.

101   *Dalstroi*   Dalniy Vostok Stroitelstvo, the department in charge of construction in the labor camps in the Far East.

Labor

104   *the Tatar horde went out of ancient Rus*   The Mongol hordes first invaded Russia in 1237 and were defeated about one hundred fifty years later, although their influence lingered for another two hundred years.

Devil's Wheel

106   *jolly hut*   The merry or jolly hut was a euphemism for the hut where prisoners and guards drank and partied together.

108   *Konstantin*   Kostia is a nickname for Konstantin.

109   *a doubled sentence for three years*   Perhaps Sliozberg means that the sentence was extended by three years.

110   *vy*   The polite form of *you* in Russian.

113   *kulich*   Russian Easter cake.

113   *izba*   A log cabin

Hatred

115   *a state of alimentary dystrophy*   Dying of starvation, with at least a 20 percent loss of normal body mass.

115   *Rolland*   Romain Rolland (1866–1944), French novelist, critic, historian, and pacifist; he was a Nobel laureate in 1915.

115   *Veresaev*   V. V. Veresaev (1867–1945), Russian writer and medical doctor. His book *Notes of a Doctor* (1901) was extremely popular.

115   *Garshin*   V. M. Garshin (1855–88), Russian writer with a keen sensitivity to social injustice.

115   *Korolenko*   V. G. Korolenko (1853–1921), Russian writer, publicist, and member of the St. Petersburg Academy of Sciences who defended Beiliss in an antisemitic trial in 1913. He also took a stand against revolutionary terror in 1921.

117   *Petipa*   Marius Ivanovich Petipa (1818–1910) was a dancer, teacher, and choreographer, often called the Father of Classical Ballet.

117   *Ilinskoye*   A Moscow suburb.

Skeleton in the Closet

120   *Dickens*   This story is probably not by Dickens but may refer to one of several stories ("The Cask of Amontillado," "The Fall of the House of Usher") by Edgar Allan Poe.

Mirage

122   *Kalinin*   Member of the Politburo and head of the Soviet Red Cross.

122   *Peshkova*   Maxim Gorky's first wife and a member of the Red Cross.

123   *Elgen*   A town in the Kolyma region.

123   *Kazan station*   The terminal in Moscow for trains from Siberia.

123   *MGB*   Secret police.

124   *article 58, section 12*   Article 58 of the Soviet Criminal Code identified political crimes. Section 12 had to do with enemies of the people.

The Goner

125   *reduced from six hundred grams to five hundred*   The bread ration was reduced from about twenty-one ounces to about seventeen and a half ounces a day.

Nadezhda Vasilevna Grankina

132   *Tsarskoe Celo*   This was a village outside St. Petersburg where the royal court had a country palace.

132 *Petrograd*   The revolutionary name for St. Petersburg, later Leningrad.

132 *Lugansk*   A medium-sized town in the Donbass region.

132 *They named her Kina—a nickname for Kommunist International!*   Kinusia is an affectionate version of Kina.

133 *Samara*   Samara is a large city on the Volga River in south-central Russia.

133 *Orenburg*   Orenburg is a city on the Ural River near the border with Kazakhstan.

134 *both died in 1943*   Or possibly during the German siege of Leningrad, 1941–42, when almost half the population of the city died of starvation.

136 *Roshchino*   A small town outside Leningrad where there were many little country houses or dachas.

136 *pirogi and shashlik*   Pirogi are meat pies, and *shashlik* is shish kebab.

137 *Till My Tale Is Told*   Nadezhda Grankina, "Notes by Your Contemporary," in *Till My Tale Is Told: Women's Memoirs of the Gulag,* ed. S. S. Vilensky (Bloomington: Indiana University Press, 1999), 111–41. Some of Sliozberg's memoir is also included in this collection.

137 *Memorial*   A citizens' initiative established in 1987 to honor the victims of Soviet state terror.

Freedom

139 *Irkutsk*   Irkutsk is a city in East Siberia.

142 *Karaganda*   Karaganda is a city is Kazakhstan where Sliozberg was later sent into exile.

142 *Twentieth Party Congress*   The 1956 Party Congress, at which Khrushchev granted amnesty to all political prisoners.

Nikolai Vasilevich Adamov

143 *ten years without the right to correspondence*   This euphemism indicated that the prisoner had been put to death within twenty-four hours of his arrest. Families often didn't receive this information until many years later.

143 *Donbass*   Donbass is a coal-mining region in Ukraine.

143 *Whites*   After the end of World War I, the White Russian Army fought the Red or Bolshevik-led Army in a Civil War that lasted until 1922, when the White Army was defeated.

144 *Colonel Garanin*   An NKVD operative personally responsible for the execution of hundreds of political prisoners.

144 *Serpantinka*   An extermination camp several hundred kilometers west of Magadan.

144 *Then Garanin disappeared somewhere* After less than a year at Serpantinka, Garanin was arrested as a Japanese spy and shot.
145 *provincial gymnasium* Russian state schools at all levels were called
gymnasiums.
145 *Krylov* The Russian fabulist I. A. Krylov (1769–1844) wrote more than
two hundred fables adapted from Aesop and La Fontaine, as well as
many of his own.
148 *Guilty Without Guilt* A play by nineteenth-century playwright Alexander Ostrovsky.
148 *Alla Tarasova* An actress with the Moscow Art Theater in the 1930s.

Verochka
153 *Sonka Kozyr or Mashka Torgsin* *Kozyr* is a trump card in gambling.
Torgsin is a shortened name for *Torgovlia s inostrantsami*, special currency
stores used by foreigners. These names imply that Sophia Mikhailovna
gave medical work releases to women who gambled or bribed her.
154 *beyond Tashkent to the east* When the Germans invaded the Soviet
Union, many families and institutions moved east to Central Asia, where
they could be safe during the war.
154 *fifty kilometers* thirty-one miles.
156 *Gosplan* The central government planning office.
156 *nonpoliticals* Real criminals.
157 *Dantès* The man who killed Pushkin in a duel.
158 *Negoreloye* A location on the Brest–Moscow railway line not far from
Minsk, in what was then Belarus.
159 *Kuban* The Kuban is a region of southern Russia surrounding the Kuban River valley on the Black Sea.
161 *ZAGS* Civil Registry Bureau.

Return
162 *port of Nakhodka* The port for the city of Vladivostok.
162 *My militia protects me.* A line from a poem by Mayakovsky.
162 *Riazhsk* A village outside Moscow.
164 *Bolshevo* Another village outside Moscow.
165 *House on the Embankment* An apartment complex in downtown Moscow, built to house the Soviet elite in the early 1930s.
166 *Gus-Khrustalny* A city about two hundred kilometers from Moscow
that was famous for its crystal.
168 *Stalin's Seventieth Jubilee* Stalin's seventieth birthday celebration.

Second Arrest

173 *Mikhail Romanov* Grand Duke Mikhail Romanov, cousin of Czar Nikolai II. Quite a few Russians came forward after the Revolution and pretended to be members of the deposed czarist Romanov family.

174 *very important criminals* Political prisoners.

174 *Kosior* S. V. Kosior (1889–1939), politician, member of the Politburo, purge victim.

174 *Kosarev* A. V. Kosarev (1903–39), politican, secretary of the Komsomol, purge victim.

174 *Vesioly* Artem Vesioly (1899–1938), novelist, purge victim.

174 *Rakovsky* Kh. G. Rakovsky (1873–1941), politician, diplomat, purge victim.

176 *an exhibit of gifts* There was a large exhibit of gifts to Stalin in Moscow, arranged as part of his seventieth birthday celebration, or Jubilee, in 1949.

176 *Pushkin monument* In Pushkin Square in central Moscow.

178 *Bulakhov* Piotr Petrovich Bulakhov (1822–85), Russian composer of songs during the romantic period.

181 *Morozov* Pavlik Morozov (1918–32) was a Soviet child-hero who denounced his own father to the secret police and was killed by his peasant neighbors.

Prisoners' Transport to Karaganda

183 *Karaganda* The second largest city in Kazakhstan

183 *Stolypin* Freight cars named after the prerevolutionary Minister of the Interior Pyotr Arkadevich Stolypin (1862–1911). Its compartments were designed for eight prisoners.

183 *Kuibyshev* The Soviet name for the ancient town of Samara (on the Volga River) where Sliozberg was born. The town is halfway between Moscow and Karaganda.

184 *Banderite* A member of the Ukrainian nationalist movement of Stepan Bandera (1909–59) or, loosely, any Ukrainian nationalist who fought against the Soviets.

185 *in 1905 she was arrested on the Krasnopresnensky barricade* In a precursor to the Revolution of 1917, a spasm of violence including strikes and street demonstrations swept Russia in 1905.

185 *Krasnopresnensky* A street in Moscow.

186 *trachoma* Trachoma is a leading cause of blindness worldwide, afflicting more than four hundred million people.

187 *Novorudnia* A region in Kazakhstan.

187 *I hope to God you were still alive in 1954 or 1956.* Years of amnesty for political prisoners after Stalin's death in 1953.

In Exile

188   *Yura Aikhenvald*   Yuri A. Aikhenvald (born in 1928), a writer and poet. Yura is the nickname for Yuri.

189   *old Soviet money*   This was before the currency reform of 1961 and would have been very little money.

191   *Alik Volpin (Yesenin)*   Son of the poet Yesenin, Alik Volpin is a mathematician now living in the United States.

191   *the army right before the war*   Many of the top leadership officials of the Soviet army were victims of the Great Terror in the late 1930s before the beginning of the Second World War.

192   *He recited "Jacobin," "Ode," "Bride of the Decembrist," "The Banners," and much more.*   Poetry by Emanuel Mandel (born in 1925). His pseudonym is Naum Korzhavin.

193   *ty*   The intimate form of *you* in Russian.

194   *Emka*   Nickname for Emanuel

194   *Novosibirsk*   Novosibirsk is the third largest city in Russia and the administrative center for the Siberian Federal District.

194   *Kislovodsk*   A spa in the Caucasus.

195   *Ogonyok*   A popular Soviet magazine.

196   *This letter I carry with me to this day*   At the present time the handkerchief on which the letter was written is preserved in the Andrei Sakharov Museum in Moscow.

198   *To a dear Tiger Daughter-of-a-Lion*   This is a play on words, since *Lvovna* (Sliozberg's patronymic) means "daughter of Lev." *Lev* not only is a man's name but also means "lion" in Russian, so *Lvovna* also means "lion's daughter."

Kerta Nourten

199   *exile in Siberia*   Many of the early Russian revolutionaries were sent into exile by the czars.

199   *"The Snow Queen"*   A fairy tale by Hans Christian Andersen.

199   *Petrozavodsk*   A town in Karelia, a province in northwest Russia that adjoins Finland.

200   *Finnish War*   Sometimes called the Winter War, this struggle between the Soviet Union and Finland took place during the winter of 1939–40

204   *Otto Kuusinen*   Otto Ville Kuusinen (1881–1964) was a Finnish and Soviet politician, historian, and poet. At this time he was secretary of the Central Committee of the Karelo-Finnish Republic, a Soviet republic that included Finland and Karelia and was incorporated into the Soviet Union after the Winter War.

The Doctors' Plot

205 *the arrest of a group of doctors* Jewish doctors were accused of poisoning Soviet leaders, including Stalin. The Western press called it the Doctors' Plot.

205 *Joint* Joint, or the American Jewish Joint Distribution Committee (JDC), was founded in 1914 in order to provide relief and welfare programs for Jews who were victims of antisemitism around the world. Joint was expelled from Eastern Europe and the Soviet Union at the beginning of the Cold War in 1946.

206 *Red Corner* A cultural corner (with a table and chairs) in most Soviet factories and other workplaces that contained Communist reading materials.

208 *Riumin* Mikhail Riumin (1913–54) was a representative minister to the MGB of the Soviet Union in 1951 and 1952 and was in charge of investigating Professor Ettinger before the Doctors' Plot trials. Riumin was put to death in 1954.

The Death of Stalin

210 *Malenkov* G. M. Malenkov (1902–88), along with Khrushchev and Bulganin, was briefly one of Stalin's three successors. He was premier of the Soviet Union from 1953 to 1955.

210 *Beria* L. P. Beria (1899–1953) was a member of the Politburo, minister of the interior, and one of the organizers of the Great Terror in the 1930s. After Stalin's death he was involved in the succession struggle and then was executed for treason.

Nikolai Adamov—The End of the Road

212 *Jezkazgan* A town in Kazakstan.

214 *He was sixty-two years old* Nikolai died in 1964.

Rehabilitation

216 *eighth of March* International Women's Day, often celebrated with gifts for women.

216 *fifty years old or older* Sliozberg was 54 years old in 1956.

217 *one hundred fifteen rubles* Calculated according to the currency devaluation after his execution.

218 *corpus delicti* This is a principle from Western law stating that a person cannot be convicted of commiting a crime unless it has first been proved that the crime has taken place.

My Relatives' Struggle for My Children

221 *I want to describe this struggle* Sliozberg added these family stories to her Gulag memoir after the original memoir had been widely distributed in the Soviet Union through samizdat.

222 *Petrovka Street* A residential street in Moscow.

222 *the room belonging to them was unenviable* It happened frequently in the Soviet Union during the 1930s that if your neighbor was envious of your apartment, your neighbor could denounce you and take over the apartment.

222 *Frunze* A Bolshevik military hero, a commander on the eastern front during the Civil War, and later a Politburo member.

222 *Kuibyshev* A Member of the Politburo who died in 1925.

Elena Lvovna Sliozberg

226 *"Baba"* Granny.

Yudel Ruvimovich Zakgeim

234 *Vitebsk* An ancient, predominantly Jewish city north of Minsk and between the Lithuanian and Russian borders. It was once part of the grand duchy of Lithuania.

234 *received a five* According to the Russian grading system, five is the highest mark, equal to an A.

235 *the degree of candidate* The Russian degree of candidate at that time was between the academic equivalent of an American master's degree and a Ph.D. The next degree was the doctorate of science, the equivalent of an American Ph.D., but requiring a substantial monograph in addition to the dissertation.

236 *a temperature of thirty-eight degrees* Thirty-eight degrees centigrade is about one hundred degrees Fahrenheit.

238 *Mendeleev* Dmitri Mendeleev (1834–1907), Russian chemist and creator of the first version of the periodic table of elements.

238 *Pavlov* Ivan Pavlov (1849–1936), Russian physiologist, psychologist, and physician who is famous for first describing the phenomenon known as classical conditioning.

238 *Timiriazev* Kliment Timiriazev (1843–1920), Russian botanist and physiologist.

The Origin of a Family Name

239 *the name Juda* Yuda means "Judas" in Russian.

240 *"fifth point"*   This was the fifth point in all Soviet internal and external passports that indicated the bearer's nationality, in this case Jewish.

240 *Ruzhany*   A small town in Belarus.

About National Feeling

242 *a Jewish woman*   In the Soviet Union, a person's ethnicity was often considered the person's nationality.

242 *Smolensk*   One of the oldest cities in western Russia, founded in 863 and situated on the Dnieper River.

243 *Herzen*   Alexander Herzen (1812–70), a Russian writer, often called the father of Russian Socialism.

243 *Here is an account of a conversation*   Adapted from Alexander Herzen, *My Past and Thoughts: The Memoirs of Alexander Herzen*, trans. Constance Garnett (Berkeley: University of California Press, 1982), 169–70. Originally published as *Byloe I Dumy: Detskaa literatura* (1976), 218.

243 *versts*   A verst is an old Russian unit of distance equal to about a kilometer.

244 *before I was born*   Sliozberg was born in 1902.

244 *Uncle Tom's Cabin*   The best-selling novel by abolitionist Harriet Beecher Stowe, published in 1852.

244 *pogromshchiki*   People who conducted pogroms.

245 *Marshak*   Samuil Yakovlevich Marshak (1887–1964) was a Russian writer, translator, and children's poet.

245 *Mayne Reed*   Thomas Mayne Reed (1818–88), English adventure writer. Translations of his novels were popular with Russian children of Sliozberg's generation.

246 *"The Crow and the Fox"*   "The Crow and the Fox" and "The Dragonfly and the Ant" (based on "The Ant and the Grasshopper" by La Fontaine) are popular Russian fables by Krylov.

246 *Beiliss Affair*   For a full history of this event, see M. Samuel, *Blood Accusation: The Strange History of the Beiliss Case* (New York: Knopf, 1966).

246 *Black Hundreds*   The Black Hundreds was a reactionary right-wing movement in Russia in the early twentieth century. The members were strong supporters of the czarist regime.

247 *Korolenko*   Vladimir Galationovich Korolenko (1853–1921) was a Ukrainian-Russian writer and human rights activist.

247 *Rootless Cosmopolitans*   An antisemitic euphemism used throughout the Soviet period.

247 *Pamyat*   A Fascist antisemitic organization founded in the 1980s.